THE WEBBS AND THEIR WORK

A STUDY OF SIX SOCIALISTS

From a drawing by H. G. WELLS

THE WEBBS
AND THEIR WORK

EDITED BY

MARGARET COLE

LONDON
FREDERICK MULLER LTD
29 *Great James Street*
W.C. 1

FIRST PUBLISHED BY FREDERICK MULLER LTD.
IN 1949
PRINTED IN GREAT BRITAIN BY
W. & J. MACKAY & CO., LTD.
CHATHAM

CONTENTS

ILLUSTRATIONS

PREFACE

This group of essays on Sidney and Beatrice Webb and their work is intended to be something rather different from the ordinary run of collective eulogies which appear after the death of eminent persons—as different as the Webb partnership was from the life of the typical eminent person.

There has never been a couple like Beatrice and Sidney Webb in British history; it seems very improbable that there will ever be another. There have been great men who were very much helped by their wives and great women—like Queen Victoria—who owed an immense amount to their husbands. But there has never been a married partnership which was so complete and so equal in its achievement—so equal and so intertwined that as Bernard Shaw says in this book no one can completely separate the contributions or judge which was the more dominant or the more gifted partner. One can say that the London County Council was mostly Sidney, as the Poor Law Commission was Beatrice; one can observe that he had a talent for committee work and quick drafting which she lacked, or that she had a natural gift of vivid description to which he could lay no claim; but that is all. One cannot say which gift was the more important, or detach the L.C.C. or the Poor Law from the living body of the Webbs' work and purpose as a whole; it is all part of the " design for living " which they evolved between them—and never, perhaps, needed to express explicitly—during the months preceding their marriage. From that June, 1892, onwards, they translated their design into practice, according as opportunity offered. Opportunities varied, and what they actually did was not, in all cases, what they had originally thought of doing. But whatever they did was part of the Webb design, and completely consonant with their habits of thought. There was no person, no institution, having experience of the Webbs over sixty years, that had the slightest doubt about the individual and unmistakeable nature of their influence.

This is what made the Webb partnership unique in our history and, I venture to say, in that of any country in the world. But there are two other factors which must be mentioned, partly because they go far to explain the reason why this book has been written.

The first is their remarkable influence on British society and British institutions. These two persons, neither of whom ever wielded political power—Sidney's brief membership of two Labour Cabinets is quite beside the point—or controlled blocks of money-power, yet built up institutions and initiated social changes, of great importance and *permanence*. One need only mention the Fabian Society, the London School of Economics, State education, the *New Statesman*, and Social Security—all described in the following pages—to realise the truth of this statement. Not all the suggestions that they made came to pass ; not all the ventures they set in train were successful—who of mortals could hope for such hundred-per-cent success ? But the extent to which they observed the social necessities of their time and devised institutions which turned out solidly suitable to them is astonishing, and is commemorated in half the chapters of the book.

The second point is the duration of the partnership. It has often been pointed out that the vitality of that generation of Radical thinkers and workers which started its effective life during the 'eighties of last century was unparalleled—Bernard Shaw and Edward Pease are still with us and writing ; the Webbs, John Burns, Will Thorne, Ben Tillett, and Tom Mann all lived on until the 'forties, and Annie Besant, older than any of them, was over eighty when she died. The causes of this longevity may perhaps be concern for biologists ; the result to the historian, however, is that, apart from the final half-dozen years of retirement—during which, none the less, the Webbs were exerting a good deal of influence upon members of younger generations—there is, up to the publication of *Soviet Communism*, over fifty years of activity to chronicle, much of which is outside the memory of all but one or two now living.

This is one of the reasons for this book today. It is not a definitive Life of either Beatrice or Sidney ; nor does it profess to cover all the activities of fifty years—only the major ones. Its purpose is to collect essays upon the Webbs and their influence in the modern world from writers who as far as possible can write

at first hand from their own personal recollections of what the
Webbs were like when they knew them, what—within the limits
of the subject-headings of the several chapters—they were trying
to do, and how far they succeeded or failed. There are two
chapters, and two only, in whose case it proved to be impossible
to enlist the services of a contemporary, but where the subject was
too large and vital to be omitted. In those cases—the London
County Council and the Break-up of the Poor Law—the editor
was fortunate enough to be able to secure the co-operation of
younger research workers who had devoted a great deal of time
and study to the question.

The chapters, it will be seen, are not all of one kind; this is
deliberate policy. The contributions of Shaw, Edward Pease, and
F. W. Galton are mainly personal recollections of the Webbs'
early days, as Desmond MacCarthy's is of their middle years,
Jack Lawson's of their impact on a young miner, and Kingsley
Martin's of the Webbs in retirement. Some chapters are mainly
appraisement and criticism; thus R. C. K. Ensor discusses their
policy of " permeation," Leonard Woolf their political thought,
and G. D. H. Cole writes on Beatrice as an economist. Others
describe a particular activity, such as Beatrice's on the Poor Law
Commission (Joan Clarke) or Sidney's on the L.C.C. (Alan
McBriar) or as a Minister (Sir Drummond Shiels), or the final
spectacular journey to the U.S.S.R. and its results (Mrs. Drake).
Others again deal in detail with one or other of the institutions
they created or helped to create—Lord Beveridge with the London
School of Economics, S. K. Ratcliffe with the *New Statesman*,
J. S. Middleton with the Labour Party, the Editor with the one-
time Fabian Research Department, and John Parker with the
New Fabian Research Bureau. This distribution between
personality, thought, institutions and administration is intended
to illustrate the distribution of the Webbs' own interests in life;
and if one or two chapters seem to contain more about the institutions than about the Webbs, their founders, I am sure, would have
approved. For they never tried to prevent the children of their
brains from growing up, and they continued to show great interest
in them when they had. All the chapters, with the exception of
the two named above, are written by contemporaries, by those who
were actually in contact with the Webbs during the period of

which they write ; and I should like to take this opportunity of expressing my very deep gratitude to those writers who might very reasonably have pleaded age and its infirmities as a valid excuse, but who preferred to put their tribute upon public record now, before it is too late.

One other word. In December, 1947, the ashes of Beatrice and Sidney Webb were buried in Westminster Abbey. This means that their place in the nation's history is now secure, and none can deny it. Therefore, there is no need now for a professionally eulogistic picture—one that omits all the criticisms and concentrates upon " selling " the Webbs to an unappreciative country. All that is over ; the Webbs can be portrayed now as they really were, with the blemishes and errors of judgment from which no human creature is immune ; and that is the intention of this book. Every contributor has been encouraged to write, uncensored, exactly what he thought about the Webbs in the circumstances of his own contribution—to be severely factual or mainly reminiscent ; and no criticism has been removed. It is my belief—as I am sure it would have been Beatrice's—that such honest evaluation can do nothing to diminish, and much to enhance, their final reputation in the country which owes so much to them ; I can say, at least, that under no other conditions would I have consented to edit these essays.

Hendon, November, 1948   MARGARET COLE

TABLE OF DATES

The following brief table of the principal dates in the long life-history of the Webbs may be of service to readers in following the separate chapters :—

1924   First Labour Government. Sidney Webb President of
       the Board of Trade
1926   *My Apprenticeship*
1928   Sidney Webb retires from Parliament
1929   Second Labour Government. Sidney Webb (as Lord
       Passfield) Colonial Secretary
1931   Fall of Labour Government
1932   The Webbs visit the U.S.S.R.
1935   *Soviet Communism*
1939   Beatrice Webb becomes President of the revived Fabian
       Society
1943   Death of Beatrice Webb
1947   Death of Sidney Webb

NOTE ON CONTRIBUTORS

N.B. This is not a set of biographies ; it is intended merely to indicate the connection of the contributors with the subject-matter of their contributions.

G. BERNARD SHAW needs no identification.

EDWARD R. PEASE was Honorary Secretary of the Fabian Society for a brief while in 1886, and paid General Secretary from 1890–1913. In 1916 he wrote its official *History*.

F. W. GALTON was personal secretary to the Webbs from 1892–98, and General Secretary of the Fabian Society from 1920–39.

LORD BEVERIDGE, author of the *Beveridge Report* and Director of the London School of Economics from 1919–37, knew the Webbs in and before the days of the Poor Law Commission of 1905–09.

R. C. K. ENSOR, author and publicist, was specially intimate with the Webbs from about 1897–1914, and Sidney's colleague on the Fabian Executive for many years during that period.

ALAN McBRIAR, lecturer in Modern History, University of Melbourne, made post-graduate studies at Oxford in the history and influence of the Fabian Society.

JOAN SIMEON CLARKE, B.A. (Cantab) was Research Secretary of the Fabian Society from 1941–43, and recently Research Secretary to Lord Beveridge.

DESMOND MacCARTHY, author and journalist ; dramatic critic of the *New Statesman* from its first issue in 1913 to 1944 and Literary Editor, 1920–27.

S. K. RATCLIFFE, journalist and publicist ; sometime editor of *The Statesman*, Calcutta ; regular contributor to

The *New Statesman*, 1913–31 ; first editor of the *Blue Book Supplement*.

MARGARET COLE, Honorary Secretary of the Fabian Society since 1945, was employed in the Fabian—later Labour—Research Department from 1917–26.

J. S. MIDDLETON, Assistant Secretary of the Labour Party from 1903–35, and General Secretary from 1935–45, became Secretary of the War Emergency Workers' National Committee in 1914.

JACK LAWSON, M.P., D.C.L., member of Durham Miners' Executive's Wages Board, was returned to Parliament for Chester-le-Street from 1919 onwards, and was a member of all three Labour Governments.

SIR DRUMMOND SHIELS, M.C., M.B., Vice-President of Royal Empire and Royal Africa Societies, was Labour M.P. for East Edinburgh, 1924–31, and Labour Under-Secretary of State for India and then for the Colonies.

BARBARA DRAKE, L.C.C., niece of Beatrice Webb, accompanied Sidney to the U.S.S.R. in 1934, when he returned to check up on their findings of two years previously.

JOHN PARKER, M.P. since 1935 and present Vice-Chairman of the Fabian Society, was General Secretary of the New Fabian Research Bureau from 1933–39 and of the Fabian Society from 1939–45.

LEONARD WOOLF, Chairman of the International Bureau of the Fabian Society, and Editor of the *Political Quarterly* since 1931, wrote the book *International Government* at the Webbs' instigation in 1916.

G. D. H. COLE, Chichele Professor of Social and Political Theory in the University of Oxford ; Chairman of the Fabian Society from 1939–46 and again from 1948.

KINGSLEY MARTIN, Editor of the *New Statesman and Nation* since 1931, was a close friend and frequent visitor to the Webbs at Passfield Corner.

EARLY DAYS

by

G. BERNARD SHAW AND EDITOR

I

EARLY DAYS

by G. BERNARD SHAW AND EDITOR

When I asked Bernard Shaw to contribute to this book, he replied in characteristic fashion that the whole project was impossible, that no sales could possibly recoup the publishers for their advance. He advised me to pay nothing at all, but to send to all the suggested authorities a questionnaire with a stamped addressed envelope for the reply ; and added

> "I did not discover Webb until he was a public man trying to ginger up the Labour Party to J. S. Mill's level. I do not think I can tell you anything printable about him that you do not know as well as I do. However, you can send me a questionnaire."

I sent the questionnaire, and reproduce it below with the replies and some supplementary notes. Its general purpose, I should add, was threefold : first, to extract some first-hand information from one of the very few people now living who knew Sidney Webb as a young man ; secondly, to obtain more light upon the political policy and methods of working of the early Fabians ; and thirdly, to get the opinion of the greatest living authority upon the greatest social partnership of our time.

Here is the result.

QUESTIONNAIRE

Q. 1. *When and how did you first meet Sidney ?*
What was the immediate impression he made on you ?

A. I think you will find this in my preface to Beatrice's book, *The Truth about Soviet Russia* (1942) :

[Following is the quotation :

"Sixty years ago, the Marxian shock was only beginning to operate in England. I had to read *Das Kapital* in a French

3

translation, there being no English version as yet. A new champion of the people, Henry Mayers Hyndman, had met and talked with Karl Marx. They quarrelled, as their habit was, but not before Hyndman had been completely converted by Marx ; so his Democratic Federation presently became a Social-Democratic Federation. Socialism, in abeyance since the slaughter of the Paris Commune in 1871, suddenly revived ; but Marx, its leader and prophet, died at that moment and left the movement to what leadership it could get.

Socialism was not a new thing peculiar to Marx. John Stuart Mill, himself a convert, had converted others, among them one very remarkable young man and an already famous elderly one. The elderly one was the great poet and craftsman William Morris, who, on reading Mill's early somewhat half-hearted condemnation of Communism, at once declared that Mill's verdict was against the evidence, and that people who lived on unearned incomes were plainly " damned thieves." He joined Hyndman, and when the inevitable quarrel ensued, founded the Socialist League.

The younger disciple had followed Mill's conversion and shared it. His name was Sidney Webb. He was an entirely un-assuming young Londoner of no extraordinary stature, guiltless of any sort of swank, and so naively convinced that he was an ordinary mortal and everybody else as gifted as himself that he did not suffer fools gladly, and was occasionally ungracious to the poor things.

The unassuming young cockney was in fact a prodigy. He could read a book as fast as he could turn the leaves, and re-member everything worth remembering in it. Whatever country he was in, he spoke the language with perfect facility, though always in the English manner. He had gone through his teens gathering scholarships and exhibitions as a child gathers daisies, and had landed at last in the upper division of the Civil Service as resident clerk in the Colonial Office. He had acquired both scholarship and administrative experience, and knew not only why reforms were desirable but how they were put into practice under our queer political system. Hyndman and his Democratic Federation were no use to him, Morris and his Socialist League only an infant school. There was no organisa-tion fit for him except the Liberal Party, already moribund, but still holding a front bench position under the leadership of Gladstone. All Webb could do was something that he was forbidden to do as a Civil Servant ; that is, issue pamphlets warning the Liberal Party that they were falling behind the times and even behind the Conservatives. Nevertheless he issued the pamphlets calmly. Nobody dared to remonstrate.

This was the situation when I picked him up at a debating society which I had joined to qualify myself as a public speaker. It was the year 1879, when I was twenty-three and he a year or two younger. I at once recognised and appreciated in him all the qualifications in which I was myself pitiably deficient. He was clearly the man for me to work with. I forced my acquaintance on him ; and it soon ripened into an enduring friendship. This was by far the wisest step I ever took. The combination worked perfectly."]

Q. 2. *Did you know his family ? Did he seem like a man who had a family ?*

A. Yes. He seemed like a man with a family because, his extraordinary ability apart, he was so completely a normal man. I knew the Keppel Street household : Sidney, Philip the collie dog, the father, an amiable and most respectable tax collector, the mother, socially extremely unpretentious with a tendency to address me as sir, and the sister, very plain and devoted to a woman friend. Charles, Sidney's elder brother, was in an India rubber business, married and out of the family. I saw nothing of him. Sidney's education in Germany must have cost his parents a good deal. Unpretentious as they were, they were essentially gentle. Webb *père* had been a volunteer, and something of a champion shot. Sidney, following his example, also volunteered and was qualified as a marksman, though he never afterwards handled a rifle. This is probably the least known and least expected incident in his career.

Q. 3. *Did he strike you as having friends, and a life of his own outside his work ?*

A. I never thought about whether he had friends or not. There was no reason to doubt that he was normal in this as in any other respect. Neither he nor I were sportsmen nor had any life apart from our work.

Q. 4. *How much were you and he together in the ensuing years ? i.e., did you play as well as work together, and at what ?*

A. We were together a good deal until my marriage. In the

interval between his marriage and mine I spent my holidays with them. This involved much bicycling with them until one day he fainted and fell off his machine, after which Beatrice never let him bicycle again. But being a tireless walker she kept him walking daily for exercise, and, incidentally, me too.

Q. 5. *Was Sidney a Socialist when you met him, or did you con-*
vert him?

If a Socialist, what kind of a Socialist? If not, what was
he politically?

A. I made him read Karl Marx after my own conversion. He probably got through the first volume of *Capital*, the only one then available, in an hour; for he was a miraculously quick reader. When I said " Well ? " he replied, " Scotland stands where it did," the only time I ever heard him quote Shakespeare. He was a disciple of Mill, and was saturated with Mill's demonstration that under private property and free contract everybody except the proprietors would be reduced to bare subsistence wages. Like Mill himself later on, and Morris, he concluded that Mill's anti-Communist verdict was against the evidence ; and, as an upper division civil servant, he saw that in State enterprise and owner-ship there was an alternative to Capitalism. He was therefore a ready-made Socialist, and had nothing to learn from Marx theoretically or from me. His later contribution to Socialist theory was his demonstration that interest is a form of rent and should be socialised as well as land. But he began politically as a Millite Liberal with pamphlets urging the conversion of the Liberal Party to Socialism, stressing the fact that there was no difference between the Liberal and Conservative programmes except that Randolph Churchill (Winston's father) had, as a Disraelian Tory Democrat, got ahead of the Liberals by advocating free education.

Q. 6. *Was he interested, then or thereafter, in other than Fabian*
brands of Socialism—e.g., Morris, Hyndman, Hardie
—or did he ignore or despise them? Had he read, or
did he read, Marx?

To what extent did his arrival in the Fabian Society have
an immediate effect on it?

A. Webb knew far too much about practical administration to imagine that societies like those of Hyndman and Morris, with their programme of enlisting members at a penny a week until they were numerous and rich enough to take the field and carry out a catastrophic revolution in one day, could come to anything. We were both strong on " the inevitability of gradualness." We were both at a loss for an organisation to join. We knew that we could collaborate at full speed solely with our own class and not with casual artisans and labourers with a different mental background and rooted class prejudice against us. A Scottish Rosminian philosopher named Davidson had formed a group of middle class suburban Utopians. When Davidson emigrated, the dominant personality among them was that of Hubert Bland, a Blackheath Tory Democrat and Coleridgian, with literary talent enough to end as a successful journalist-preacher. When the group proposed to found a colony in Brazil as a Fellowship of the New Life, and live on one another's passbooks, Bland revolted and formed a political group to stay at home and engage in political action. This he called The Fabian Society. It issued a leaflet entitled " Why Are the Many Poor ? " It fell into my hands, and the happy and clearly educated name Fabian suggested that this might be the society that Webb and myself were looking for. I joined ; took my place on the front bench at once ; and wrote two leaflets for it.

It was a silly business. They had one elderly retired workman. They had two psychical researchers : Edward Pease and Frank Podmore, for whom I slept in a haunted house in Clapham. There were anarchists, led by Mrs. Wilson, who would not hear of anything Parliamentary. There were young ladies on the look-out for husbands, who left when they succeeded. There were atheists and Anglo-Catholics. There was Bland's very attractive wife Edith Nesbit, who wrote verses in *The Weekly Dispatch* for half a guinea a week, and upset all the meetings by making scenes and pretending to faint. She became famous as a writer of fairy tales. Bland was in financial straits, militarist and very censorious, though he was living with two women besides his wife.

After about a year of this I made Webb join. I knew that what these people needed was *Facts for Socialists*, and that Webb alone could write it. Marx was at the back of this ; for I knew from my own experience that *Das Kapital* had changed the mind of Europe not by Marxist dialectics translated into a pseudo-Hegelian jargon that only philosophers could understand and nobody could read, but by the terrific battery of official facts dug out by Marx in the British Museum Reading Room from the reports of the factory inspectors.

It came off as I planned. Webb joined and wrote *Facts for Socialists*. He formed a Parliamentary League within the Society which soon enlisted the whole membership and revealed the secret that Mrs. Wilson's following of anarchists was imaginary. Then the Society became itself as you know it. Olivier joined in the wake of Webb. Wallas came later on, but was never quite comfortable, and finally resigned to write books and flourish as a University Extension lecturer. Olivier was taken away to British Honduras and Jamaica by the Colonial Office. But for a while Webb, Olivier, and Wallas were the Three Musketeers of Fabianism, with myself as D'Artagnan. Bland was hopelessly outmatched; and it taxed my diplomacy to the utmost to keep the peace between him and the musketeers, as it did long afterwards between the Webbs and G. D. H. Cole in his very combative phase of Guild Socialism.

In short, Webb and I made and led the Fabian N.E.P.; and as joint authors of *A Plan of Campaign for Labour* laid the foundation of the I.L.P. under Keir Hardie. I had to supply him with its programme.

Q. 7. *When you embarked on "Fabian Essays," were you intending to produce a classic, or merely a straight statement of principles? Did you realise, in effect, what you were doing?*

A. Read the first preface to the *Essays*. We were out for immediate propaganda, not for abstract planning.

[The 1889 preface to *Fabian Essays* says :

"The essays in this volume were prepared last year as a course of lectures for delivery before mixed audiences in London and the provinces. They have been revised for publication, but not recast. The matter is put, not as an author would put it to a student, but as a speaker with only an hour at his disposal has to put it to an audience. Country readers may accept the book as a sample of the propaganda carried on by volunteer lecturers in the workmen's clubs and political associations of London. Metropolitan readers have the advantage of making themselves independent of the Press critic by getting face to face with the writers, stripping the veil of print from their personality, cross-examining, criticising, calling them to account amid surroundings which inspire no awe, and before the most patient of audiences. Any Sunday paper which contains a lecture list will show where some, if not all, of the seven essayists may be heard for nothing ; and on such occasions questions and discussions form part of the procedure.

The projection and co-ordination of these lectures is not the work of any individual . . . The writers are all Social-Democrats, with a common conviction of the necessity of vesting the organisation of industry and the material of production in a State identified with the whole people by complete Democracy. But that conviction is peculiar to no individual bias ; it is a Capitol to which all roads lead ; and at least seven of them are represented in these *Fabian Essays* ; so that the reader need not fear oppression here, any more than in the socialised State of the future, by the ascendancy of one particular cast of mind.

There are at present no authoritative teachers of Socialism. The essayists make no claim to be more than communicative learners."]

Q. 8. *Why did the Society wait until the end of* 1888, *when it was nearly five years old, before producing the " Essays " ?*

A. A senseless question. Why did we wait ten minutes ? Why did we not wait ten years ? We waited until we were ready.

Q. 9. *Why did the work of the Society cost so much less, right up to* 1914, *than it does today ?*

A. We began with no money at all except what we could extract from our own pockets : say £40 a year and no bank account. For everything beyond our own work we had to wait until the I.L.P. brought the trade unions in. When Keir Hardie chucked me out of the Labour Representation Committee, and Pease, whom he tolerated as harmless, told me triumphantly that the opulent Miners' Federation had joined and enriched us, I said " Yes ; but if the trade unions pay the piper the Socialists will no longer call the tune."

[On this one point, and on this alone, Shaw only answered half

my question. He showed why it was better for a young organisation of opinion not to have a large income contributed by out-
siders, but to rely upon the unpaid services of its own members.
(For some years, the Fabian Society had no paid servants at all ;
it then gave a salary of a pound a week to Edward Pease as General
Secretary.[1]) What he did not explain was how the members of the
Society were able to give so much unpaid time to the work ; in
one year there were recorded fifty-seven meetings of the Executive
Committee, the members of which were also engaged in writing, lecturing, reading and criticising pamphlets, advising and answering
questions—as well as in earning their own livings. Beatrice Webb,
we know, had an independent income ; but not so the others, who
managed somehow to do, or get done, for nothing, the work which
under modern conditions involves the Fabian Society of today in
a basic salary bill of comparatively enormous size. It is not merely
a question of increased prices ; it would be impossible nowadays
even to start, let alone to carry on, a Fabian Society for twenty
times the £40 mentioned by Shaw. The cause is partly, no doubt,
the much more strenuous working day now " enjoyed " by the
upper strata of professional—the Civil Servant who, like the
fountains in Trafalgar Square, " played every day from ten to
four " is a thing of the past ; and partly to the immense increase
in knowledge and *expertise*, which makes the formulation of
detailed schemes of policy a much more formidable job. But it
would have been interesting to have had the comment of one who
served in the early care-free days.   M.I.C.]

Q. 10. *Why does early Fabian literature contain so little
      reference to Joseph Chamberlain ? Wasn't the
      " Unauthorised Programme " (1885) very much
      of a Fabian policy ? Did you regard him as a rival,
      or a dangerous influence ?*

A.   Why should they refer to Chamberlain any more than to
Balfour or Randolph Churchill or Asquith or any other of the
pre-Marxist figureheads ? Ruskin had declared that Gladstone
and Disraeli had no more importance for him than two old bag-
pipes whistling in the wind. Beatrice in her girlhood had some
private relations with Chamberlain which her *Diaries* may reveal.

[1]See p. 18.

But you must bear in mind that she did not come into the Society until years after it was in full sail, and that she began with an intense contempt for it as a rabble of silly suburban faddists.

Q. 11. *In 1891, in the manifesto " To Your Tents, O Israel,"*
        you and Sidney proclaimed that the existing parties
        were useless and that the working classes would have
        to form their own. Why, then, did Sidney turn back
        to " permeation " and continue with it for so many
        years ?

A.   There was no turning back. The organisation of the Labour interest as a political party in no way suspended nor reversed the necessity for permeating all parties with the Socialist outlook. This was the point on which we were opposed by Blatchford and the supporters of the Manchester Fourth Clause which excluded and ostracised all Conservatives and Liberals. At the initial I.L.P. Conference in Bradford I defeated Blatchford on this question, though he had all the applause and I most of the votes.

[Shaw's answer to this question is a marvel of brevity. I have ventured to supplement it with the following quotation, taken from a 1906 reply of the Fabian Executive Committee to the campaign of H. G. Wells and his friends, which explains more fully the official Fabian view on both " permeation " and the young Labour Party. The document is unsigned ; but the style seems to me so unmistakable as to justify its inclusion. M.I.C.

"When we first began to try and permeate Parliament in 1885, there was no separate Labour Party there : the Liberals were in opposition, and the Conservatives in office. Now, Permeation as applied to Parliament means wire-pulling the Government in order to get Socialistic measures passed, and stimulating the Opposition to denounce the Government for neglecting the grievances of the people. All parties are revolutionary in Opposition. Therefore the Permeation of the Opposition is a far more public and clamorous affair than the wire-pulling of the Government, which must necessarily be carefully concealed not only from its party but as far as possible from the Government itself. Thus in the 1885–92 Parliament our Permeation of the Government was represented by the County Government Act, in which our hand was not seen, whereas our Permeation of the Opposition was represented by the Newcastle Programme. Now it was perfectly well known to us that the Liberal leaders resisted with all their might the foisting of this programme on the National Liberal Federation by Fabians who had joined the Liberal Federations in all directions with this object. But without the Newcastle Programme they would have been defeated : as it was, they scraped through with a very small majority. Having scraped through, they promptly threw over the Programme. We had foreseen that they would do this. Our plan was to use their disregard of the Programme and their breach of its pledges to Labour, as a proof of the need for an Independent Labour Party. Accordingly, in 1894, we unmasked our battery and delivered the most smashing attack on the Liberal Party that has ever come from the Labour side. A storm of denunciation of us as traitors and Tories burst on us from the Liberal Party and Press. . . .

This kind of Permeation was abandoned thirteen years ago, when it had served its turn ; and since then there has never been the faintest suggestion of its revival. Its purpose, which was achieved with the most astonishing completeness, was to force a number of Socialist and Labour measures into a Parliamentary programme ; to win an election on them ; and then, on their being dropped by the victorious party the moment they got into power, to use that as a proof that only a new Labour party, entirely independent of the Liberals and Conservatives, could possibly carry out such a programme. The virtual repudiation of the Newcastle Programme by the Liberals ; the subsequent attack on them by the Fabians with the cry 'To your tents, O Israel ! ' ; and the publication by the Society of a detailed electoral Plan of Campaign for Independent Labour at the polls, was planned and foreseen by us from the beginning. After the publication of the Plan of Campaign, we had no further use for the Liberal and Radical Associations ; and we need hardly add that they had no further use for us. Our cards were on the table then ; and from that time our business was to get our Plan of Campaign carried out, leaving the Liberals to get along as best they could without the ideas they had proved themselves incapable of assimilating. We won the 1892 election for them : they lost the subsequent elections by themselves ; and when 1906 came, Independent Labour was at last fairly in the field, organised by a Labour Representation Committee which had come into existence partly on our initiative, and on which the Fabian Society was from the first represented."]

Q. 12. *Did you foresee the Webb marriage?*

A. I foresaw it. Sidney used to come out in spots when he fell in love, which he did first with a lady who did not reciprocate and married a politician named Duncan Grant. When Sidney recovered from this infatuation he was heart-free for a while ; and then it was Beatrice. She quite deliberately sampled the Fabians as possible husbands by inviting them down to Gloucester for week-ends one after another. I refused, alleging facetiously that I could not afford the journey, really because I had discovered that Sidney was in love with her and I would not take a chance of cutting him out. After that she thoroughly disliked me ; and it is enormously to her credit that she forced herself to have me in the house because I was Sidney's loyalest and most useful friend. But we soon became the best of friends, though to the end nothing annoyed her so much as being suspected of any sexual attachment to me.

Q. 13. *What difference did it make to Sidney's activities or ideas? Did Beatrice's private income and higher social provenance have any effect in withdrawing Sidney from Fabian " comradeship? "*

A. None whatever. Neither of them had the least taint of snobbery. Beatrice really liked hobnobbing with trade union secretaries over their pipes and drinks.

Q. 14. *Do you think that their individual contributions to The Partnership can be separately valued? If so, what were they?*

A. No. It was a perfect collaboration. But until Beatrice's diary is published nobody can pretend to answer.

Q. 15. *What do you, looking back, believe to have been their greatest contribution to (a) the thought of their time (b) the political and social organisation of their time? i.e., on what would an intelligent historian of 1980 lay most stress?*

A. I cannot tell you anything about 1980, nor can anyone else. Like everyone else, the Webbs had their limitations ; but they were limitations not of ignorance of the things they did not write about, but of time to concern themselves about them. *The History of Trade Unionism* and its sequel *Industrial Democracy* with its minimum wage conclusion were epoch making. Their death blow to the Poor Law (Beatrice did the fighting) was immensely important. Meanwhile their historical investigation of local government went on. Finally, the book on Russia proved that they had all along been far more deep in the Socialist faith than those who classed them as bourgeois. But with such a record to choose from it is quite impossible to say what they will be most and best remembered by when we are all dead.

This is the best I can do with your questionnaire.

G.B.S. 1st May, 1948.
To MARGARET COLE.

WEBB AND THE FABIAN SOCIETY

by

EDWARD R. PEASE

II

WEBB AND THE FABIAN SOCIETY

by EDWARD R. PEASE

Writing in my ninety-first year, unable to leave home in order to consult records in the Fabian Office, I can only rely on a second-rate memory and on my *History of the Fabian Society*, the only source available. This is my excuse for any errors of fact which may be found.

When Sidney Webb was born on the 13th July, 1859, Bernard Shaw was three years old, I was a year and a half, and Beatrice Potter a few weeks younger than I. Only in legal infancy and in second childhood do such small differences in age count for anything. Shaw came to a Fabian meeting at 17 Osnaburgh Street, on the 16th May, 1884, when the Society was four months old ; he had, I believe, made the acquaintance of Webb at a debating society, and on the 20th March, 1885, Webb, who had probably attended one or more meetings previously, read a paper on " The Way Out " : he was elected a member on the 1st of May following.

The infant Fabian Society passed through three phases. At first it was ethical, sentimental and vague, thinking of " reconstructing society in accordance with the highest moral possibilities." Frank Podmore began pointing out the right road, and then came Shaw, still abstractions salted with wit. Lastly came Webb, with his passion for precise facts, and he led the Society to the path which it has followed ever since. His first Fabian Tract, *Facts for Socialists*, has gone through sixteen editions and after sixty years still sells.

About this period, Webb was something of a geologist, the only case, so far as I know, in which he was interested in any form of " natural " science. I do not think that he ever spoke to me, then or afterwards, on the subject, or showed any interest in it when we were in America : I know because when I was working as a cabinet maker in Newcastle in 1887, I made to his order, a geological cabinet. Galton, who was the Webbs' secretary after their marriage, tells me that the cabinet was gradually emptied of fossils, which were thrown away, and was filled with papers. When the Webbs gave up their house in Grosvenor Road, Sidney gave the cabinet to the Fabian Society, and it is still in the Fabian Office.

In the autumn of 1888 he and I went for a three months' tour in the United States and Canada. We sailed in the *Queen Elizabeth* of that time on her second voyage ; one engine failed and the crossing took ten days. We often played chess, both then and on railway journeys ; both of us were mere drawing-room performers with no knowledge of books or openings, and strange to say, Webb played no better than I did ; we ended up all square. One would have thought that he would be a born chess-player, and the game would have just suited his make of mind. I never heard that he played any other game.

We went to learn what the Americans were thinking about social problems. We took out a vast pile of introductions, mostly his, and travelled about nearly all the time in the area between Chicago, Richmond and Quebec, calling on people in one city after another. America, we thought, was then a generation behind Europe, but that of course was sixty years ago. He made all the plans and I kept the accounts.

In 1890 I had married and returned to London and was appointed Secretary to the tiny Fabian Society at £50 a year for half-time. At the members' meeting this proposal was unexpectedly opposed by Mrs. Bland and her followers, who alleged that a paid secretary was undesirable. In his autobiography, H. G. Wells describes how in his time, about 1908, the Executive Committee was dominated by a feud between Bland and myself partly because Bland wanted to be paid secretary in my stead. Wells spends more than a page on explaining how " the larger purposes of the Wallases, Webbs and Shaw had to defer continually " to this Bland v. Pease feud. It is all a case of the fertility of Wellsian imagination. For a few weeks there was a slight coolness owing to the way in which Mrs. Bland acted in the matter. And that is all. The statement that it was remembered for eighteen years is fiction. I am sure that Bland never wished to be paid secretary ; I never heard it suggested till I read it in Wells's autobiography ; the payment was far too small for him and he never took any interest in office work. All he ever did for twenty years in my time was to sign as many blank cheques as I asked for. He never looked at the accounts. There was no feud between Bland and the rest of us. He was a sound Socialist, but otherwise a Tory, and the rest of us were born Liberals. He was a little difficult, and a little of an outsider, but that is all there was to it.

Webb engaged me as his secretary for the other half of my time. He did not arrive at Whitehall until noon, and every morning I went to Park Village East, where he lived with his parents, to work with him. I did not feel then and I do not think now, that the work I did had any value to him or to anybody else. I think he made the plan in order to help the Fabian Society out of a difficulty. They could hardly engage me for half-time unless I had work for the other half, and I think the £50 Webb paid me was actually a gift to the Fabian Society. After a year the society paid me £100 a year for full time and I carried on its activities at my flat in Hyde Park Mansions.

Henry Hunt Hutchinson[1], I believe, started his career as an office boy, and although not a solicitor, ended it as clerk to the Justices of Derby. He was a great admirer of Herbert Spencer, a native of that town, and about the time of his retirement he read *Fabian Essays* when they first were published.

On the 16th June, 1890, he was elected a member of the Society, a matter of which Webb was hardly aware, although in the event it dominated some, and coloured much of the rest of his life. A few weeks later Hutchinson offered us £100 or £200, and approved of our proposal to spend it on lectures in the provinces. Webb, no doubt, took the lead in planning the successful and important "Lancashire Campaign," and gave many of the lectures.

About this time occurred one of the extremely few difficulties we had with Shaw. Hutchinson complained to the Society that Shaw did not answer his letters, no doubt about Spencerian doctrines; Shaw said he could not be bothered to write to the old fool. We urged him not to offend our benefactor, I think successfully, but perhaps this was the reason why Shaw was not one of Hutchinson's trustees.

About 1892, Hutchinson and his wife were living in London, and they used to come to little Fabian evening parties at our flat.

[1]See also Chapter IV.

Webb did not know him personally, and I think few if any of the rest of us made his acquaintance. The next thing that happened was that in 1894, he shot himself, and left a will appointing Webb his sole executor, leaving him the whole of his property, about £10,000, including his goods and chattels, and creating a trust of which Webb was to be chairman ; the others were his daughter Constance, De Mattos, William Clarke, and myself. He also left Webb £500 for the publication of his MSS. if Webb thought fit. Webb paid me £25 to examine and report on them. I think they were all about Herbert Spencer, and they appeared to me to be completely useless. Webb used some of the money to endow the Hutchinson Medal at the London School of Economics.

Webb found that Mrs. Hutchinson had only £100 a year and we agreed to his proposal to buy her an annuity of £100, partly because the will seemed to be unfair to her, partly because the family might very plausibly have contested it. In fact the family behaved with very great magnanimity in the matter and I do not think that they ever raised the slightest objection to Webb's management of their affairs. Moreover, Constance was apparently not quite happy over our small departure from her father's plans, and when she died about a year later, she left all her money, about £1,000, to Webb and me, thus almost exactly replacing what we had spent on the annuity.

Of the five trustees, Constance, I think, never attended a single meeting. De Mattos went to America and took no part in the trust. William Clarke was no good on committees ; he belonged to the class that attend seldom and late, go early, and sit in silence betweenwhiles. At first therefore the trust was managed by Webb as chairman and myself as secretary. The records are preserved in two big volumes now in the library of the London School of Economics.

One last word about the Hutchinson family. There were at least two sons besides Constance; one of them joined the Fabian Society, and many years later, when he was farming, he asked Webb to guarantee his overdraft. I agreed to come in and we had to pay up £300.

Webb's plan to use part of the fund for founding the London School of Economics was approved by Constance and also by the Fabian Executive and he acted with the friendly advice of Lord (then Mr.) Haldane ; about half the fund was spent on the School, and the other half went to the Society for provincial lectures and for book-boxes. It was to be expended in ten years but a little was left when the term expired. This was transferred to the Constance Hutchinson trustees for this reason.

Webb never quarrelled with anybody, but sometimes a few people were hostile to him. His rule was that enemies were better inside than outside : therefore Bland, who might have made trouble, was co-opted as a Hutchinson trustee and Ramsay MacDonald, when his colleague on the L.C.C., was put on the Technical Education Board, of which Webb was Chairman. Possibly MacDonald's long one-sided feud with Webb began because he was not appointed to a post in the London School of Economics. Graham Wallas covered the subjects for which MacDonald was fitted. MacDonald intrigued against Webb for years. He incited a person to allege that Webb was using public money, the grant of the Technical Education Board, to teach Socialism, and for this reason Wallas for years was paid his School of Economics salary by the Hutchinson Trust direct and not through the School. Fear of trouble from MacDonald made us technically close the fund at the expiry of ten years. Thirty years later another Fabian, a bachelor, left his property, several thousand pounds, to me and Webb for the Society ; this time therefore I took the lead and Webb duly signed on the dotted lines.

For the first fourteen years of the Labour Party, I represented the Fabian Society on the Executive Committee, and Webb took very little interest in it. Shaw was fond of saying that the Labour Party was not Socialist, and Webb, I think agreed with him, tho' I do not recollect his saying so. In this matter Shaw disregarded the Fabian doctrine laid down by him in the report to the International Socialist Congress of 1896. " No person can obtain the support of the Fabian Society or escape its opposition merely by calling himself a Socialist or Social Democrat." The Labour Party at that time did not call itself Socialist, and Shaw attached too much importance to the name. In fact it was from the first purely Fabian in its policy, both in the measures it advocated and in its tolerance of Liberalism. It was then deliberately maintaining the Liberal Government in office, and on one occasion it actually voted against a resolution of its own—I think about wages at Woolwich—because the Tories intended to vote for it, and the Government might have been defeated.

In 1914, William Sanders succeeded me both in the Fabian Society and in the Labour Party, and one day in the autumn of 1915, he told me at the office that he had been called up, and must resign from the Labour Party Executive. By the rules at that time when a seat on the executive fell vacant, the executive committee of the body to which the late member belonged, appointed his successor. I said to Sanders at once, " we must get Webb to take your place." So we promptly went to 41 Grosvenor Road, and persuaded Webb to accept nomination. Of course the executive gladly appointed him, and thence followed much. I consider this my second-best day's work. My best was when I invited the future Fabians to meet at my rooms.

It is not for me to describe how Webb took the lead in re-moulding the Labour Party, both in its constitution, and in its published policy, so that it became at last in words as it always had been in deeds, a Socialist Party.[1] How widely his action was approved in the Party, is shown by the fact that in one annual election of the Executive Committee he obtained the highest vote, no doubt partly on account of his conduct of the miners' case on the Royal Commission on Coal Mines. During the first World War there was a large War Emergency Committee representing the Labour Party, Trade Unions, Co-operative Societies, Socialist Societies, and in fact the whole of the working class. We had to appoint a small sub-committee for some important purpose. Each of us wrote a list of half a dozen names. When these were examined every list contained Webb's name, the next was a long way down.

In the first thirty years of the Fabian Society, Webb dominated the Executive Committee, not because he was in the least dictatorial, but because he was always wise and right. All the initiative came from him. Shaw drafted most of the documents, but, if my memory is not at fault, Webb proposed the plans. Of the first sixty Fabian Tracts he wrote twenty-five. I can recollect only one occasion on which he failed to get his way. There was a joint committee of the three Socialist Societies, the I.L.P., the Social-Democratic Federation and the Fabian Society, formed to pre-

[1] See Chapter XI.

vent clashes in elections. Our Society was out of place because we did not as a Society run candidates, nor did we pretend to control our members in this or any other respect. Webb wanted to withdraw, but the Executive voted against him. At the next meeting of the Joint Committee the S.D.F. said they would withdraw if the Fabians remained, so we walked out, leaving the other two in possession of our offices where the meeting was held.

Webb was a member of the Fabian Executive from 1886–1935, a much longer period than any other member except myself. He was at the head of the poll, at most, perhaps at all the elections, and he was a thoroughly regular attender. Indeed he was an ideal committee man. As I wrote in my *History*, if he were a member of a committee, it may be assumed, unless there is evidence to the contrary, that any report or resolution adopted was drafted by him. He was at his best in committee work : he was not a great orator, and in his later years his voice was weak, but I do not recollect that this was the case in earlier days. He was of course an admirable lecturer, and spoke with very few notes. I remember his once saying to me, " I have to lecture tonight, I can't at the moment remember what it is about," and that not because, as in the case of some lecturers, the lecture, whatever the title, was always the same. His lectures were always full of matter, admirably expressed.

He was a very easy person to work with. For something like thirty years I worked with him, or, when he dominated the Fabian Executive, in a sense under him, and I cannot recollect that he ever complained or scolded, or grumbled, or interfered. He sometimes devised schemes for increasing the Fabian income. One was a suggestion that members might properly pay as subscriptions half of one per cent of their incomes. He at this time paid £7 7s. od., and so I infer that his family income was about £1,400 a year.

The Fabian Executive was a wonderfully friendly and united body. In all my fifty years' experience of it there was nothing that can be called a quarrel, and very few resignations on differences of opinion, and this harmony was largely I think due to Webb's good temper and persistence in conciliation. Annie Besant left the Society because she became a Theosophist, and regarded poverty and misfortune as punishment for sin in a former incarnation. Graham Wallas dropped out really because he disliked Webb's tolerance of religion in the Church of England schools. Webb proposed to improve the education in these schools by grants of public money, regarding good education as more important than anything else. Webb, as far as I can judge, was quite uninterested in religion, having none of his own, and feeling no concern to interfere with that of other people. Wallas was an ardent secularist. Ramsay MacDonald and J. F. Green resigned because the Society—not only in this case the Executive— refused to pass a resolution on the Boer War. The Society did not like resolutions opposing or advocating this, that, or the other. They involve futile discussion, and perhaps disputes, and they achieve nothing. (By an odd coincidence, twenty years later, Green, an ardent supporter of the Government in the first World War, defeated MacDonald at Leicester, and turned him out of Parliament because he—MacDonald—was opposed to that war also.) We were greatly rejoiced to get MacDonald out of the Society. Somebody said that the Boer War was a great evil, but there was one compensation : for us, it got rid of MacDonald. The only other resignation was that of G. D. H. Cole, who left because we would not alter the Fabian Basis, in order to suit the Guild Socialists. Years later he gave up that heresy and was brave enough to say publicly that he was wrong and the Old Gang, led by Webb, was right. Guild Socialism infringed the rule, first laid down by the Webbs, that " Industry must be controlled by the consumer, and not by the producer."

Webb was one of the few people who think for themselves ; a dangerous thing to do. It is given only to a very few to add more than a tiny brick to the great edifice of knowledge. Most original thought is rubbish. Even very great thinkers often adulterate their wisdom with occasional folly. August Comte, a philosopher highly regarded by J. S. Mill, and by many of Webb's generation, though not, so far as I know, by Webb himself, proposed not only a priesthood of the religion of humanity, but government, if my memory serves, by six bankers. Webb has often been compared to Bentham. That wisest of thinkers suggested putting skeletons along country house drives, as memorials of the dead, said that punishments for crime should be such as would give pleasure to the community, and wished civil service posts to be sold by auction. Neither Webb nor the Webbs ever proposed anything silly, and only one of their many projects has so far proved to be abortive. This was their plan for duplicate parliaments, a new one for industry, and the old one for the rest of the business of the State.[1] Many no doubt regard their enthusiasm for Russian Communism as excessive and uncritical; but when they wrote their massive book, Trotsky's policy of capturing Europe for Communism was denounced as heresy, and it is only, for the most part, after the second World War, that the heresy has been transformed into Communist orthodoxy.

Webb's outstanding moral quality was modesty: he never talked in my hearing about Rosebery or Balfour or any of the other important people who consulted him; he never laid claim to be the founder of British Socialism, or the intellectual parent of the I.L.P. in the days of its political greatness; he liked to do things and write things, and did not care who took the credit. One curious example of his preference for privacy is that he never wrote to The *Times*. Some important people like this way of expressing their opinions or knowledge. G.B.S. appears at least once a month. I cannot recollect a single letter from Webb, and his name appeared seldom or never attached to collective letters. No doubt this reticence was a valuable asset. The people who sought his advice were aware that he would not give them away.

One of his chief gifts was the power of extremely rapid reading. He told me once that he had read through the *Encyclopaedia Britannica* for a prize offered by the proprietors: I think he came out sixth. When we were going to America he took from the steamer's library a big volume of a history of the United States, and read one volume a day; each of them would have taken me weeks. It is said that when he and Shaw took a holiday in Germany, Shaw had a book which lasted him throughout the tour: Webb read it whilst Shaw was writing a letter.

This is almost the only story I know about Webb, and hence it is not possible to make a biographical notice amusing. Stories arise when people do silly things, or wrong things or eccentric things, or even amusing things. Webb always did the right thing in the right way, and said the wise thing without circumlocution. This article is a long eulogy. Is there no other side to be recorded?

[1]See pp. 95 and 275.

B*

Had he no faults, no weaknesses ? He had limitations. So far as I know he took little or no interest in any form of aesthetics, or even in natural as opposed to social science. But I cannot think of any moral faults or weaknesses which can be attributed to him. I knew him for sixty years, and for much of that period had constant dealings with him, and if anyone says that I seem to regard him as a perfect character, I will not gainsay it. He had his reward ; he was the only English social reformer who had the good fortune to live to see his policy adopted by his country and nearly all his proposals actually embodied in Acts of Parliament.

INVESTIGATING WITH THE WEBBS

by

F. W. GALTON

III

INVESTIGATING WITH THE WEBBS

by F. W. GALTON

It was my good fortune to be closely associated with Sidney and Beatrice Webb from the year 1891, before their marriage, until 1898 when they had completed and published their first two joint books the *History of Trade Unionism* and *Industrial Democracy*. In 1898 they left this country for a tour round the world, and my direct and personal work for them came to an end. During the seven years or so in which I was so closely associated with this remarkable couple, I had ample opportunities of watching them at work and noticing the methods they employed. Some account of these at first hand may prove of interest to all who knew the Webbs or have read their books or followed their work in other fields.

First, however, I ought perhaps to explain how I came to be so closely associated with them in the early years of their partnership, as it throws some light on the very methodical plans they had made even before their marriage. In 1890 I was a young man working as a journeyman at my trade as a heraldic and general engraver and metal worker, for the employer to whom I had previously served seven years apprenticeship. On coming " out of my time " as the saying is, I had joined the little Trade Union in the trade and was shortly afterwards elected its secretary. At that time Socialism was very much " in the air," it was in fact the *dernier cri* of the dying century and like many other young fellows I was caught up in the new ideas, largely through reading Henry George's well-known book *Progress and Poverty*. At the Working Men's College, then in Great Ormond Street, which I had joined as a student some years before, a group of young men had formed a college Socialist Society in which I took an active part. I had also joined various existing Socialist Societies, but had found the talks and discussions at their meetings too ill-informed and impractical to be of use, and in fact to lead nowhere at all.

Then I was introduced by a friend to the Fabian Society and

heard Bernard Shaw and Sidney Webb speak and realised that this was what I had been looking for. Shaw of course fascinated me with his wit and audacity, but it was Webb who really impressed me most. Early in January, 1892, Webb came to the Working Men's College to lecture to the little Socialist group which had now been reorganised as the Working Men's College Group of the Fabian Society. The subject he chose for his talk was " Some problems of Trade Unionism," which indicates that he and Miss Potter, as Mrs. Webb then was, had already begun to plan the work they intended to do together. As I was the only secretary of a Trade Union in the group, I was elected chairman for the meeting and this was my first personal contact with Webb. A few days later I was invited by Graham Wallas to supper at his rooms in Great Ormond Street, to meet Miss Potter of whom I had heard and whose book on the *Consumers' Co-operative Movement* I had read. We had a very agreeable evening, Shaw and Webb and another young Fabian friend joining in a lively talk. The following week, after attending a Fabian meeting, Webb spoke to me and asked me to walk home with him to his mother's house in Park Village East, Regents Park, where he was living at that time. On the way he told me of his engagement to Miss Potter, which I had already guessed, that he was leaving the Colonial Office to take up a career as writer and in political life, and invited me to become their secretary and assistant in the work they proposed to undertake on the *History of Trade Unionism*. As I had already made up my mind to get out of my trade, and had in fact begun to find employment in writing for the press and was getting known in Fleet Street, I was glad to accept the invitation and arranged to begin the new work almost immediately.

So I began my new work at the end of January, 1892. My first task was to assist in Webb's election campaign for the London County Council in which he was one of the Progressive candidates for Deptford. He was duly elected in March and so began his long service of eighteen years on the L.C.C. For the next few years my time was taken up with a regular routine. In the early spring I went off into the country making my headquarters in one of the large cities and interviewing the local trade union officials, collecting any kind of printed matter they issued, attending meetings of local branches and Trades Councils wherever I could get permission to do so, and writing full reports of all these activities. The printed matter after perusal was all sent to Webb. My reports of interviews and meetings were all written on sheets of paper of uniform size with strict attention to the necessity of using separate sheets for separate subjects. This paper was all supplied to me ready for use and I was enjoined to see that matters relating to, say, the history of a Union should not be mixed up with matters relating to trade practices, regulations, etc. My instructions in this and other details of the work came from Miss Potter at first as I saw and heard from Webb only occasionally.

My first visit was to Manchester where the Co-operative Union lent me the use of a room in their building as an office. Miss Potter came down to that city several times in the three months or so I spent there, staying usually in apartments in Ackers Street off the Oxford Road. Here she entertained to dinner some of the leading officials of the Cotton Trade Unions, and of the Co-operative Movement; and attended meetings of the Textile Workers' Unions and of the Manchester Trades Council. She came also to my office and was able to superintend my work and to give me some hints and directions as to its improvement. The Webbs were married in July, 1892, and subsequently they came together to Birmingham and Nottingham when I was in those cities in 1893, staying at hotels. It is perhaps worth noting as a sign of the change in manners since then that on such occasions, when I had been to lunch with them at their hotel, they always retired to their bedroom after lunch for Mrs. Webb to smoke a cigarette! For a woman to smoke in any of the public rooms at that time was considered highly improper and would have labelled her as " fast " at once.

After their marriage they lived for a few months in a furnished flat in Fitzjohn's Avenue, Hampstead, and in the autumn of 1892, when I returned to London from the provinces for the winter, I spent some time there. However, Mrs. Webb was busy house-hunting and work on the book did not make much progress that autumn. After deciding to take the house at 41 Grosvenor Road, Westminster, which afterwards became so well known, there was the business of furnishing it and moving into it. All this was accomplished about the end of 1892 and then began the regular work of writing the books, which I must try to describe.

The house was not a large one. There were the usual kitchens in the basement ; on the ground floor a single large room overlooking the river which served as dining room and workshop. On the first floor a similar room for rest, receptions, etc. On the half-landing between the two floors was a small room, looking out to the back on a builders' yard, with writing desk for use and its walls lined with nests of drawers of various sizes. This was my workshop for the autumn and winter months when in London. Here all the papers and documents were filed away under various headings and it was my business to keep them in order, to produce the necessary documents about any particular trade union or industry as and when required, and to replace them in proper order when done with. The system worked quite satisfactorily on the whole, but could not have done so without Webb's remarkable memory. He had read or perused everything in the files and had an almost uncanny way of recalling where and about what trade union he had read and noticed some out of the way but relevant fact mentioned, or some pertinent idea referred to and explained.

Frequently during the autumn and winter months I went to breakfast with them at 8 a.m. in the dining room mentioned above. After breakfast, not a long or heavy meal, we all smoked a cigarette together and discussed the coming morning's work, while the table was cleared. By nine o'clock the Webbs had started to work, seated each at one end of the table facing one another with the necessary books and papers at hand. Meanwhile, I went up to my room and began to sort out any fresh documents required for the day's work which I took down to them. Unless required to stay and discuss any points that arose I returned to my room to file away again any papers left over from the previous day's work. Very often, however, I was called down to join in the discussion with them and to help in elucidating points in my reports which were vague or inconclusive. Sometimes these discussions became so interesting and absorbing that, even in winter, the fire in the room would go out and have to be relighted by one of the servants.

As to the actual writing of the various chapters and the book, when, after discussion, the general scheme had been settled upon, this was done entirely by Webb in the large flowing handwriting which he wrote with great speed. Mrs. Webb disliked the labour of writing and in any case her script was so bad as to be practically unreadable. As to the plans evolved for the outline of the book, and for its separate chapters, however, Mrs. Webb was fertile in suggestions and often made really brilliant ones which were adopted and used in the book being written. She had a very considerable faculty for seeing how questions stood towards each other, and of recognising a common thread of use between things and ideas apparently unrelated to each other. And she could, and often did, make suggestions, sometimes founded on abstract ideas, which threw light on obscure points in trade union regulations and practices. When she had made a suggestion of this kind it was discussed by us all three together, and if accepted by Webb, and the evidence available appeared to support it, he would then proceed to write the chapter or section of the book with his usual speed.

Once written and completed the work was seldom subjected to much further revision. They would finally read it over again together and sometimes get Shaw and Graham Wallas to read particular chapters and make use of their suggestions and criticisms. But in the main when once written and read over by themselves the section was put aside as complete and done with, and the next one began and carried through in the same systematic and workmanlike way.

The discussions which arose about particular sections of the book were carried on in a lively and often high-spirited way. I remember one occasion when Mrs. Webb had made a particularly bold and somewhat far-fetched suggestion which Webb had smilingly dismissed, I ventured to quote the well-known remark by John Morley that " Abstract thinking is thinking withdrawn from the concrete and particular facts. But the abstract thinker should not withdraw too far."[1] Mrs. Webb laughed gaily at this sally, and even Sidney so far unbent as to chuckle quietly to himself for some time afterwards.

Work was interrupted at one o'clock for lunch, again a light and not very prolonged occasion. Afterwards the inevitable cigarette and then Webb would go off to a meeting at the L.C.C. or of some other of the numerous bodies and committees through

[1]In the essay on " Maine on Popular Government," republished in *Studies in Literature*, pp. 129—130. Macmillan & Co., 1890.

which he was promulgating his Fabian ideas. Mrs. Webb generally rested a while and then went for a walk or to call on some of her many friends and relations. They seldom if ever worked on their books after lunch.

So far as the *History of Trade Unionism* was concerned everything was carried through rapidly and it was published in 1894, less than two years after its inception and the beginning of the inquiries. On the other hand their second book *Industrial Democracy* proved a longer and harder task and was not published until 1897. Many people still consider it the best of the books they wrote, with its clear and precise analysis and statement of some of the most complicated and obscure problems and practises of British Trade Unions.

Of the two of them engaged in their work Mrs. Webb with her striking, rather aristocratic and somewhat Jewish appearance, was the more prominent. Besides possessing great industry and determination, and a keen intellect she had a talent amounting almost to genius for devising plans and schemes. This faculty she no doubt inherited from her father who was similarly endowed, as she describes him in her autobiography. In his case of course this talent was used to promote business interests and money-making, but Mrs. Webb turned it to social and political questions. Like her father also, as she describes him, she was not so good at carrying out the plans she evolved, or perhaps, to put it another way, she was more interested in their inception than in their execution. Hence it was a remarkable stroke of luck that through the chance remark of a mutual friend she was led to meet Sidney Webb and to marry him. He possessed in a high degree the very quality in which she was deficient—great executive power and driving force—and thus by their combination the plans often devised by her in collaboration with him were carried to fruition in many directions.

In their joint enterprises, the long list of books published, and other directions Mrs. Webb was largely responsible for the plans and so to speak the architecture, while all the actual construction was done by Sidney. The general plan and outlines were of course discussed by them jointly, and sometimes with others also, but Mrs. Webb contributed most to the general scheme and outline so far as my experience went. Seeing and hearing them at work from day to day on one or other of their books it is difficult to decide on the separate contributions they made to it. Their minds worked so closely and harmoniously together that it is hard to disentangle the parts played by each of them individually in the final result.

John Stuart Mill has described in his autobiography in clear and precise terms the somewhat similar relations that existed between himself and his wife in the writing of some of his books. I once sent a copy of the paragraph to Sidney Webb saying it seemed to me to fit their case also. He spoke to me about it later and did not demur to what I had said, though at the same time strongly deprecating any attempt to write biographical notes or details about them and their private lives. Those who have read Mrs. M. A. Hamilton's book about the Webbs will recall the statement in the preface that " On undertaking this work, an inquiry was addressed to them as to whether they could bear the idea, the reply to which was that ' They would rather not have a book written about them, but if it had to be done they did not mind.' "[1]

What Mill actually said on the subject seems so pertinent and so much to the point that it is worth quoting here. He wrote :—

> "When two persons have their thoughts and speculations completely in common ; when all subjects of intellectual or moral interest are discussed between them in daily life . . . when they set out from the same principles and arrive at their conclusions by processes pursued jointly, it is of little consequence in respect to the question of originality which of them holds the pen ; the one who contributes least to the composition may contribute most to the thought ; the writings which result are the joint product of both and it must often be impossible to disentangle their respective parts and affirm that this belongs to one and that to the other."[2]

This seems to me a fair and precise summary of the working of the partnership between Sidney and Beatrice Webb as I saw it.

Mrs. Webb had not the physical strength and stamina of Sidney. She was more easily tired and needed change of occupation and interest. She threw herself strenuously into such activities as those

[1] *Sidney and Beatrice Webb.* A study in Contemporary Biography. By Mary Agnes Hamilton. Sampson Low, 1932.
[2] J. S. Mill. *Autobiography.* The World's Classics, 1924, p. 204.

of the Fabian Society, the founding of the *New Statesman*, the work of the London School of Economics, and above all with the work of the Royal Commission on the Poor Law. This body presented exactly the right mechanism for the display of her talent of planning.

As to Sidney and his methods of work many of those who co-operated with him in the various public duties he undertook will have vivid recollections. He possessed a remarkable memory so that after once reading a book or memorandum he could remember it and where he had read it instantaneously. With this he combined a great faculty for marshalling all he knew or had ever heard or read of any subject almost at a moment's notice. This combination of qualities made him a most successful examinee, and it is not surprising he should have passed any examination and carried off any awards or degrees for which he entered. It made him a most interesting companion for a walk as he could and did pour out a stream of information on any topic that happened to arise. It also made him a very formidable member of any committee or body and he could generally succeed in persuading his colleagues that his view of any subject under discussion was the correct one.

Besides all this, he had a very great faculty for devising a form of words which embodied the general view of a committee or meeting, a most valuable gift for anyone engaged in public affairs, and one not sufficiently recognised. It has been said, and it is safe to assume that practically all the decisions on important matters reached by any body at which he he was a member were in form drafted or suggested by him. This faculty is no doubt what the late Professor W. E. H. Lecky was thinking of when he referred to Webb as :

" A plausible writer and adroit tactician, who, in the London County Council and elsewhere has played a considerable part in contemporary English Socialism."[1]

Apart from these, so to speak, public qualities, Webb possessed very great power of self-control and was scarcely ever excited, or even ruffled. In the fifty years or so in which I was in active association with him in various political and other movements I

[1]W. E. H. Lecky. *Democracy and Liberty*. Vol. II, p. 375. Popular ed. 1918.

can only recall two or three occasions on which he showed any sign of being annoyed or flurried. I never heard him speak an angry word, and he was a model of courtesy and kindness to all with whom he came in contact regardless of rank or position. It was a great privilege to know them both and to work with them from day to day for five or more years was a liberal education in itself. Perhaps I ought to add in conclusion that while I carefully respected their wishes not to have articles about their personal and private lives written, now that they are gone I feel it is really a public duty in those who knew them to describe to the best of their ability the kind of people they were, and the methods they pursued in the many fields of work they cultivated.

THE LONDON SCHOOL OF ECONOMICS
AND THE UNIVERSITY OF LONDON

by

LORD BEVERIDGE

IV

THE LONDON SCHOOL OF ECONOMICS AND THE UNIVERSITY OF LONDON

by LORD BEVERIDGE

" The School of Economics is the favourite child of the Webbs." Most of us, whose own work has lain in the School, and who are old enough to have known the Webbs there, have said something like this at one time or another. We felt like that, and I believe that we were right.

The School of Economics came in the early years of the great partnership beginning in 1892, when both the partners were in their thirties, making through the *History of Trade Unionism* and *Industrial Democracy* their first large contribution to building social science on a new basis. They had turned from theory to description and analysis of institutions. They turned as deliberately from central organs of Government to examination of voluntary and, later, of local institutions, as important as central government in their influence on the lives of individual citizens, though hitherto little regarded by students of politics. What they were doing thus personally, as researchers and writers, to place social science on a new basis, they set out at the same time to make possible for others, by founding the London School of Economics and Political Science. The School was a way to the object which always lay nearest to the hearts of the Webbs, the bringing about of improvement in social conditions, not by revolution or violence, but by application of reason and knowledge to human affairs.

The foundation of the School at the time it happened was made possible by an accident.[1] In August, 1894, the Webbs were staying

---

[1] In what is said here as to its early days I have drawn freely on the interesting article on the School prepared by Professor Hayek for its Jubilee in 1945 and printed in *Economica* of February, 1946. I have had access also to early Calendars and Prospectuses in the School Archives. I have drawn largely on *Our Partnership* by Beatrice Webb (Longmans Green & Co., 1948). But I have made no attempt to write here a documented early history of the School. That would require not one chapter but many.

at Borough Farm near Milford in Surrey, with Bernard Shaw and Graham Wallas as visitors. The account given thirty years after by the last of these of what happened there is as follows :

> So many causes go to every effort that it is generally impossible to assign the invention of any important institution to a precise date. There is no such impossibility in the case of the School. It was invented at Borough Farm early in the morning of a certain day in August, 1894 . . . Mr. and Mrs. Webb, Mr. G. B. Shaw and I were staying at the little farm. The day before, Mr. Webb learnt that, by the will of Mr. Henry Hutchinson, he had been given the duty of directing the expenditure of a sum of money. He and Mrs. Webb woke up early, had a long discussion, and at breakfast told us that part of the money would be used to found a School in London on the lines of the *École Libre des Sciences Politiques* in Paris.

This account contributed by Graham Wallas to the Handbook of the Students' Union of the School in 1925 is printed in *Our Partnership* and therefore is clearly authentic.

The Hutchinson Bequest of about £10,000, noted by Beatrice Webb in her diary as "An odd adventure!", led to what she described as the "biggest single enterprise of Our Partnership."[1] The bequest itself and the use proposed for it were not free from difficulties. In the first place, as is stated in *Our Partnership*, the will, owing to its extreme informality, and the suicide of its author shortly after its signature, probably could have been upset if the testator's widow and children had chosen to dispute it. But, with a public or a family spirit which Beatrice Webb recognises, they with one accord demanded that the will should be carried out. In the second place, while the will gave discretion to Sidney Webb as to the manner of spending, it was to be spending for a named purpose. After making Sidney Webb and his daughter Constance executors and giving family legacies, the will proceeded :

> I request Webb to use not exceeding One hundred pounds in employing a literate person to examine such original manuscripts as I leave and if aught thereof is found worth publication after selection and free editing I devote not exceeding five

[1] *Our Partnership*, p. 84.

hundred pounds more to the effecting of that purpose and that if it may be under the auspices and for the benefit of the Fabian Society of London. I place my manuscripts of all sorts and my few books entirely at Webb's disposal for use distribution or destruction at my Cost. The Residue of my property I bequeath in trust and jointly to said Constance and Webb together with their colleagues of said Society William H. De Mattos, William Clarke and Edward R. Pease, that they may apply the same at once gradually and at all events within ten years to the propaganda and other purposes of the said Society and its Socialism and towards advancing its objects in any way they deem advisable. Webb for the first year to be President and as long as he remains such to have except in his own re-election a casting vote, such election to be annual and the President for the time being to be always removable but until removed to be Administrator of the Trust Fund. Witness my hand this tenth day of October, 1893.

This was the document that launched many thousand students of Economics.[1]

Henry Hutchinson in making his will desired Sidney Webb to have increased power to spread Fabian Socialism. But Sidney wanted even more to do something that on the face of it was different—establish a School of Economics and Political Science where men should be free to study and teach scientifically, pursuing truth as they saw it in independence of any dogma, whether of Socialism or the reverse. The story, as he told it to me later, is

[1]Henry Hutchinson had never seen Sidney Webb, but had been a member of the Fabian Society since 1890 and one of its chief financial supporters. His will has not, to my knowledge, been published before. In describing his first consultation with Sidney Webb, W. A. S. Hewins who became the first Director of the School, states the purpose of the bequest : it " could be used at Webb's discretion for the promotion of the objects of the Fabian Society " (*Apologia of an Imperialist*, vol. i. p. 24). The purpose of the bequest is not stated directly in *Our Partnership*, though there are several references which make the purpose clear, including Ramsay Macdonald's objection to " diverting Socialist funds to education " (p. 132). Most revealing both of the will, and of the Webbs, is the discussion on pp.85–86 of possible ways of spending the money. The alternatives of placing it all to the credit of the Fabian Society for ordinary propaganda and of making " a big political splash " by the whole Fabian Executive standing for Parliament are both ruled out. " Mere propaganda of the shibboleths of collectivism is going on at a rapid rate through the I.L.P.—the ball has been set running and it is rolling down the hill at a fair pace. It looks as if the great bulk of the working-men will be collectivists before the end of the century. But reform will not be brought about by shouting. What is needed is *hard thinking*."

that he consulted R. B. Haldane (later Lord Haldane), who asked whether he remained a convinced Socialist. On the answer " yes " followed the further question : " Do you believe then that the more that social conditions are studied scientifically and impartially, the stronger does the case for Socialism become ? " To this, also, came the answer " yes." " Very well, if you believe that you are entitled to use the bequest for the starting of a School for scientific impartial study and teaching." In the event, about half of the bequest was spent on lectures and propaganda for the Fabian Society ; the other half met deficits in running the impartial School of Economics.

The School became in due course one of the most heavily endowed of modern academic institutions in Britain. It began— probably in this respect unique among colleges or universities— without any endowment at all. It lived from hand to mouth on a vitalising purpose.

The purpose embodied several distinct ideas. First, there was the general idea of increasing, out of all proportion to anything attempted hitherto, the resources devoted to scientific study of society. In place of a single Professor of Political Economy, as in Oxford or Cambridge, or two very part-time professors each giving a few lectures, as in London, there must be many professors with adequate junior staff, research funds and so forth, each specialising on one side or other of the immense varied field to be covered. But, second, while each of the professors should specialise, as is the nature of professors, they should live and work together in one institution, bringing about the essential cross-fertilisation of ideas and techniques. And, third, the new institution was to do something new.

> While much attention will be given to the study of economic and political theory, the special aim of the School will be, from the first, the study and investigation of the concrete facts of industrial life and the actual working of economic and political institutions as they exist or have existed, in the United Kingdom or in foreign countries.[1]

---

[1]This is the third paragraph of the School's first Prospectus preserved in one of its Archive Volumes (Papers, 1895–96). The first and second paragraphs are as follows :—

> The growing importance of social and economic subjects has drawn atten-

The first prospectus of the School thus paid lip service to theory, no doubt by way of ensuring that " cordial co-operation of the leading economists and students of political science in the United Kingdom " with which it claimed to start. But its heart was else-where: in the study of institutions, where the heart of the Webbs was.

Fourth and finally the new departure included not merely the setting up of the School of Economics, but the securing for its studies of their proper place in the University of London. The new constitution of the university emerged at last in 1900, after a dozen years of controversy, two Royal Commissions, an Act of Parliament, and a Statutory Commission with legislative powers. Sidney Webb was one of its two chief artificers, with R. B. Haldane as the other.[1] As he said to me once, he was not particularly proud of the constitution : it was merely the best compromise that could

tion to the need of further provision for systematic training in economic and political science, and the promotion of original investigation and research. While success has followed the organisation of economic and political studies in certain foreign universities, in the *École Libre des Sciences Politiques*, Paris, Columbia University, New York, and other institutions in foreign countries, no similar provision has been made for these subjects in the United Kingdom. Funds have been placed at the disposal of trustees for the establishment of a LONDON SCHOOL OF ECONOMICS AND POLITICAL SCIENCE, which will be organised under the direction of Mr. W. A. S. Hewins, M.A., of Pembroke College, Oxford, and will begin work in October, 1895.

The London School starts with the cordial co-operation of leading economists and students of political science in the United Kingdom, and with the support of the Society of Arts and on its commercial side, of the London Chamber of Commerce. It will be organised to meet the needs of different classes or students. In the lectures on higher commercial subjects which will be given under the auspices of the London Chamber of Commerce, and the classes in connection with them, students will be able to acquire that wider knowledge of modern commercial conditions which is every day becoming more necessary for the successful conduct of business. Those students who have already, by means of university extension lectures or otherwise gained some acquaintance with economic or political science, will be able to pursue their studies under the direction of experts, and the advanced courses will supply that scientific training which is likely in the future to become essential as a qualification for the civil service, municipal employment, journalism or public work.

In the copy of this Prospectus, as preserved in the Archive Volumes, there is an obvious misprint in the third paragraph, in the substitution of " economic and political *relations* " for " economic and political *institutions* " as given above. Other contemporary statements about the School in the Archive Volume give the aim as stated in the text above.

[1]See *Our Partnership*, pp. 100–01 and 234–35.

be reached between equally strong and determined opponents.[1] But it gave to London, first among British Universities, a separate Faculty for the Social Sciences, "The Faculty of Economics and Political Science (including Commerce)" with its own degrees, of Bachelor of Science in Economics, and so forth. The five-year-old School was recognised as a School in the Faculty and became for many years the only School setting out to cover all the work of that Faculty.

Webb, of course, was not the only or the first person to emphasise the need for a science of society. As I pointed out in one of my first addresses as Director of the School in 1920, T. H. Huxley nearly seventy years before had made an eloquent plea for a School of Economics, and Plato in the *Protagoras* 2,000 years before had foreshadowed the same need.[2] And in the very month in which Sidney Webb in Surrey received the solicitor's letter telling him about the Hutchinson bequest, the British Association in Oxford was discussing a Committee Report emphasising the deplorable state of economic studies and the need for remedial action. Ideas may come to many men. Sidney Webb had the master gift of making ideas viable.

In their foundation of the School the Webbs were curiously close to Huxley, who had seen social science as a completion of

[1]The University of London, established in 1836, had since 1858 become an examining body merely, treating identically those who had studied in the great teaching colleges of London and those who had never been attached to any academic institution anywhere. The controversy of the eighties and nineties was between those who wished to set up a second and separate teaching university in London and those who thought that the old examining university and the teaching colleges might be married to make a single university. The compromise of 1900 established one university, but provided that it should give two kinds of degree, one " external " depending simply on written examination, and one " internal " where admission to examination should be conditional on having studied in a recognised institution or under a recognised teacher and where the teaching and the examination should to some extent be related to one another. The later stages of this controversy, through another Royal Commission in 1909–13 and a new constitution of the university in 1926, fall outside the scope of this chapter.

[2]See *Economics as a Liberal Education* printed as the first article in the first number of *Economica*, January, 1921. The address of Huxley referred to by me is that given by him in St. Martin's Hall in 1854 on *The Educational Value of the Natural History Sciences* and printed in *Science and Education*, p. 38. For the myth in the *Protagoras* and Webb's appearance in the character of Hermes, reference should be made to my address in *Economica*, pp. 11–12.

the natural history sciences. After five years, at the beginning of 1900, Beatrice wrote in her diary in the following terms.

Meanwhile our little schemes with regard to the new University of London prosper. We have got the School recognised as a Faculty of Economics, we have secured a site and a building free of cost, and an income of £2,500 devoted to economics and commercial science. Sidney will be a member of the Faculty and will probably represent the County Council on the Senate. Best of all he has persuaded the Royal Commission to recognise economics as a science and not merely as a subject in the Faculty of Arts. The preliminary studies for the economics degree will therefore be mathematics and biology. The divorce of economics from metaphysics and shoddy history is a great gain. We have always claimed that the study of the structure and function of society was as much a science as the study of any other form of life, and ought to be pursued by the scientific methods used in other organic sciences.[1]

Economics and Political Science did not in practice develop in the School or in the University just on the lines suggested in this passage. The degrees of the new Faculty were called degrees of Science in Economics, but the connection with Natural Science was never more than a name. For practical purposes the Faculty and its teachers in the University came to be grouped with those of Arts and Laws rather than with the scientists and medicals. Mathematics and biology did not become the preliminary studies for the economics degree. Meteorology, noticed by Professor Hayek as making an unexpected appearance in the teaching of the School in 1909–10, disappeared again.

Thirty years later I found the Rockefeller Foundation ready to give to the School a large endowment to be used if desired for cultivating the borderland between the social and the natural sciences, and I persuaded the Governors to devote part of this endowment to the establishment at the School of a Department of Social Biology. As the passage just cited from *Our Partnership* shows, in making this proposal, I was nearer to the early intentions of the Founders than I, or perhaps they, realised at the time. This second attempt to affiliate social science in London with natural science has failed, as the first attempt did. Perhaps thirty years after it a third attempt may come to lasting success.

[1] *op. cit.*, p. 195.

The School did not develop in every detail just as the Webbs had thought of it at first. They would never have expected it to do so. It became a creature with a life of its own. But it remained always the dearest of their creations, an extension of their own personalities, an institution for getting done permanently on a large scale the thing that lay nearest to their hearts—the application of reasoned knowledge to human relations.

Though the foundation of the School at the moment when it took place was made possible by an accident, it was not in any true sense an accident. Before ever he received the solicitor's letter Sidney had been thinking of a research institution to serve social science. As Chairman of the Technical Education Board of the London County Council, controlling its " whisky money "[1]— another fortunate accident—he was able to secure vital financial help to the new venture. In the same capacity and as himself a London graduate, he was in the thick of the controversy about university education in London that raged through all the nineties; as Beatrice observed about the School, by the beginning of 1897 Sidney had " contrived to edge it into any possible London University." The School would have been launched somehow before the twentieth century began, even if Henry Hutchinson had never lived and died. The School of Economics was a consequence of the Webbs so natural as to be all but in-evitable, once they were there, with social science as their major interest and with his constructiveness and love of contriving.

The School of Economics was the Webbs embodied in an insti-tution. In his dealings with it, Sidney's qualities of super-human industry, breadth of view, ingenuity and absence of personal egotism were illustrated again and again.

In the earliest days of the School, the Webbs did nearly every-thing. As Professor Hayek observes, the " Administrative Com-mittee " which till incorporation of the School in 1902 nominally looked after its finance, " was little more than another name for Sidney Webb." Nothing was too small for him, nothing to

[1]The Conservative Government's budget of 1890 increased the duties on spirits with a view to creating a fund for purchase of publican's licences deemed to be redundant. Temperance opposition to recognising property in annual licences compelled the Government to abandon this proposed use of the money, but the duties had been imposed and the money was there. Enthusiasts for technical education managed to get it allocated to that purpose through the County Councils.

laborious, nothing too large, if by doing it he could help the School. Again and again anyone turning over the early records of the School finds a memorandum or letter in Sidney's handwriting dealing with some practical detail of furniture, or building plans, or how to get books or of who might be worth approaching for money. When, just before the opening of the second session, the Director, W. A. S. Hewins, fell ill, both the Founders had to throw themselves into the breach and take his place at the School. " Poor Sidney trudges over there directly after breakfast and spends his mornings with painters, plumbers and locksmiths."[1] Beatrice took charge of the housekeeping, becoming for a while " Lady Visitor." Both of them lectured at the School. By receptions and informal gatherings of many kinds in their own home and elsewhere they kept the staff and students together and they kept the School in the public eye.

As the organisation grew, its authors naturally stepped back. But for many years, Sidney did all the important things : chose the successive Directors ; secured for the School its place in the University, in hard bargaining with other Colleges; got the Army Class to the School in 1906 through his friendship with R. B. Haldane ; got the site of the School from the London County Council and the money for the Clare Market Building from Mr. Passmore Edwards ; got £250,000 from Sir Ernest Cassel after the first World War to endow the teaching posts needed for the Commerce Degree ; filled the gap when for a while in 1918 there was no Director.

Sidney's breadth of view in judgment of persons appeared conspicuously in the appointment of Directors. The first four Directors—W. A. S. Hewins, Halford Mackinder, Pember Reeves and myself—were all chosen in effect by Sidney. He made the search, conducted the interviews and clinched the bargain ; the Trustees or Governors of the School said " agreed " to his recommendation. Sidney never wavered in his Socialism ; yet only the third of these four Directors to whom he entrusted his creation could be described in any way as a Socialist. Each of the first two became in turn a Conservative Member of Parliament.

Sidney's breadth of view appeared, in a yet more important way, in relation to the scope of the School. The besetting danger

[1]*Our Partnership*, p. 94.

C

of nearly all academic persons is specialism, the tendency to believe that no study is really indispensable except their own. Sidney Webb had a specialty of his own, but no idea of keeping the School to it. Very early in my own time at the School one of those who had been there from near its beginning, said to me how impressive had been Webb's determination to draw the circle of the School wide, not narrow. So he had held on to Law, not simply to Economics. So he brought in Sociology and Anthropology, despite the doubts of an old guard who wondered why a School of Economics should concern itself with the " nasty habits of dirty savages." So, though or perhaps because the Webbs always engagingly admitted their personal incapacity for statistical inquiry[1], they made Statistics from the beginning, in the person of Professor Bowley, one of the cornerstones of their institution.

Professor Hayek in his article mentions the comment attributed to Alfred Marshall that the early lecture list of the School was determined more by the sort of people who were available than by educational considerations. Of course the School in its beginnings, with no endowments and no assured income, had to be conducted on the most economical lines. That meant getting people who had some other source of income to give their spare time to the School : in its first twenty years the School had no full-time professor. Its poverty gave unlimited scope to Sidney's love of frugal devices.

When he discovered that under the Scientific Societies Act of 1843, passed at the instance of the Prince Consort, libraries could escape payment of local rates, he established the British Library of Political Science whose Director was also the Director of the London School of Economics and Political Science and in the former capacity allowed himself in the latter capacity to conduct lectures and classes on the library premises. Sidney would probably have done this, for the fun of the device, even if the School of Economics had had the money to pay the rates. As it was, escape from this burden proved of great value to the infant institution. It was several years before the School of Economics grew too large to be hidden from the rating authorities of Westminster in the interstices of the British Library of Political Science.

[1] " We are not competent, either by mental equipment or by experience, to deal with what is sometimes termed the Statistical Method." (*Methods of Social Study*, p. 202.)

It was thirty years before the latter changed its name and acknowledged that it included economics as well. The presentation of the library as something apart from the School had another advantage more permanent than escape from local rates by grace of the Prince Consort. The Library set itself from the beginning to make the most complete collection possible of the official papers of as many countries as possible. It was easier to ask for this for the " British Library of Political Science " than for the library of a particular teaching institution.

The same characteristic of ingenious frugality appeared in the incorporation of the School as a Company limited by guarantee under the Companies Acts. Academic bodies of the standing which the School aspired to and attained normally receive a Royal Charter. Sidney Webb was content with the simpler if less conventional procedure of the Companies Acts; a Company, authorised to leave the word " limited " out of its name, the School remains today. In the dry form of its Articles of Association, Sidney entrenched a fundamental principle : that no teacher in the School should suffer any disadvantage merely for the holding or expression of any opinion whatsoever.[1]

The most important of all Sidney's qualities for securing that co-operation of others without which great things cannot be done was unselfishness. It was characteristic that on the starting of this Commerce Degree, Sidney did the most important work and left all the limelight to others. He was without personal vanity. And if it helped the School he was ready to go completely into the background. There was a crisis once when the Railway Companies threatened to withdraw their subscriptions because of a speech about railway wages which Sidney had made : he was at that time Chairman of the Governors. This would have been little short of financial disaster : the steady income from the Railway Department and the Army Class made at one time a vital contribution to meeting the School's overheads. As one personal contribution towards appeasing the Railway Companies, Sidney retired grace-

[1] " No religious, political or economic test or qualification shall be made a condition for or disqualify from receiving any of the benefits of the Corporation, or holding any office therein ; and no member of the Corporation, or professor, lecturer or other officer thereof shall be under any disability or disadvantage by reason only of any opinions that he may hold or promulgate on any subject whatsoever." These words, forming Article 28 of the Articles of Association, deserve today all the prominence that they can receive.

fully, though a little sadly, from the Chairmanship of the Governors and was succeeded by a rising young Conservative Member of Parliament. But it remained true of the Governors, as of many other gatherings, that wherever Sidney Webb happened to sit, there was the Chair—the source of ideas and practical expedients and reconciling compromises.

The first Director of the School, W. A. S. Hewins, has placed on record, in words which deserve to be repeated, what it was like to work with the Webbs.[1]

> Outside the School I was often warned by uneasy economists of the danger of my association with Sidney and Beatrice Webb. Nothing could have been more absurd. I have worked with many different colleagues, but never with any two people so free from prejudices or so absolutely loyal and devoted to the main objects of what we were doing and so indifferent to the ordinary prejudices to be found in academic circles as Mr. and Mrs. Webb.
>
> *   *   *   *   *
>
> I shall always look back on the period during which I worked with them as one of the happiest and most productive of my life. We met almost daily and never had a dispute during the eight years I was so closely associated with them.

For myself who became in 1919 the fourth Director the story is the same. The School had grown and continued to grow beyond the daily care of its Founders. But they and particularly Sidney continued to be ideal colleagues, advisers and friends for any Director. From them came an inexhaustible stream of ideas and projects, great and small. To them every major problem would be put naturally. They were the power which every one would want behind his throne. They were power which could always be trusted, for they sought no purpose of their own.

Sidney Webb loved inventing devices. But his determination to make and keep the School of Economics independent of any political and economic dogma was not a device. It was fundamental in his outlook and that of his partner.

The Webbs in their glorious prime were anti-Marxist in a sense

---

[1] W. A. S. Hewins, *op. cit.*, pp. 31 and 26. The first of the two passages cited proceeds to an account of the Webbs' freedom from bias in the selection of staff for the School.

more important than any disagreement as to the nature of rent or as to procedure by revolution. They rejected utterly that dictation of opinion which has come to be the mark of Marxism in practice. They were sure that whatever form of Government men had, men could not be governed well without science. They knew that social science, like every other science, is nothing if it is not free.

In their own writing they had a bias and they knew it. They were reformers as well as scientists, and, as I have suggested elsewhere, the reformers in them gained on the scientists.[1] But this happened in their own writings only. It never affected by one hairsbreadth their attitude to the School of Economics. They believed that the impartial scientific study of society would further the Socialism which was their practical aim, but they were prepared to take the risk of being wrong in that belief. The School of Economics was their favourite child, dearer even than Fabian Socialism.

[1]See my obituary notice of Sidney Webb in the *Economic Journal*, September, 1948.

PERMEATION

by

R. C. K. ENSOR

V

PERMEATION

by R. C. K. ENSOR

"Permeation" as a political term may have several meanings. In countries which have a well-established two-party system, like Great Britain and the United States, the natural thing for the champions of a new cause to do is not to found a new party, but to bring organised influence to bear on the old. That is what the Anti-Corn Law League did in Britain, or the Prohibitionists in America, and what a large number of " pressure-groups," especially in the latter country, are doing every day. It is what the trade-union movement did for a long time in both countries, and still does in the United States. It is what the Fabian Society called " permeation " from about 1886 onwards.

This kind of pressure may sometimes be applied to both parties indifferently. Early in this century, for instance, the National Union of Teachers had as its spokesmen in Parliament two able ex-teachers, of whom one sat as a Conservative and the other as a Liberal. They thus could rely on their voices being heard in both camps from within. This is the earliest and simplest form of permeation. A second stage may be reached, when it becomes apparent that one of the two parties is very much more accessible to the desired influence than the other. Permeation may then take the form of concentrating upon the preferred party, and trying to get established in its councils as many as possible of the cause's champions. That is what the trade unions did in Great Britain during the fifteen years following the death of Disraeli, and especially during the last ten of them, after the Home Rule split had removed from the Liberal Party its most obviously Right-wing elements.

There may be yet a third stage of permeation, when the permeators, after obtaining a strong position inside Party A, find that for carrying a particular policy there are possibilities of working through Party B. Cleverly executed, this kind of permeation may succeed in carrying the particular policy, and, if it is a very important one, the success is to that extent important. It may probably, however, destroy all the future influence of the permeators, who risk forfeiting Party A's confidence for ever without, save in the particular matter, creating any compensating tie with Party B.

In *Fabian Essays*—published, it must always be remembered, two years and a half before the Webbs were married—there is an extended reference to " permeation " of the second type. The passage occurs in the middle of Hubert Bland's essay, entitled *The Outlook*, which deals with the party-political aspects of Socialism as distinct from the economic, historical, ethical, industrial or ideological aspects treated by the other essayists. Why Bland was selected for this has never, I think, been explained ; for his point of view on such matters was apt to differ widely from those of his colleagues. On this occasion he launched out into a very definite attack on " some of our brightest and otherwise most clear-sighted spirits," who " have begun to base high hopes upon what they call the ' permeation ' of the Liberal Party." Who in particular were these " bright spirits " ? Bland naturally gives no names, but two allusions in his diatribe were clear to all Fabians. One was to " the successes which Radical votes have given to some of our candidates at School Board elections." That is, in particular, Graham Wallas. The other was : " These of our brothers have a way of telling us that the transition to Socialism will be so gradual as to be imperceptible." That is, in particular, Sidney Webb ; who throughout the 'nineties was constantly emphasising what twenty years later he called " the inevitability of gradualness."

If anyone should feel surprise at finding that within the four corners of *Fabian Essays* one of the essayists makes an onslaught on two of his most prominent colleagues, several things might be pointed out to him. First, that the *Essays* were originally lectures given at the meetings of the Fabian Society—features of which in the old days of Willis's Rooms and Clifford's Inn were cut-and-thrust debates with quarter rarely asked or given. Secondly, that, as the preface expressly tells us, in editing the lectures into essays there was " no attempt to cut out every phrase and opinion the responsibility for which would not be accepted by every one " of the essayists.

Bland's view was not typical of the Society. On the Executive his particular line had little support, save intermittently from

Bernard Shaw, and twenty years later more regularly from Cecil Chesterton. Regarding party tactics his evolution resembled Hyndman's. Both had been Conservatives before they were Socialists; and as they disliked Liberals and at the same time, after Disraeli's death, could see no Socialist future inside the Conservative ranks, they rejected permeation and went instead for a separate Socialist Party—not, be it understood, a Labour Party, not the broad-bottomed Keir Hardie idea which has carried Socialism in Great Britain to the position which it holds today, but the narrow idea which Hyndman tried to embody in his little Social-Democratic Federation, and which never really got anywhere.

The ordinary Fabians, with Webb, Graham Wallas and Pease at their head, had evolved quite differently. Their sympathies had been Radical, and they naturally inclined to permeate the party which they knew, and which at that time, following the Home Rule split of 1886, was in a peculiarly fluid state favourable to the admission of new ideas. Hence in the late 'eighties Fabian " permeation," which originally had conformed to what above was called the earliest and simplest type, moved on to the second type —i.e., became a definite attempt to capture for Socialist ideas the Radical wing of the Liberal Party. The Radicals themselves welcomed the Fabian approach. Their two newspapers, the *Star* and the *Daily Chronicle*, gave generous space to Fabian writers. And the " L. and R.'s," i.e., the Liberal and Radical Associations in the London constituencies, freely allowed Fabians to lecture to them. The 1889 preface to *Fabian Essays* mentions that in the twelve months ending in April of that year the number of lectures delivered by members of the Fabian Society exceeded 700. How many of them were delivered to " L. and R.'s," it is not possible to say, but certainly a large number; and more fruitful soil for the seed to fall on there could hardly be, for in those days, while the Liberals found the money for these bodies, the Radicals found the membership. The result of it all was the Liberal-cum-Socialist combination in London local politics which came to be known as the Progressive Party. It was as a member of this party that Sidney Webb sat on the London County Council from 1892 to 1910, and it was through it that he obtained his eventful chairmanship of the Technical Education Board.

But was the membership of a local body, albeit the greatest, or the achievement of a far-reaching administrative task, like that of the Technical Education Board, all that Webb looked for from his permeation of the London Radicals ? Assuredly not. He and Beatrice may in later life have come to think so, for it was his nature never to let his mind dwell on what his destiny had denied him, but always on what it had vouchsafed to him—a pleasant trait to which Beatrice pays repeated and well-merited tributes in *Our Partnership*. Nevertheless, if we ask whether what he was aspiring to before (and for some while after) his marriage was what he actually attained in the twenty years following, the answer is No. He was aspiring to a career in Parliament and as a Minister.

The present writer asked him in 1900 why he left the Civil Service. His answer was that the longer he was in it, the more clearly he became conscious of the great gulf fixed between two orders of men—the civil servants who carry out policies and the politicians who as Ministers determine them. However influential a civil servant might be, his position precluded, as a rule, his initiating large changes, such as a Socialist policy would involve. While in the service, Webb had felt this increasingly, and decided, as soon as he was able, to put himself on the other side of the gulf.

For a man with the gifts which Webb had at the time, this was the only natural conclusion. He then was, among other things, a very remarkable speaker. In later life he entirely ceased to be ; his voice failed him, and he took to gabbling ; and by the time that (at 65) he was a Cabinet Minister in the first Labour Government in 1924, he was a byword in the House and the Gallery for inaudibility and ineffectiveness. It is curious that by 1926 (as her sketch of him in *Our Partnership* would suggest) Beatrice herself had come to suppose that he had always been rather like that. But it was not so. In the 'nineties he was quite effective on the most popular kind of platform, as his hold on his Deptford L.C.C. seat showed. But on another kind of platform he was much more. When he gave an address at Oxford, hearers hung on his lips. The Fabian Society's meetings at that time had a very high standard of debate. The numbers attending were not great—forty or fifty ; but there was no passive " audience," for nearly all present were themselves practised speakers and debaters, many of them trained, as Bernard Shaw had been, in the very exacting but bracing school of open-air propaganda. The war of argument was gladiatorial ; and if Webb could not be claimed as the arch-gladiator (probably Shaw was that), it remains true that he always held his own with distinction, and on the score of disarming his opponents and winning agreement to his views was the most *successful* debater of them all. Even Beatrice in the passage referred to above admits that on the platform he was singularly apt at answering questions. But the same qualities, which enable a man to answer questions brilliantly and convincingly on the spur of the moment, are those that will contribute most to his success as a Parliamentary debater. Moreover there was a peculiarly persuasive side to Webb's debating, which would have profited him just as much in the House of Commons as it did at Clifford's Inn. It was that his triumphs left no sting. If he proved you completely wrong, you never felt that it had been done to score off you, and it was always made as easy as possible for you to agree with him without loss of face. Where policies were so skilfully pleaded, they usually prevailed ; and this had been going on around Webb's personality for some years before he met Beatrice.

Down to that date their paths had been extremely different. Beatrice had already attained great distinction as a social researcher. The work that she had done in East London, both for Charles Booth and on her own account, was expert, authoritative, and highly original ; so was her book *The Co-operative Movement in Great Britain*, in some ways more brilliant, perhaps, than any of the books that they afterwards wrote jointly. Webb had nothing of that sort to his credit ; he had as yet never done any scientific social research ; his few books were little more than large pamphlets of the kind that clever politicians write, especially in their ambitious youth. For the rest, he was an exceptionally able young man, who had risen very rapidly in the Civil Service, but who, as we have seen, wanted to get out of it into politics, if only he could afford to do so. An even bigger " if " then than now, in those days before Payment of Members.

But there were other differences. Beatrice had for years acted as hostess to her wealthy father in entertaining the leading politicians of the day. She had thus met many, and knew some intimately. One certainly (and perhaps another) she might have married ; and her almost unique combination of rare beauty and charm with a piercing intellectual capacity made it easy for her to exert social influence in the highest circles. Sidney Webb, an adventurer, with no capital, no family influence, no powerful friends, and few friends at all outside the early Fabian circle, lived in a different world. Except perhaps occasionally in the course of his civil service duties, he had never spoken to a Front Bench politician. Nor had he even any connections in the universities.

Now when these two people came together and fell in love and decided to marry, the respective roles which they contemplated within marriage were naturally determined by their antecedents. Beatrice's money would enable Sidney to leave the Civil Service and go into politics, for she would have enough for him to live without earning. At the same time she would use her wide political knowledge and influence to introduce him to the Parliamentary world and pull wires for him in it to the best of her ability. But her own role could not possibly be in politics, for at that time women could not sit either in Parliament or on county or borough councils. She, therefore, would continue writing books of social research on lines that she had made her own. Sidney with his uncanny felicity in quick drafting would be—as from the first he was—a very real help to her ; but the books would be hers, and not, as they eventually became, a joint effort over joint signatures. In *Our Partnership* (p. 26) Beatrice quotes a very revealing extract from her diary of 15th September 1891, not many months after their secret engagement. She, who was preparing to follow up her book on the co-operative movement by one on the trade union movement, had been getting Sidney to do quite a lot of work for her (as a young man will work for his fiancée) ; and she thus excuses herself.

And for Sidney this inquiry will be of untold use. The politician of the future must understand all the details of industrial life ; he must be, before all things, a practical economist. For economics in the widest sense are rapidly becoming the technical side of the politician's work. Also, he is learning, through this wider intercourse with facts and men, a more proportionate sense and a wider judgment than was possible to a London civil servant. Thus, from a strictly personal point of view, an acquaintance with the leaders of working-class organisation throughout the country will be a highly desirable

connection, not to be despised. So that, in helping me, he does
not feel, nor am I conscious, that this work is my particular
concern.

In spite of the self-excusing self-accusing last sentence, the
purport of this is clear enough. Sidney's role is to be " the
politician of the future." For that (and not, be it noted, for its
own sake) he needs " practical " economics (at which Beatrice had
long been working, and he not) ; a wider outlook on society than
that of the civil service (from which her engagement has enabled
him to emancipate himself, but which has kept him hitherto in a
much narrower world than hers) ; and wide personal acquaintance
with Labour leaders (which she already has and he is only now,
through her, coming to get, and which will be for him, in a political
sense inapplicable to her, " a highly desirable connection.")

The choice of their first house, 41 Grosvenor Road, was significant. It was within a short walk of Parliament, and had Webb
become an M.P. that would, in the pre-motor age, have been an
enormous boon to him. As it was, it enabled Beatrice most conveni-
ently to attract her Parliamentary friends and acquaintances to lunch
and dinner, and she at once set about doing so, quite simply and
naturally, in her husband's interest. So originated what became
the celebrated Webb *salon*. It was to develop, as time went on,
away from its origins. Anyone who wrote about it ten years later,
or thereafter (as H. G. Wells did in *The New Machiavelli*), was apt
to figure it as a sort of parlour, into which two remarkable spiders
invited political flies. " Permeation," but in the doctrinal rather
than the party-political sense, had become its end-all and be-all.
Gone was the notion that Webb's career was to be that of a
brilliant House of Commons man graduating to become a Socialist
Minister in a Radical Cabinet. Instead had come the conception
of him as a man purged of any desire to enter Parliament or hold
office at all ; a man personally disinterested in politics, yet sharing
with his equally disinterested wife a treasure of political wisdom
(attested by a growing row of very solid books), which it was their
delight to impart to anyone deemed capable of utilising it.

The picture would be incomplete, unless one added that everybody knew they held a certain broad view on economics and government, which was called Socialism, and were also apt to hold
elaborately argued special views upon almost any subject in

domestic affairs—views very often connected with something which they had set their hearts on getting done. Thus, though grown disinterested in regard to personal gain, they were never disinterested in the game of politics, but intensely anxious to score practical points in a dozen different directions at any given time. These special policies were usually slipped forward under cover of general principles ; and people who assented to the latter without realising what corollaries would be drawn from them, sometimes found they had bitten off more than they could chew.

Now how did this change-over take place, from permeation in the sense of permeating the Liberal Party and capturing it for a wide programme of Socialistic reform to permeation in the more promiscuous sense which has sometimes seemed to justify a comparison between the Webbs' influence and Jeremy Bentham's— not, of course, in regard to its direction, but in regard to the mode of its exercise ? The fact is that Webb as " the politician of the future " failed. No fault can be found with him for entering politics by courting Liberal votes, for in 1892 there was no other way in which a middle-class Socialist could. Keir Hardie's way at West Ham in the same year was only possible because he was a working man. Nor was it bad tactics to begin with a few years in local government before entering the House of Commons. Joseph Chamberlain, the most powerful politician of the day, had done so ; so had Fowler, one of the two most successful Ministers in the 1892–5 Cabinets. In 1892, W. T. Stead even hailed Sidney Webb as the coming Socialist Chamberlain.

True there was always a difficulty on the side of the Fabian Society itself. The Society could have practised permeation much better, had it been the only Socialist body in the country. But it was not ; it had a rival in the Social-Democratic Federation, which opposed permeation and preached joining a Socialist party. Hence in order to keep their end up with their Socialist public the Fabians had publicly to boast the successes of permeation. But that is just what a wise permeator should never do. If anyone looks up *Fabian Tract No.* 41 (by Bernard Shaw), published in August, 1892, he will see the point. Nothing could be better calculated to make London Radicals repent their support of Webb and think that they had been hoodwinked by him. Shaw, who usually bowed to Webb's logic and often gave most valuable

support to his policy, was yet with his mischief-loving temperament—part Puck, part *enfant terrible*—a serious impediment to
Webb's progress. The famous anti-Liberal Fabian manifesto of
November 1893, " To Your Tents, O Israel ! " was drafted and
largely inspired by Shaw, though Webb also lent a hand in it. It
damaged incalculably Webb's relations with his Radical allies on the
London County Council (as more than one of them told the present
writer many years afterwards), and removed for ever the prospect,
till then thought a real one by many, of his becoming " the
London Chamberlain."

Another force militating against his success in Parliamentary
politics was, paradox though it may seem, the influence of Beatrice
herself. So long as he was engaged with her in research and
writing and the *salon*, she had a great deal of him—so much that
she could afford to let him spend afternoons at the London
County Council. But Parliament, in which she could never join
him, would mean an end to much of that ; and the more he
succeeded there, the more she would fall into the background of
his life. As early as July, 1894, a passage in her diary (quoted in
Our Partnership, on p. 117) shows this unmistakably. In it she
admits that, when offered this or that constituency, he refused
" largely because I discouraged him." And after elaborating some
rather artificial arguments against a Parliamentary career she comes
down to bedrock :

> A Parliamentary career would destroy our united life ; would
> cut at the root of a good deal of our joint effort. Perhaps that
> is why I distrust my dislike of his going into Parliament ; it
> would take so much away from me personally, would add so
> many ties and inconveniences. Sooner or later, I suppose, he
> will have to make the sacrifice—but better later than sooner.

Yet the main cause of Webb's failure as a politician lay in himself. He evolved away from the front-stairs to the back-stairs in
politics, because he really had more genius for the latter. From
the achievement of front-stairs success he was hindered by two
possibly fatal defects ; he was a bad judge of men, and he often
strangely failed to appreciate the bigness of big issues. Beatrice,
who alone might have corrected these defects, unfortunately
shared them. The fact was that between 1895 and 1905 the Webbs
had a clear opportunity of placing Sidney in a position, where

the office of President either of the Local Government Board or of the Board of Trade would have been his for the choosing in the Campbell-Bannerman Cabinet. They lost it, not for want of trying, but because they tried in the wrong way and put their money on the wrong horses. Think what might have happened, if they had not, and if Webb instead of Burns had obtained the Local Government Board. Most and perhaps all, for which they asked in Beatrice's 1909 *Minority Report on the Poor Law*, could have been put through before that by Sidney in office.

The Webbs' evil genius in dealing with the Liberal Party was Haldane. He cared for Beatrice before her marriage, and might perhaps have married her. He had, though it was not always obvious, a truly noble side to his character, as more evidently had she ; and each of them was conscious of this nobility in the other. When she married Webb, Haldane at once took to him ; their temperaments had much in common, and they pursued many objectives in close co-operation, notably the reconstitution of the University of London. But in Liberal party politics Haldane was then an intriguer, always plotting away at a scheme which did not come off. He took to himself, perhaps rightly, the credit for having wirepulled the assent of Liberal Ministers and Parliamentarians to Queen Victoria's nomination of Lord Rosebery as Prime Minister in 1894. After the Rosebery Government's fall in July, 1895, an unhealed division within the Liberal Party between Roseberyites and anti-Roseberyites rankled for ten years, Haldane being the arch-intriguer for the one and L. V. Harcourt for the other.

If the Roseberyites had won, Haldane would have wielded great influence and could have put Webb into high office. But there were two fairly evident reasons why they never could win. The first was the character of Rosebery, who had lost his health and his nerve, and rarely emerged from seclusion except to puzzle and disappoint his friends. The second was the fact that, essentially, the Roseberyites were the Whigs and the anti-Roseberyites the Radicals, and the future lay with the Radicals. Haldane sought to disguise this from Webb by representing the Roseberyites as the " collectivist " wing of the party. He was only too successful, and Webb's fortunes were cast with the Roseberyite group. On 28th July, 1901, he took part with them in an anti-Campbell-

Bannerman dinner, and this was followed in September by Webb's much-noted review article, " Lord Rosebery's Escape from Houndsditch," which caused him to be definitely ranked with the " Liberal Imperialists " in the public eye. For months thereafter the Webbs were in almost incessant contact with the leaders of this group—not liking them the better, the more they knew them, but too far engaged to draw back. To estimate the effect one has to remember that the sentiment throughout the country of Radicalism—not merely Liberal Radicalism, but that of the Independent Labour Party, of the Social-Democratic Federation, and of the more political trade unionists—was by then almost unanimously pro-Boer, with that exalted sensitive conviction which comes from having faced and surmounted much hostile persecution. Thus the Webbs fatally antagonised all shades of Radicals ; who were, after all, the only people through whom Socialism could look for popular support, and who were destined soon afterwards, in 1905–14, to dominate the domestic policies of the Government.

Both the Webbs' defects were exemplified in this episode. The ablest of the Liberal Imperialists, with whom they had thrown in their lot, was, as the event soon showed, Asquith. Yet for him they early conceived a personal repugnance, which naturally came to be to some extent reciprocated. At the same time they developed, on the Radical side, a similar repugnance to Lloyd George ! The present writer has notes of a conversation as late as 8th June, 1904, in which they described him as " absolutely apathetic " towards social reform. Graver, perhaps, than these personal misjudgments was their blindness to the meaning of the South African issue for Radicals and Socialists the world over, as involving supremely the issue of liberty. The circumstance that they were already on other grounds somewhat suspect in regard to liberty made the effect all the worse.

The same points were equally exemplified in their attitude to the nascent Labour Party. When the I.L.P. was formed in 1893, it was not easy for them to support it, since Sidney was working with the Liberals. But they absurdly underrated it, describing Keir Hardie in private as a mere poseur, and totally failing to grasp the scale of his appeal. Even after the L.R.C. movement was launched, they argued to the present writer as late as 1904 that the Labour Party would never come to anything. Their views in each of these cases were supported by a wealth of clever arguments. But the point is that for all their cleverness they (as the sequels showed) were entirely astray.

And there was more to come. What completed the estrangement between the Webbs and the rising popular forces was their action in regard to the Education Acts of 1902 and 1903. It was " permeation " of the kind which at the outset above we distinguished as the third—that which occurs when a permeator of Party A, turns over to " permeate " Party B. As a piece of highly skilled wire-pulling it marked perhaps the summit of Sidney's achievements. The subject was one which, thanks to his chairmanship of the London County Council's Technical Education Board, he had explored exhaustively. The Conservative Prime Minister, A. J. Balfour, was a politician of high and flexible intelligence, who had long known Beatrice and through her Sidney.

The Acts—a national one for England and Wales in 1902 and a special one for London in 1903—had been pioneered in 1895 by the report of a Royal Commission on Secondary Education presided over by James Bryce. The Webbs were then friendly with Bryce, and another prominent member of the Commission, Henry Hobhouse, was one of Beatrice's brothers-in-law ; so between the two there was some Webbian permeation, though it is difficult to say how much. The Commission reported in favour of a single central authority for education and a single local unit (an education committee of the county or county borough council) for secondary education. The first recommendation was adopted in the Board of Education Act, but the second was much more difficult. Two rival sets of local authorities disputed the claim to provide secondary education. On the one side were the *ad hoc* elected School Boards, which the Education Act of 1870 had set up to provide and run the State's elementary schools, and which since then had developed a good deal of secondary education in " higher grade " schools. On the other were the county and county borough councils, interpreting the Technical Instruction Act of 1889 in a sense which covered all kinds of secondary education, and acting through Technical Instruction Committees, the London edition of which (Webb's " Technical Education Board ") set the most advanced and conspicuous example. In 1899, the Cockerton decision declared the School Boards' " higher grade " efforts *ultra vires* ; and as it was upheld in 1900 and 1901 on two appeals, legislation became inevitable.

But the Acts did more than confirm the removal of secondary education from the School Boards. They abolished the School Boards altogether, and transferred their elementary schools to the education committees of county and county borough councils, or (under certain conditions as to area population) of borough and urban district councils. This wipe-out of the School Boards was accompanied by a wipe-out, to a considerable extent, of the distinction between " Board " (i.e., publicly provided) and " voluntary " (i.e., privately provided) elementary schools. Both came alike under the umbrella of the new local authority, though with certain differences as to finance and management, which enabled denominational schools to remain denominational. The effect was to give a new lease of life to denominational education ; in particular enabling Church schools to retain their monopoly in the multitude of " single-school areas." On this and some other grounds the Free Churches fiercely and unanimously opposed the Bills, and their resentment was a powerful factor in Radical opinion for many years afterwards.

Now Webb was not the parent of these Bills (as far as any single person was, it was R. L. Morant, the head of the Board of Education) ; but he played a very active part in advising and guiding Balfour, who himself piloted them through Parliament. It was the second Bill, that for London, which called out his highest powers. After the national Act was passed, there was a very strong movement to appease opposition by sparing in London the great London School Board. Feeling ran very high within the Fabian Society itself, for Graham Wallas and Stewart Headlam championed the Board of which they were members. But to Webb with his L.C.C. point of view it was even more important to make the change in London than elsewhere. He played every move in his game with bewildering ability, and in the upshot scored a complete victory. It is always difficult to assess one man's contribution in a complex struggle ; but it seems likely that, if he had not been there, the London School Board might not have been abolished.

Whether this was great statesmanship depends on whether the

abolition was a good thing. Historically now, as politically then, two views may be taken about it. But as politicianship Webb's skill, industry, courage, quickness and resource could hardly be over-praised. The effect, however, upon what was left of his status with Liberals was shattering. Though he sat on the London County Council till 1910, he never again filled a chair there. And here again he had shown some want of the larger vision. He failed to realise how genuine was the Nonconformist grievance in regard to the single-school areas ; or, again, how much the School Board had meant to a great many Londoners. Had he done so, and shown a little more generosity towards the losers, his course might have been less resented ; and, incidentally, Graham Wallas might not have left the Fabian Society.

The result of this whole record was that, when in 1905–14 the great tide of social reform started flowing, and the Webbs with their massive treasure of knowledge and thought about the administrative problems involved stood ready and willing to dispense help and advice, few of those in charge were inclined to seek it from them. Haldane of course remained faithful ; but first as War Minister and then as Lord Chancellor, he was fully busied with affairs outside their scope. In 1907, the present writer heard the late L. G. Chiozza Money give them some rather remarkable advice. He said : " There are two Ministers in this Government who, on account both of their abilities and their comparative youth, must go to the very top. They are Lloyd George and Winston Churchill. You have neglected them both. Cultivate them." As Lloyd George was then only at the Board of Trade and Mr. Churchill Under-Secretary at the Colonial Office, this showed prescience on Chiozza Money's part. And (though not for some time) the Webbs acted on it. Lloyd George was now beyond them, but Mr. Churchill welcomed their advice and help, with memorable results during his too brief tenures of the Board of Trade and the Home Office. Their only other important disciple in high places was Herbert (now Lord) Samuel. Himself endowed with a trained intelligence much above the ordinary Minister's level, and studying politics with an industry scarcely inferior to the Webbs' own, he made fruitful contacts with them over a considerable period. But unfortunately the 1914 war cut short too soon his work in high places.

For the rest it has to be recorded that, for all their rare gifts, the Webbs made relatively little impression on the reforms *of that period*. On the merits it might seem inexplicable, but in the light of the foregoing narrative it can be understood. Only so, again, can be explained the fate of Beatrice Webb's *Minority Report* and the brilliant campaign which she waged in the country on its behalf. It is significant, but not surprising, that Balfour and other intelligent Conservatives were much more favourably impressed by it than were the heads of the reforming Government. The latter almost inevitably distrusted it because of its source.

But let us not end on the note of failure. Hard and disinterested work for high ideals, pursued as the Webbs' was over a long period of years, is never thrown away. In certain directions, particularly in regard to education, the pair achieved a series of very solid successes. But minor successes—a spoke in this little wheel, a screw in that—accrued to them all the time ; and the cumulative result must have been very great. There was, however, yet another effect—an imponderable. H. G. Wells has put on record his impression of the Webb *salon*. The present writer would like to state a very different one. He cannot recall a single one of the very many visits which he paid to that *salon*, from which he did not return with heart and mind enriched, encouraged and braced. Often he may have disagreed with his hosts' arguments ; but even disagreement stimulated. It is tragic to think how much goodness, beauty, nobility and wisdom may appear in this world, and then drop out of it almost as if they had never been. May one surviving unforgetting witness enter this plea against oblivion.

SIDNEY WEBB AND THE LONDON COUNTY COUNCIL

by

ALAN M. McBRIAR

VI

SIDNEY WEBB AND THE LONDON COUNTY COUNCIL

ALAN M. McBRIAR

" Beneath the surface . . . there runs a continuous
controversy between an Ego that Affirms and an Ego
that Denies."

(The opening sentence of *My Apprenticeship*.)

In these words, Beatrice Webb described a dialectical conflict
between Hypothesis and Doubt that she was conscious of in
her own mind when she attempted to solve important problems. Is this a common experience of an historian faced with any
of the really important problems of history ? Whatever the general
answer may be, it certainly seems as if the conflict could never
rage more fiercely than it does when an attempt is made to estimate
the Webbs' own influence on the politics of their age. As one turns
the pages of the heavy Minutes of the London County Council in
the library of County Hall, the " Ego that Affirms " searches
hopefully for some trace of the Fabian hand, gently pushing History
along the Collectivist path. The " Ego that Denies," meanwhile,
encouraged by the paucity of the information to be found there,
raises the doubt whether, after all, even great Fabians do not drift
fairly helplessly, like most of us, on history's dangerous flood. In
the case of Sidney Webb, the decision is made more difficult by
the political method he adopted of " permeation," and yet still
more by his extreme modesty about his own achievements. To
him, it was the attainment of the objectives that mattered ; the
" personal element " he deemed " contemptible." No one could
have been more willing than he to work in the background and
allow others to take the personal credit ; no one could have been
more anxious than he to stress the continuity of historical change
and the manifold influence of the " Spirit of the Age." At last, his
very self-effacement became suspect, and a myth was created of
Webb as the Machiavelli of County Council politics, the manipu-

lator of all the wires behind the scenes. And if Webb steadfastly refused to make any such claims for himself, his friends (particularly Bernard Shaw and R. B. Haldane) were prepared to make them for him, boldly claiming the whole of Progressivism to be of Fabian origin, until by way of reaction a counter-myth of Fabian ineffectiveness emerged once more. Eventually an attempt must be made to decide between the rival hypotheses.

Webb's principal work on the L.C.C. was in the field of technical education, and it would be possible in this chapter to concentrate entirely on the administration of the Technical Education Board, avoiding all the more controversial problems of Webb's general influence on the Progressives. But this, though no doubt important, would be comparatively dull, especially as the story of Webb's influence in many major decisions of educational policy is told in another chapter of this book. And no estimate of Webb's work on the L.C.C. could be complete which did not attempt some assessment of his more general influence. He was a member of many other committees besides the Technical Education Board, and he wrote extensively about the whole range of L.C.C. activities. Certain questions demand an answer : *Can* Webb be called the founder of Municipal Socialism ? To what extent *was* he the initiator of the programme of the Progressive Party ? An examination of the evidence for the assertions and denials made in answer to these questions might serve to bring out what really were Webb's substantial contributions of original ideas or driving energy, of intellect or of will.

Was Webb the founder of Municipal Socialism ? Let us take this question first. It can be shown, I think, that any claim that he was the " onlie begetter " of Municipal Socialism breaks down under criticism. But this much truth will appear in it : that Webb did add a couple of important ideas to the London reform programmes of his Radical predecessors.

The claim that Webb was the " founder " usually springs from the fact that the name of the Fabian Society is always associated with the words " Municipal Socialism." From the early 'nineties of the last century, the Society made itself the chief propagandist of Municipal Socialism, for at least the next two decades. And within the Fabian Society itself, Sidney Webb was recognised as the man who had first turned his colleagues' attention to the importance of local politics. The Fabian Society's first Tract on Municipal Socialism, published in 1889, the *Facts for Londoners*, was substantially Webb's work. It was followed in 1891 by the important booklet *The London Programme*, which appeared under Webb's own name. Both works were extremely successful, and the Fabians were tremendously impressed with their success. Undoubtedly Webb had opened the eyes of his fellow-members of the Fabian Society to what was *for them* a whole new field for propaganda and activity. As a result the Fabians and those who became influenced by them were perhaps inclined to overrate the originality of Webb's proposals for London reform.

The criticism of this claim began early. The Liberal-Radicals of London in the early 'nineties were not prepared to admit the novelty of Webb's proposals for London reform. The Liberal journal, *The Speaker*, reviewing the *London Programme* in its issue of 3rd October, 1891, declared : " On this occasion Mr. Webb writes more as a Radical than as a Fabian, and, except on one subject[1] . . . every reform he advocates is certainly included in the programme of every Liberal and Radical in London." The basic point of this criticism is that the movement for London reform had a long history behind it before Webb joined in the campaign. That movement dated back to the time when London had been excluded from the Municipal Corporations Act of 1835, which had reformed the government of the other cities of England. The next fifty years of London government were an era of Anarchy and Private Enterprise, which the miserable degree of centralisation introduced by the Metropolis Management Act of 1855 did little to alleviate. In general, the local government authorities of London remained limited in size and power—inefficient, undemocratic, sometimes corrupt— and the public utility undertakings were necessarily left in the hands of profit-making companies. Such was the state of affairs until the Local Government Act of 1888 established the London County Council. This fact—that London reform had been so long delayed behind that of the other cities of England—had two

[1] The " one subject " was Leasehold Enfranchisement, a proposal that lease-holders of houses built on land let for ninety-nine years should be empowered to purchase the freehold at a valuation. It was popular amongst some Radicals, but the Fabians opposed it. They considered it the urban equivalent of the Chamberlain-Collings " three acres and a cow."

results : *first*, that the other cities of the Kingdom had already pioneered many extensions of municipal government ; and *second*, that the demands for reform in London had already been carried to great lengths before the L.C.C. came into being. Naturally the Radicals had carried their demands furthest, but by the 'seventies and 'eighties the need for reform was so great that many Conservatives, even the august *Times* itself, lent approval to many of the demands. To some extent London reform initially was non-party, and many a Royal Commission report provided useful ammunition for the reformers. The material was all ready for the English Socialist organisations, reborn during the trade depression of the 'eighties, to take over and extend the Radicals' demands. Sidney Webb and the Fabians were chiefly active in this. But the Fabians had come late to London reform. The L.C.C. had been established not long after Mrs. Annie Besant had dragged the Fabians from one another's drawing-rooms and plunged them into London's Radical politics. They had had no real share in bringing the L.C.C. into existence, but they aimed at *completing* the reorganisation of London's government machinery, and extending the scope of municipal enterprise. Their task was to agitate for the reform of the lesser government bodies of the Metropolis, for an extension of the L.C.C.'s power, and for the carrying out by it of a " progressive " policy.

What then was Webb's relationship to his predecessors in municipal reform, and what was new about his Municipal Socialism ? His predecessors, as has been suggested, were of two kinds : the practical administrators of the other cities of England, and the Radical theoreticians of Birmingham and London. It is necessary only to look at the early Fabian Tracts to see how much " Municipal Socialism " was a fact before it was a theory. It was indeed a feature of Webb's propaganda that most of the reforms he was advocating were neither new nor untried. It was not even necessary to stress that many Radicals already advocated some of them, for in many towns of England they had already been introduced for purely " practical " reasons. Webb and the Fabians took up the attitude that they were demanding, for London, institutions which had been successful elsewhere. When the Fabians first recommended the municipal supply of gas in London, they did not fail to point out that 170 different towns in England already owned their own gasworks " to save the cost of share-holders." Similarly, when they urged municipal trams for London, they were careful to say that thirty-one towns already owned their own trams, and one (Huddersfield) worked them without employing a contractor and was the only tramway at that time which granted an eight-hour day to its employees. It was the same with the water supply (where they could also use the recommendations of Royal Commissions and Departmental Committees that London's supply should be taken out of the hands of the water companies). It was the same with the Docks, and Housing. So also was it with their lesser demands : the abolition of the Guilds of the City and the transfer of their property to the control of the representatives of the people of London, the control by the L.C.C. over the markets of London, the provision of "amenities," more baths, wash-houses, libraries, parks . . . all these things amounted to a claim that London should enjoy the " freedom and social activity " of the most progressive provincial cities. Their demands for the simplification of the governmental machinery of London, and for introducing a certain measure of centralisation under the L.C.C., also followed along Radical lines, which sought to obtain for London the advantages that the other cities of the Kingdom had secured in 1835.

Sidney Webb's forerunners as theorists were, principally, Joseph Chamberlain and J. F. B. Firth. Though his name is today the less well known, Firth in the 'eighties undoubtedly had the greater influence among the London Radicals. Firth was a lawyer and politician of considerable ability, and his London Municipal Reform League, which had been founded in 1881, had become the principal organisation of the London Radical reformers. Until his death in an accident in 1889, Firth, not Webb, was the intellectual leader of the London " Progressives." The books and pamphlets on London government which he wrote in the 'seventies and 'eighties represented the chief theoretical material in circulation amongst them. The majority of the Progressives of the first L.C.C. owed allegiance to Firth's Municipal Reform League, while not a single Fabian was elected to the first L.C.C. Firth was appointed the first deputy-chairman of the L.C.C., and became the recognised leader of the Progressive Party, which he was accused (by those who wanted to keep party politics out of the L.C.C.) of having " created." Webb certainly derived a great deal from Firth. A comparison of Webb's earliest works with Firth's writings reveals many striking similarities, both in the proposals for reorganising the machinery of London government, and even in the proposals for the control of public monopolies. Firth, like Webb, saw no reason for the preservation of the rights of the liverymen of the City Guilds ; he wanted the two police forces of London amalgamated and placed under the control of the elected representatives of London ; he recommended that London's central authority should purchase the assets of the water and the gas companies and " have control of " the markets and tramways and " give full consideration to " the question of acquiring them, as other cities had done. In one of Firth's pamphlets—*The Gas Supply of London* (1874)—there is an examination, more comprehensive than anything in Webb's early writings, of the different conditions under which gas companies' assets had been acquired by other municipalities, leading to some conclusions about the best methods of " municipalisation." The only major service about which Firth made no recommendation, and Webb did, was the London Docks, and this was simply because the condition of the Docks was only brought to the attention of the reformers by the agitation amongst the dockers in the late 'eighties.

Such is the criticism of Webb's claim to be the " founder " of Municipal Socialism. It is formidable, and fatal to any crude claims. But when the criticism has done its worst, it is necessary to point out that Webb's programme for London reform really did differ in important ways from those of his predecessors. The novelty of Webb's proposals can best be demonstrated by mentioning Joseph Chamberlain's conflict with Firth. In his Unauthorised Radical Programme of 1885, Chamberlain had gone out of his way to attack the kind of plans advocated by Firth. The difference between them was a profound one ; it was a difference that had run throughout the whole history of the London reform movement : the conflict between centralisation and decentralisation. Firth wanted a centralised system for the Metropolis, with extensive powers in the hands of the central authority and " District Councils " (to replace the Vestries) strictly subordinate to it. Chamberlain on the other hand, thinking he had learnt from " practical experience " as mayor of Birmingham that Birming-

DEBATE BETWEEN BERNARD SHAW AND HILAIRE BELLOC,
JANUARY, 1913

Those depicted include E. R. Pease, Hubert Bland, Hilaire Belloc, Sir John
Cockburn (in the chair), G.B.S., Beatrice Webb and Sidney Webb

Cartoon by Will Dyson

41, Grosvenor Road,
Westminster
(now 41, Millbank)

Passfield Corner, near Liphook, Hants

THE WEBB HOME IN TOWN AND COUNTRY

ham was the ideal size for local administration, wanted London split into several " cities " of this size, federated merely for common purposes in a central body.

When Sidney Webb entered the lists as a theorist of London reform, he attempted to take a middle position between these champions of centralisation and decentralisation. Throughout his whole career as a theorist of Municipal Socialism he preserved a middle position between the extremes, though he tended on different items of policy now towards one side and now towards the other, and occasionally changed his ground as the result of his experience of London government. Thus in *Facts for Londoners* Webb appears more a disciple of Firth than he later appears in *The London Programme*. In *Facts for Londoners* he recommended that the smaller authorities should be under " the control, supervision and audit " of the L.C.C., while in *The London Programme* he anticipated that the new " District Councils " would " undoubtedly be bodies of independent authority, having power to raise their own rates, expend their own funds, and settle their own questions in their own way." In the latter work Webb can also be observed making his discovery that the principle embodied in " Grants-in-Aid " provided a very satisfactory relationship between higher and lower authorities, giving the necessary degree of central control for ensuring efficiency while also permitting a large measure of local autonomy. Even in *Facts for Londoners*, however, Webb was much less of a centraliser than Firth : indeed, he was much less of a centraliser then than he himself became in later years. Whereas Firth wanted the functions of the London School Board and the Poor Law Guardians taken over by the new central body, Webb, in his earliest works, showed little objection to the continued existence of these and other *ad hoc* authorities. At that stage he said nothing against the machinery of the School Board, and he apparently contemplated with approval the establishment of a new *ad hoc* " Charities Board " or " Poor Law Council " to take over and " humanise " the functions of the Guardians and the Asylums Board and to administer public hospitals and other charities. Nor did Webb appear greatly concerned whether the Docks should be taken over by the L.C.C. or by a special public Trust or Board— in fact, in *The London Programme* he expressed a slight preference

D

for a Board. In later years, as is well known, Webb came back to a point of view similar to Firth's concerning the *ad hoc* authorities, and came to recommend the transfer to the L.C.C. of the functions of the School Board and the Guardians. Consequently it is not possible to label Webb a " centraliser " or " decentraliser " without qualification. After the time of *Facts for Londoners* he became somewhat less of a centraliser where the smaller governing bodies were concerned, but never a decentraliser like Joseph Chamberlain ; on the other hand, after the time of *The London Programme* he became rather more of a centraliser in his growing hostility to the *ad hoc* authorities. Only in one thing was Webb a fairly uncompromising centraliser throughout : he thought the different authorities should have basically the same electoral areas and the same electoral register. He favoured (so far as was possible, having regard for local sentiment) the Parliamentary electoral area as the basic unit. He believed, with much reason, that overlapping areas for different authorities, and different electoral registers, were highly confusing to the ordinary citizen, and that their " centralisation " would increase the participation of the ordinary citizen in local affairs, and foster that active local patriotism which he prized so highly.

That represented the most distinct difference between Webb and his predecessors. But Webb was a Socialist, while Firth and Chamberlain had been Liberals, albeit Radical-Liberals. Surely that made a difference ? It did ; but it was a difference more of ends and objectives than of immediate demands.[1] Webb wanted Socialism ultimately, but he thought of it primarily as a vast administrative task, only capable of being accomplished gradually, and he was willing to begin with those concerns that the Radicals were ready to take over. His Socialism was largely an optimism

[1] I do not wish to underrate the importance of this difference, however. There seems no doubt that Webb's presentation of particular reforms as part of a whole scheme of " Municipal Socialism " gave the Fabians a feeling of superiority to the Liberal-Radicals, who had no such comprehensive outlook : a feeling of leadership, a feeling of knowing the way the world was going. This was the Fabian " myth," as important in its more limited sphere as the Marxian " myth," which it somewhat resembles. One can test its *validity* either (as a political scientist) by examining the causal factors claimed to be influencing the movement of history in that direction, or (as an historian) by looking in retrospect at the extent to which history *did* move in that direction. (The second procedure is adopted in this chapter). But its *emotional value* for those Fabians who participated in the events of this time cannot be doubted.

that these experiments would prove a success and would pave the way towards further extensions of municipal and government ownership and "trading." Firth and Chamberlain (though Chamberlain had certainly toyed with the word " socialistic " in the Unauthorised Programme) clearly desired no general inroad into the private ownership of the means of production, but were willing to take into public ownership certain monopolies in the interests of " efficiency." Other Progressives sometimes justified these extensions of municipal activity on the ground that the reform of a few abuses whose existence could not be denied would deprive the Socialists of much of their support. But the usual Progressive attitude was Lord Rosebery's : " Those things are not Socialism at all. They are a vital necessity for a great city." This difference over ultimate objectives and the borderlines of definition is important in considering the intellectual leadership that Webb and the Fabians were supposed to have given the Progressives. Did Webb manage to persuade the Progressives to go any further than they had already resolved to go ? Certainly his phrase " Municipal Socialism " caught on. This was rather against the will of many of the Progressive leaders, but it was a striking phrase, and its constant use both by Socialists and by Conservatives popularised it. In addition there *was* a borderline of practical difference : the Fabians were confident that the L.C.C. would not only be able to own but also to manage the concerns it took over, whereas Firth in his writings showed the Liberal distrust of public management. He appeared to favour the municipality letting out its monopoly to a contractor, under fairly strict conditions ; but he was cautious and tentative about it, he seemed willing to be open to conviction, and on this point the Fabians may have had some success in persuading the Progressives. There were, finally, certain specific " labour " demands which the Socialists supported enthusiastically —demands for " fair wages " and the eight-hour day for Council employees, for the payment of Councillors, etc. But the Progressives also relied to a considerable extent on a working-class electorate, and the majority of them found they could agree to these " labour " demands without moulting too many feathers of their faith in private enterprise.

This inquiry into the novelty of Webb's proposals for London reform is necessary in an historical evaluation, but of course absolute originality is far from being the only thing that is important in politics. Even more important, perhaps, is " he who says it so long and so loud that he compels mankind to hear him." This brings us to our second, and even more important question : What was the extent of Webb's influence upon the Progressives ?

There is strong evidence for the claim that Webb's influence was very considerable. Even if it is allowed, as it must be, that Firth's influence was paramount amongst the Progressives in the first year of the L.C.C., yet Webb did become, in a very real sense, the *successor* of Firth as the Progressive Party's theoretician. Firth's death occurred in 1889, at the end of the first session of the L.C.C., and his organisation, the Municipal Reform League, over-confident that its work was done once the L.C.C. had been established, appears to have faded out of existence soon afterwards. Webb stepped into the vacant place, and his influence with the Progressives really dates from the time of the publication of *The London Programme* in 1891. It was in that year that the Fabian Society distributed the greatest flood of leaflets it has ever put forth in its whole lifetime, each leaflet dealing with a different point of *The London Programme*. This propaganda had its effect. At the time of the second election for the L.C.C. in 1892, the Progressive Party definitely recognised *The London Programme* as the most up-to-date statement of its objectives. In October of the same year the Fabians consolidated their position when the London Reform Union was founded, as the main propaganda body of the Progressive Party, on the basis of a programme which reads like a paraphrase of Webb's booklet. Lord Rosebery, as its first President, made a graceful figurehead for the London Reform Union, but Webb saw to it that the organisation was always well-staffed with Fabians. Webb himself in its early days was a member of its committee, and Tom Mann, who at that time was a member of the Fabian Society, and was working closely with the Webbs, became its first secretary. Later, when Tom Mann retired from this position in 1898, his place was taken by F. W. Galton, who up to that time had been the Webbs' private secretary. Other Fabian names appeared on the Union's list of public lecturers, and there were Fabians on nearly all its subcommittees. In consequence, it is hardly surprising to discover that the character and format of the pamphlets issued by the

London Reform Union bear a marked resemblance to the Fabian Tracts.

In addition to this propaganda through the London Reform Union and the Fabian Society, there was the personal share that Webb and the other Fabians took in the actual work of the L.C.C. The Fabian representatives on the L.C.C. were very active, even if their number was never great. In fact, their result at the 1892 election was a portent of their later results : at the 1892 election six Fabians were elected (out of a total of 118 elected Councillors), and this number continued to be the average Fabian representation on the L.C.C. right up to the end of the 1920's. While Webb was on the L.C.C., the only fluctuations from this number occurred at the 1895 election, when the number of Fabians returned was reduced to three, and after the 1907 election, when the Fabians did not suffer in the Progressives' debâcle, but actually increased their number to eight (including two Aldermen). Webb was steadily returned by Deptford so long as he chose to stand (that was until 1910). While he was on the Council all the Fabian representatives were members of the Progressive Party, which was continuously in power from the first election until the election of 1907, and continuously out of power thereafter. During the period of Progressive ascendancy the Fabian representatives were, then, a small but very active group inside the dominant party. Webb himself during this time was a member of more than a dozen committees, covering a vast range of L.C.C. work : the mere list of them is impressive (see footnote)[1]. His principal Committee throughout was that dealing with education, but he was also for a continuous period of nine years a member of the Local Government and Taxation Committee—twice he had the Vice-Chairmanship and once the Chairmanship of it—and he was also a

[1]List of Webb's Committees :
1. EDUCATION :

Technical Education Committee (chairman)	1892–3
Technical Education Board	1893–1904
(Chairman 1893–8 and 1901–2. Vice-chairman 1899–1901)	
Education Committee	1904–10

2. FINANCE :

Local Government and Taxation Committee	1892–1901
(Vice-chairman 1892–5 and in 1900. Chairman 1900–1901)	
Corporate Property Committee	1895–1904
Finance Committee	1893–5 and 1904–9
County Rate Committee	1896–1901

member for the same length of time of the Parliamentary, the General Purposes, and the Corporate Property Committees.

At this stage there should follow a detailed description of Webb's work on all these Committees, in order to overwhelm the " Ego that Denies " with facts. This, however, is not possible, both for reasons of space, and because the minutes of the L.C.C. (both the general minutes and the Committee minutes) tend, like Webb, to eschew personalities. The influence of an individual emerges most clearly only when he is in disagreement with his colleagues. As Webb was a superb committee-man, much of his work is hard to disentangle. The following observations on Webb's work for technical education and the reorganisation of the lesser authorities of London are made, therefore, not as an attempt to do justice to all his hard committee work, but simply as a statement of his most notable achievements, and an account of his relations with the Progressive Party.

To begin, Webb can be called the creator of the Technical Education Committee and the Technical Education Board that grew out of it. This achievement was less a matter of overcoming opposition than of just getting the thing done, and Webb did it. By the early 'nineties the actual opposition to the development of technical education under L.C.C. control was comparatively slight. There was, of course, the usual dead-weight of apathy and stupidity, but by that time, a sufficiently large number even of vested interests had become alarmed about England's trade and industrial position relative to Germany's—a disadvantage which was freely attributed to the better German system of technical education—

3. OTHERS :

Parliamentary Committee	1892–1901
General Purposes Committee	1892–1901
Thames Conservancy Committee	1893–4
Rivers Committee	1894–5 and 1899–1901
Water Committee	1892–5
Public Health and Housing Committee	1892–3
Establishment Committee	1892–3 and 1899–1901
Appeals Committee	1892–3
Historical Records and Buildings Committee	1901–4

4. SPECIAL COMMITTEES AND APPOINTMENTS :

London Government	1894–5
New Offices	1900–4
City Parochial Foundation	1899–1909
Senate of London University	1900–9
Metropolitan Water Board	1904–5

to make the path of the reformer smoother than it might otherwise have been. In fact, a considerable move had been made before Webb was elected to the L.C.C. The Conservative Government in 1889 had introduced a Bill to provide for Technical Education, and the Bill gave the power of levying the rate and providing for this technical education to the County Councils. The London School Board protested, claiming that in London it should have the rating power. But Goschen, a convinced centraliser who looked to Germany for his model, forced the Bill through, and it became the Technical Instruction Act, 1889. In the following year, as the result of a conflict between the Government and the forces of Temperance, the " Whisky Money " (the customs duty on beer and spirits levied under the Local Taxation—Customs and Excise— Act, 1890) was diverted by Goschen from the " compensation of decayed publicans " to the subsidy of technical education. Thus both the power and the funds for technical education had been placed in the hands of the L.C.C. However, nothing was done about it during the lifetime of the first L.C.C. : the opportunity was wasted in a futile squabble with the City Corporation, when the L.C.C. tried to wrest from the Corporation still more money for educational purposes.

Webb determined to end this state of affairs. Shortly after his election he moved that a committee be appointed to examine the needs of technical education and the ways in which the Council could best make use of its powers. He also suggested a list of names for a committee of twenty, including himself and three other Fabian Councillors. The Committee was appointed and unanimously elected Webb its Chairman. He continued to hold this position when, early in 1893, the Technical Education Committee was converted into the Technical Education Board, with fifteen nominees of other organisations added to the twenty L.C.C. members. Once again this change was made on Webb's advice, to avoid the antagonism of these other bodies to exclusive L.C.C. control.

Webb's first actions were characteristic. He employed H. Llewellyn Smith to make a full survey of existing facilities, and of London's needs, for education above the primary level. Then, with the help of A. H. D. Acland, he secured the widest possible definition of the meaning of " technical education," until, in his own words, it included " the teaching of every conceivable subject, other than ancient Greek and theology." Finally, he engaged a particularly able secretary—Dr. William Garnett. Equipped with these advantages, the Technical Education Board went vigorously to work, under Webb's minute supervision and guidance. The permeative method was displayed in its activity. New establishments were certainly provided where they were needed—the London Day Training College and the Central School of Arts and Crafts being the chief of these—but the Technical Education Board preferred to subsidise existing educational institutions, encouraging them to improve and extend their teaching and equipment. This policy avoided delay in building up completely new institutions, avoided the friction which the competition of the new with the old would have created, and established a " unity in diversity " by introducing a measure of central supervision and control over otherwise autonomous bodies. In the final report of its ten years' work from 1893–1903 which the Technical Education Board handed to its successor, it was able to give an impressive list of its work along these lines.

But it was the creation of his " scholarship ladder " that Webb had perhaps even more at heart. When Llewellyn Smith reported in 1892, there was an elementary school roll of 680,000 pupils, yet the total number of scholarships available for them was only about 1,000, and many of these had onerous qualifications and obligations attached to them. Webb in 1893 got a resolution passed by the L.C.C. allowing the Technical Education Board to provide scholarships, and shortly afterwards got the Board to agree to the award of 500 junior county scholarships annually. These scholarships entitled pupils at elementary schools to further education at secondary or higher grade schools, and in addition (a wise addition) provided a maintenance grant of £10 a year " to compensate parents to some extent for the loss of their children's earnings." In later years, this " scholarship ladder " was extended, and at the time the Technical Education Board handed over to its successor in 1904, the number of junior county awards had risen to 600, and there had been added to them 100 intermediate scholarships for pupils of sixteen to nineteen years, five senior scholarships, three teachers' travelling scholarships, thirty art scholarships, some 350 other scholarships for those taking technical, evening or continued instruction, and 800 odd domestic economy scholarships for women and girls. Administratively, this widespread scholarship system had the same result as the Board's grants; as Beatrice Webb has put it : "What had previously been a chaos of isolated institutions, largely unaware of one another's existence, became gradually welded—without suppression of local administration by separate bodies of governors—into a graded educational system covering every part of London."

The success of Webb's administration of the Technical Education Board helped to convince the officials of the Education Department (if they needed convincing) to centralise the control of education under the County Councils. What is more, the success of the Technical Education Board's work may have convinced Webb himself of the need for this step. Mrs. Webb wrote, many years after, that Sidney Webb had decided on this step as early as 1892. If such was the case, he certainly did not take the Fabian Society into his confidence until some years later. Is it possible that Mrs. Webb has mis-remembered slightly, and that Webb came to recommend the centralisation of education under the L.C.C. more as a result of his practical experience of the difficulties of divided control than purely on grounds of " principle " (which the early date would suggest) ? Certainly, it was his experience of the practical difficulties that Webb insisted on— the conflicts of authority which wasted time and money ; the bad effects of the cleavage between elementary and higher education on teachers, scholars and administrators ; the expense, etc.—in the argument that finally carried the Fabian Society against the Rev. Stewart Headlam, the champion of the School Board.

Webb's decision to throw his weight into the support of the Education Acts of 1902 and 1903 finally put an end to his popularity with the Progressives.[1] At first sight this appears surprising, considering that so many of the Progressives had been nurtured on J. F. B. Firth's centralising doctrine. And in truth the Progres-

[1]This is a generalisation which needs a little elaborating. Webb's estrangement was rather from the Nonconformist rank-and-file of the Progressive Party than from the Progressive leaders. But the large Nonconformist tail certainly wagged the Progressive dog. The Progressive leaders were obliged to placate their Nonconformist followers, whatever their real feelings were towards Webb. It was not, however, until after 1907, by which time a number of the older Progressive leaders had been elected to the House of Commons, that the Nonconformists under Scott Lidgett gained complete control of the Progressive Party.

D*

sives on the L.C.C. were placed in a cruel dilemma by the Education Acts, but this only made them dislike Webb the more for having made up his mind so firmly. If it had been a simple issue of L.C.C. control, the majority of the L.C.C. Progressives would have favoured it (though the Labour men amongst them, led by J. Ramsay MacDonald, who had come to dislike Webb, had found new virtues in the " primary democracy " of *ad hoc* authorities). But it was the intrusion of larger, national issues into municipal politics which brought about the complications. The Conservative Government had managed to tie up the issue of County Council control with the support of Church schools out of the rates. The Liberal opposition (to which the Progressives were officially allied) constituted itself the defender of the School Boards in the interests of Nonconformity. The Progressives could not, or would not, understand how a Rationalist like Webb could ally himself with " clerical reaction." They did not realise that his agnosticism was non-militant and completely tolerationist.

After the passing of the Education Act of 1903, Webb was estranged from the Progressives. Before the 1904 election the Webbs, apprehensive of Progressive intentions, were secretly hoping for a Moderate victory ! This did not occur, and the Progressives revenged themselves on Webb by keeping him out of all positions of importance and turning him off the Progressive Party Committee. But they did not proceed to the final breach. Webb thought it better to try still to influence the Progressives, and some of the Progressive leaders were reluctant to lose Webb's expert knowledge of educational affairs. Consequently, he was given the subordinate position of Chairman of the Scholarships and Higher Education Sub-Committee on the new Education Committee. Even in this position Webb nevertheless made his influence felt : the most considerable new development during the first three years of the Education Committee was the adoption of an elaborate scheme for the extension of scholarships which was planned by him. This revised scholarship scheme in turn required accommodation for an additional 11,000 pupils by 1910–11, so the Education Committee was forced to commence an extensive building programme. By 1907 it had provided sixteen new secondary schools taking 4,000 pupils. But Webb was never quite happy about the Progressives' attitude to the Education Act, during the years when the Nonconformist Liberals were vigorously agitating for its repeal, and he was probably not sorry when the position was secured, so far as the L.C.C. was concerned, by the victory of the "Moderates" (under their new name of "Municipal Reformers") in 1907. Actually it must be said on behalf of the Progressives that they showed remarkable forbearance in refraining from sabotaging the Education Act, as they well might have done, but there was a constant danger until 1907 that they might close down more of the voluntary schools than was necessary. As it turned out, the tremendous task of bringing the voluntary schools up to standard was virtually accomplished by the time Webb retired from the L.C.C. The training of the unqualified teachers had been put in hand, and of 282 voluntary schools which needed substantial alterations, only seventy-seven were closed, and all but fifty-six of the others had been brought up to the Council's standard by that time.

It is interesting that Webb's other work on the Committees dealing with the reform of London government also resulted in his estrangement from the Progressives. In fact, as this question was solved before the other, the dispute over the Borough Councils really began Webb's estrangement from the Progressives, and the Education differences merely completed it. Once again, it was a matter where national politics obtruded themselves into County politics. Before this happened, Webb had worked together with his Progressive colleagues on the Local Government and Taxation Committees for such objectives as the equalisation of rates between wealthy and poorer districts, the taxation of ground landlords, etc. The Committee Minutes show that most of these issues had been raised on the Committee before Webb was elected to the L.C.C., but proceedings *do* seem to have speeded up when he became Vice-Chairman. The controversy finally arose over the main issue of the reform of the vestries, and it was precipitated by the action of the Conservative Government. We have already seen how Webb stood between Firth and Chamberlain on the issue of " centralisation." When Chamberlain had gone over to the Conservatives he found little difficulty in persuading them to his view of Municipal Government, after two elections had convinced Lord Salisbury that the L.C.C. was nothing but a hotbed of

Radicalism and Collectivism. The violent reaction of the wealthier vestries to the L.C.C.'s plans for equalising rates seemed to provide the opportunity for a Conservative Bill which, under the pretext of reorganising the lesser authorities of London, would really split London into ten " cities " and deprive the L.C.C. of most of its power. The Progressives fought the original intentions of the Metropolitan Borough Councils' Bill fiercely, under the slogan of " Unification versus Tenification." Webb found himself in a middle position : he agreed with the Progressives in their opposition to " Tenification," but he did not want " Unification " either. Consequently he and the Fabian Society set about persuading the Progressives not to oppose the Conservative Bill root-and-branch, but rather to endeavour to amend it. In the end that is what happened ; Webb professed himself not dissatisfied with the resulting London Government Act of 1899, which set up the Metropolitan Borough Councils, and the Fabian Society took credit for having brought the Progressives to take a " sensible " attitude to it. But in truth this result was probably due less to Fabian persuasion, than to a compromise between a strong Conservative Government and a Progressive Party which had an overwhelming victory on the " Unification versus Tenification " issue at the 1898 election. The Progressives were by no means so satisfied as Webb with the compromise, and Webb fell out of their favour for applauding it.

These two examples we have taken of Webb's work reveal something of the strength and the weakness of his position on the L.C.C. —they provide material both for the " Ego that Affirms " and the " Ego that Denies." In general the " Ego that Affirms " has the best of it. Not only can it point out Webb's remarkable administrative achievements within the limits of the Progressive Party's policy, but also that, in some matters where the Progressive Party was in conflict with the Conservative Government, and Webb's views were intermediate between them, the ends he desired were also secured. And in education it could claim that Webb's influence was very real, in the sense that, if Webb had not occupied the position he did, the development of education in London might very well have been different. In the case of the Borough Councils, a similar claim could not be made with like certainty.

But the " Ego that Denies " would return to the attack by asking how far these achievements were "Socialist"? Could not Webb have done all he did on the L.C.C. if he had not been a Socialist at all ? While he could perhaps negotiate solutions that were intermediate between Liberalism and Conservatism, did he manage to achieve any result intermediate between Liberalism and Socialism ? Did he, in short, persuade the Progressives to transcend the Radicalism of J. F. B. Firth's kind ? In one sense, perhaps, these questions are illegitimate. If Socialists and Liberals both desired such things as better educational facilities, more scholarships and better municipal government, surely Webb cannot be justly criticised as a Socialist for pursuing these objectives ? Of course not ; and yet . . . the question remains : Are these things *really* " Municipal Socialism " or Radicalism ? And the answer must be that they are part of both, but that " Municipal Socialism " leads one to expect lots of other things as well.

On the specifically " Socialist " side, the final results of L.C.C. activity were disappointing. It is not altogether fair to say (as has been said) that the list of Webb's Committees shows he preferred those committees where quiet and intricate work could be done by his painstaking, expert and educated mind, to the actual " socialising " committees, where the issues were obvious and the public controversy certain. While he may have found the problems of London education, the negotiating of the L.C.C.'s parliamentary business, and the intricacies of municipal finance and government most congenial topics, he was nevertheless a member, at one time and another, of Committees dealing with the water supply, the docks, and the ill-fated Thames Steamboats. The minutes of Webb's principal Committees also show that there were many opportunities of urging the cause of socialisation on them (on the Local Government and Taxation Committee, for instance) which we can be sure he did not fail to use. And even if the leadership of the Committee dealing with the " municipalisation " of the tramways, the water supply, etc., was left to non-Fabian Progressives like (Sir) John Williams Benn and W. H. (Lord) Dickinson, other Fabians assisted on these committees.

In general, however, and apart from the question of Webb's personal share in promoting it, " Municipal Socialism " in so far as it meant bringing services under the control of the L.C.C., was not a success—certainly it was not a *permanent* success. Two points need to be made about it. First, that Webb and the Fabians had no great success in persuading the Progressives to go beyond the limits of J. F. B. Firth's proposals. Second, that in the long run " Municipal Socialism " succumbed very largely to " State Socialism." Let us consider these two points.

" Municipal Socialism " did not prove to be a non-party affair, as had been hoped by many people, including Webb, in the early days. The fact that there was a semblance of it initially was due to London's lag behind the other cities of the Kingdom in municipal administration. The history of L.C.C. politics has been the story of the development of parties as London rapidly caught up, and some groups wanted to press further forward, while others thought " progress " had gone far enough. First, the division into a Progressive Party faced with a weak Moderate opposition, then the Progressives opposed by a strong Moderate Party which soon after took the more appealing name of " Municipal Reformers," finally, in 1910—the year of Webb's retirement from the L.C.C.— the emergence of the Labour Party. For measures that in any real sense involved an extension of municipal activity in new and socialist directions, the Fabians were dependent on obtaining an avenue to power through a party. During Webb's time on the L.C.C., they were dependent on the Progressive Party's approval of their measures. Those of the measures they advocated (like municipal trading in the supply of liquor, milk, and bread, municipal fire insurance and the municipal ownership of pawnshops and slaughter-houses) which did not obtain Progressive approval never had any hope of fulfilment. In any case, these " further steps " along the road of Municipal Socialism were put forward in the last years of the nineteenth century, by which time Webb's influence with the Progressives was already on the wane. Only in their more favourable attitude to direct L.C.C. management of municipal undertakings did the Progressive Party advance seriously beyond the views of J. F. B. Firth.

In the three cases where the L.C.C. did become the controlling authority in a Socialist sense, namely in the cases of the trams, the Thames Steamboats, and the Works Department, two were ended by the " Municipal Reformers " when they came to power, and the third was finally absorbed into a new-type *ad hoc* body, the London Transport Board. The only instance in which the

socialisation came and remained *somewhat* in the way Webb originally advocated was that of the Port of London Authority—and in
that case, it will be remembered, Webb had approved the example of the Mersey Docks and Harbour Board and had not recommended direct control by the L.C.C. In the other cases where
services were socialised, the early Fabian-Progressive plan for
L.C.C. control did not come about ; new type *ad hoc* authorities
were developed here too : the Water Board, the Joint Electricity
Authority, the Transport Board. These had certainly not been
sought by Webb and the early Fabians. They had emerged partly
in response to the technical needs of the service itself (as with
Electricity) and partly as a compromise between Progressive pressure and Conservative resistance (as with the Water Board). It
remained for Mr. Herbert Morrison and a newer generation of
Fabians to give a blessing to these new *ad hoc* authorities. " Municipal Socialism " of the early Fabian type was born too late. It
must be regarded in some ways as a reflection of London's lag
behind other cities in its municipal services. It was formulated at
the very time when administrative space was shrinking and the
organisation of many services was becoming national rather than
municipal.

The Webbs recognised the difficulties that were created for
their Municipal Socialism by the growth of these new *ad hoc*
bodies, and after the first World War, they faced up to them in
their *Constitution for the Socialist Commonwealth of Great Britain.*
This work has too often been dismissed as Webb's only attempt
at an " Utopia." While the practicality of some of their plans
can be debated, it is much more interesting to regard the " Constitution " as an outcome of the Webbs' experience of the
L.C.C. For once the Webbs abandoned their usual preoccupation
with history and gave an *ideal* extension to the State Socialist level
of some of the principles which had lain behind their Municipal
Socialism. Thus their " Minty-bookcase system " for combining
units of local government was an attempt to retain their earlier
principle of " one register for all elections " and yet cope with the
fact that many services overlapped ordinary municipal boundaries.
And so with their major proposal for the splitting of the present
Parliament into two—into the Political Parliament and the Social
Parliament. The Political Parliament was to retain all the present

trappings, and so enable the young gentlemen from Oxford and Cambridge to continue their Union debates in the traditional manner on foreign affairs and other matters that Webb was not greatly interested in. Meanwhile the Social Parliament was to be *an enlarged L.C.C. for all England*, where the graduates of the London School of Economics might do the real business of governing England. The Social Parliament, they thought, would enable democratic control to be maintained over the new National Boards by a " democracy of consumers," as the Webbs never had much hope of democracy *in* industry, through the " democracy of producers."

Webb's early " Municipal Socialism " had, however, an important influence amongst Socialists themselves. It drew the attention of Socialists to the potentialities of local government, pointing out to them that the National State did not exhaust the possibilities of Socialist action, and making clear the need for detailed information on administrative problems. At a time when it was not easy for Socialists to enter the National Parliament, Webb insisted on the possibility of local work. This gave those who engaged in it valuable training in practical administration, and in course of time brought them prestige, which in some cases resulted in their subsequent election to Parliament. Most important of all, it gave Socialists something to do, some concrete objectives to work for. It supplied Works as well as Faith, the indispensable mixture for continued as well as vigorous political action. Even if Webb did tend at first to generalise from the rather peculiar London position that " permeation " could be a substitute for an independent party of Labour in local and national politics, this mistake was presently corrected by the I.L.P. and Labour Party ; and the I.L.P. and Labour Party, in their turn, learnt much from Fabian methods.

How does the " Ego that Affirms " emerge from its ordeal at the conclusion of this chapter ? We have briefly looked at Sidney Webb on the L.C.C. from three angles : as theorist of London reform, as practical administrator within the scope of the Progressive Party's programme, and as propagandist for the extension of municipal activity in new and Socialist directions. His efforts in each of these fields were outstanding, and if his *success* was greatest in the second of them, that was to be expected in the circumstances. There can be no doubt of Sidney Webb's place of honour amongst those men who by their energy and initiative converted London from one of the worst-governed cities of the Empire, which it was in the 1880's, to one of the best-governed, which it is today. But he had also a considerable theoretic triumph in anticipating the nature of the development of London's government machinery more accurately than Firth or Chamberlain had done ; and while perhaps the same cannot be claimed of the narrowly " Socialist " aspect of " Municipal Socialism," nevertheless even this had an importance of no mean order in the history of British Socialism.

THE BREAK-UP OF THE POOR LAW

by

JOAN SIMEON CLARKE

VII

THE BREAK-UP OF THE POOR LAW

by *JOAN SIMEON CLARKE*

The *Minority Report of the Poor Law Commission* seemed to the Webbs, as they wrote it, to comprise not only a plan for the Break-up of the Poor Law, but also a formula which would " ensure to the workers by hand and by brain steady progress in health and happiness, honesty and kindliness, culture and scientific knowledge, and the spirit of adventure."[1]   Beatrice, looking back on it later, recognised that the plan, already largely implemented, was sound, but considered that the formula arose from an immature appraisal of the poisons inherent in monopoly capitalism; we, reading the *Report* again after the enactment of major social legislation between 1944 and 1946, find in it wider but rather different values.   We see, first, a mammoth administrative programme for the social services, almost impeccable in breadth and in detail;   secondly, a strong and consistent moral code;   thirdly, proposals for a new method of assessment and collection;   fourthly a social study describing in careful detail the depth of early twentieth century poverty.   Perhaps it is for this last quality that the *Minority Report* will have permanent value when its prophetic qualities are exhausted;   it may secure a place in its own right as a documented work of social history.

The *Minority Report* followed Sidney Webb's earlier contribution to social service reform;   he had, for some fifteen years preceding the Old Age Pensions Act of 1908, been one of the leading people agitating for pensions for the elderly.   The 1908 Act, although it was passed while the Royal Commission was still sitting, owed much more to these years of unremitting, though unspectacular, agitation than it did to the heat which was gradually surrounding the Royal Commission.   It also bore what later came to be a hallmark of the Webbs' thinking; it was based on the non-contributory principle and did not follow the model of old age

[1] *Our Partnership*, p. 477.

pensions insurance which had been set up by Bismarck in 1889 and which was not fully reflected in Great Britain until 1925.

THE ROYAL COMMISSION

The Royal Commission on the Poor Law was appointed in 1905 to inquire :—

"(1) Into the working of the laws relating to the relief of poor persons in the United Kingdom ;

(2) Into the various means which have been adopted outside of the Poor Laws for meeting distress arising from want of employment, particularly during periods of severe industrial depression ; and to consider and report whether any, and if so, what, modification of the Poor Laws or changes in their administration, or fresh legislation for dealing with distress, are advisable."

Beatrice was a member of it. She soon discovered that the officials of the Local Government Board had already decided what line the Report of the Commission should take, and had accordingly arranged who should give evidence. She therefore enlisted George Lansbury to support her in pressing the Commission towards a deep, broad and independent inquiry. Not only did she persuade her fellow-members to set up a number of special committees, and to instigate various pieces of detailed research, but she, herself, privately undertook various research projects (helped financially by Mrs. Bernard Shaw) and presented the Commission with fully documented memoranda on points about which she felt strongly. In all this she was strengthened by Sidney, who contributed both instances and arguments and helped her to prepare her numerous memoranda so that her material reached her colleagues punctually at the peak of argument. This continuous, internal pressure from Beatrice undoubtedly built up the Royal Commission into a much more important landmark than it would otherwise have been. During its inquiries it uncovered copious facts about the Poor Law, about the few other public social services, and about the life pattern of the poverty-stricken and of the technically destitute. These horror stories, as in fact they were, could not be ignored. Even though the many proposals of the *Minority Report*[1] were shelved for many years,

[1] The *Majority Report* was never considered to be even a basis of discussion.

the facts on which these proposals were based themselves constituted a leaven of reform. They would undoubtedly not have
been so systematically collected, nor so loudly publicised, had
Beatrice not been on the Commission. She, with Sidney, did much
to create that ferment of the public conscience which must necessarily precede major social change. That the Webbs did not
approve of the direction in which Lloyd George steered the
ensuing reforms does not at all detract from the value of the work
they did in rousing public opinion about the need for change.

THE CAMPAIGN

The Royal Commission reported in 1909, both *Majority* and
Minority Reports being issued, as usual, in a single volume by the
Government. However the Webbs feared that the *Minority
Report* would be smothered in the heavy dust of Blue Books, and
quietly arranged that it should also be published separately. The
Fabian Society put out a cheap edition, annotated specially by the
Webbs.   When the Treasury threatened the Society on the
grounds that it had infringed Crown copyright, Sidney replied,
first, that My Lords of the Treasury had previously renounced
any rights of copyright in Blue Books, and, secondly, that the
manuscript of the *Minority Report* was in his handwriting, and
that presumably, therefore, he himself held the copyright.[1] The
Treasury retired, startled, perhaps, to find that the Royal Commission had acquired two such fine and complementary intellects
for the price, as it were, of only one of them.

The Webbs then saw that the principles of the *Report* needed
more publicity. They started, in 1909, a propaganda and educational organisation called, eventually, The National Committee
for the Prevention of Destitution. This body had its own magazine,
The Crusade. Both Sidney and Beatrice undertook heavy speaking
programmes, " stumping the country," only a short time before
Lloyd George started on his rounds to explain the insurance
scheme which the Webbs so much disliked. It was Lloyd George's
Parliamentary success with sickness and unemployment insurance which defeated the N.C.P.D. The public realised that
major social legislation had been introduced and that this would
do much to help the poor in times of crisis. The distinction

[1] *Beatrice Webb*, by Margaret Cole, Longmans, 1945.

between the Lloyd George and the Webb method seemed to fewer and fewer people to be worth learning or fighting for. The agitation connected specifically with the *Minority Report* died down. However, the ideas of the *Report* did not die ; they reappeared continually until today almost all have been implemented. The Webbs themselves, however, turned to other activities, notably to politics, realising that fundamental change comes only through public readiness combined with political pressure. It was not until 1917 that either of the Webbs concentrated again directly on the problem of the Poor Law. In that year Beatrice was appointed to sit on the Local Government panel of the Reconstruction Committee, under the chairmanship of Sir Donald Maclean. It was typical of the Webb methods and the Webb strength that the Report of this Committee turned out to be similar in fundamentals to the *Minority Report* of the Royal Commission. However, this document was shelved almost immediately, and its reiteration of the 1909 programme did little to advance the latter, which for another twenty years proceeded on its slow, but, as we now see, inevitable course.

PORTRAIT OF THE POOR LAW

Before examining in detail the proposals of the *Minority Report* it is worth while to look at the social conditions which inspired them. In 1905, when the Royal Commission was appointed, the Poor Law was the only statutory cash-paying social service in the British Isles. In 1908, before the Commission reported, the Old Age Pensions Act was passed, but this Act was more important for its principle—tax-provided pensions for the aged, free of Poor Law stigma—than for any widespread effects. Pensions were made available only to persons aged seventy and over (provided that these old persons were not known to be of bad character) and the maximum rate was 5s. od. a week. The Act, therefore, left to the Poor Law all those indigent and enfeebled persons who had not yet had a seventieth birthday, and the openly disreputable ones over seventy ; it also, because its rates were low, left within the orbit of the Poor Law all those who, although in receipt of pensions, could find no way of supplementing them without relief. The Poor Law was also the dominant factor, actual or potential, in the financial outlook of millions of younger people. If the wage-earner became sick, or if he had an accident, or if he lost his job, he could turn only to the Poor Law. This, too, was the prospect for his family if he were imprisoned, if he deserted them, or if he died. Unless he either had relatively rich and generous relatives, or could manage to save substantially, or to ingratiate himself with one of the voluntary societies, he was almost certain to have, sometime, to apply for Poor Relief.

The content and spirit of Poor Law administration was therefore of vital importance to a large proportion of the population. The picture which emerges from the Webbs' *English Poor Law History* and from the *Minority Report* itself, fully explains the horror which stalked behind all those who feared that they might one day become destitute. Poor Law relief was of three kinds, outdoor relief (money to spend while living at home) indoor relief (the workhouse), and medical relief (the services of a general practitioner) Receipt of relief carried with it pauper status, including deletion from the register of voters. It also rendered the recipient of indoor or of outdoor relief liable to be removed from his home under the Act of Settlement. Although by 1909 the implementation of this Act had become much modified, the Webbs found "upwards of 12,000 poor persons actually deported annually, under compulsory orders, and often against their will, from one Union to another—occasionally from one end of the kingdom to the other—a form of exile by administrative order which in some cases causes great hardship."[1]

Coupled with these uniform disabilities were others varying in nature and intensity from one Union to another. Some Unions, in pursuance of a policy of keeping down out-relief, systematically " offered the House " (i.e., institutional maintenance) even to non-able-bodied persons when there was quite obviously no question of an able-bodied worker living indolent upon the rates. This practice had two disastrous effects. First, families in the desperation of poverty refused to apply for relief for fear that they might be sent into the workhouse and their members separated one from another ; they chose instead squalor, sickness and hunger, leading eventually, if no miracle happened, to starvation or crime.

---

[1] *Minority Report*, Chapter IX, p. 402. (Page references to the *Minority Report* throughout this chapter refer to the Fabian edition of 1909, and to Volume I unless otherwise specified.)

Secondly, those who accepted indoor-relief, even to tide them over a short period of hardship only, ran the risk of separation and of losing their home while they were inmates, as well as of other hardships to be described below. This policy of " offering the House," was, in some Unions, used as a blackmailing method of forcing liable relatives to maintain their destitute kin. It was paralleled in other Unions by a policy of granting outdoor relief almost automatically on application. However, so small were the sums allowed that ill-health and slow starvation undermined all those who had no resources other than relief. In fact this relief was apparently given on the assumption that other means of sub-sistence did exist, although the Relieving Officers seemed in-capable of ascertaining the extent of these resources or even of determining whether they were or were not present. Thus, some families with moderate incomes were clever enough to achieve subsidies from the rates, while other families, entirely dependent on relief, struggled to survive on sums that were openly admitted to be insufficient for full maintenance. Nor did either the Guardians or the Relieving Officers attempt to exercise any influence on the way that the money was spent. They had no responsibility for the health or for the morals of those whom they financed, and whose vice or disease might even increase in direct ratio to the relief allowed.

The saddest feature of all is that no small proportion of the 234,000 children whom, in the United Kingdom, the Destitution Authority elects to bring up upon Poor Relief—in the course of a year probably as many as 600,000 different children—are today without any interference by these Authorities, chronic-ally underfed, insufficiently clothed, badly housed, and, in literally thousands of cases, actually being brought up at the public expense in drunken and dissolute homes.[1]

Indoor relief was equally unsatisfactory. It was the common practice to have General Mixed Workhouses in which the infirm and the able-bodied, the sick and the feeble-minded, the aged and the young were accommodated together. Maternal and infant mortality was high, not only because there was a partial and some-times a complete lack of skilled nursing, but also because the con-tinuous influx of temporary inmates was a perpetual source of

[1] *Minority Report*, Chapter II, p. 80.

infection and dirt. Some of the more enlightened Unions had cottage homes for children ; but the slight protective effects of these were nullified because at a whim of the parents (if these were also inmates) the children could be whisked from meals or even from sleep and brought to the workhouse gates for reunion with their parents before discharge. Families known as " Ins-and-Outs " habitually entered and left the workhouse in this manner, one Shoreditch family, for example, being readmitted 111 times in five years. In Kensington, of all admissions to the School District Receiving Home in 1907–8, 39 per cent were readmissions, mostly " Ins-and-Outs."[1] The General Mixed Workhouse in trying to be " General " failed in all the tasks which it undertook. Its deterrent character was irrelevant for the non-ablebodied who could not in any case work and who were in effect subjected to the hardships intended for the work-shy able-bodied. Meanwhile the latter could not be effectively treated either by training or by what we should now call rehabilitation because of the demoralising presence of those for whom work was out of the question. The workhouse could not function properly as a hospital because its main preoccupation was with the healthy, nor as either a nursery or as a school because it was basically planned and run for adults.

Medical Relief, the third element in the trilogy, was equally unsatisfactory. The District Medical Officer was a general practitioner living within the district ; he was paid a sum between £10 and £400 yearly, out of which he had to find his own dressings. He was supposed to attend cases only on the order of the Relieving Officer, no matter how urgent they were represented to be ; and he had, of necessity, to restrict the time he devoted to Poor Law cases in order to attend in good measure to those paying patients from whom he derived his livelihood. Medical attention of sick persons in the workhouses and infirmaries of the Poor Law Authorities was represented to the Royal Commission as also being quite inadequate.

The Poor Law provided the services of a leaky umbrella. Underneath this miserable shelter there were crowded maternity cases, respectable old people, children in Poor Law Schools, young persons undergoing industrial training, the sick, the mentally defective, the work-shy, and skilled men temporarily

[1] *Minority Report*, Chapter IV, p. 170.

unemployed. It is difficult now to efface from the imagination the Ministry of Labour, the Ministry of Health and the Assistance Board. In 1909 the place of all these different authorities was taken by the Poor Law, operating diversely through the policies of the various Unions as interpreted by their untrained and sometimes unsuitable Relieving Officers. The Poor Law administration was even responsible (instead of the Board of Education) for educating pauper children.

THE MINORITY REPORT

Such was the situation confronting Beatrice Webb when, with her fellow-Commissioners, she began to review the Poor Law. She decided that the inquiry should be a thorough one, and persuaded the Commissioners to adopt " the Webb method of concrete investigation."[1] As a result the *Minority Report* constantly refers to research methods, and is, in this respect, also instructive reading for later students.

> " We thought it necessary, in order to clear up this conflict of testimony, to supplement the very elaborate investigations that we set on foot . . . by the appointment of a special Investigator to make a detailed inquiry . . ."[2]
> " We were struck with the allegations that were made . . . We therefore thought it necessary to have a special inquiry made . . . in a dozen different towns and villages."[2]

The *Report* has another quality which cannot, unfortunately, be taught. It is vividly imaginative. The Webbs looked at the chaos of the Poor Law in a *laissez-faire* society and imagined, in detail, the pattern of administration which could replace the Poor Law in a society based upon social and economic planning. The *Minority Report* was not a lucky guess. It resulted from a series of brilliant deductions about existing conditions and a closely-reasoned and partly intuitive comprehension of the measures needed to solve current problems. The Webbs did not, of course, mean to prophesy the content of social legislation for almost forty years ahead ; they thought that they were putting forward a plan capable of immediate application. (They did, in fact, get a young

---

[1] *Our Partnership*, edited by Barbara Drake and Margaret Cole, Longmans, 1948, p. 464.
[2] *Minority Report*, Chapter II, pp. 68, 72.

Fabian to draft a Bill to this effect during their subsequent campaign.) It is partly our dilatory and piecemeal legislation which now gives the *Minority Report* its air of major prophecy. But its imaginative realism, and its administrative vision derive, undoubtedly, from genius.

The Webbs' programme sprang from the concept that poverty is not a unifying force. Many types of persons are poor for diverse reasons. It is therefore necessary to discover why they are poor, and so to treat the cause of poverty that the poverty itself is eliminated or alleviated. This may involve a number of provisions separate from, and supplementary to, cash aliment. Such provisions must be constantly measured against their wide social purpose so that their effect, singly and cumulatively, consistently forwards this aim. Poverty is thus seen not only as a personal problem but as a social challenge involving human waste as well as much expense to society. Random, wholesale relief is, at best, a superficial palliative which must be replaced by scientific, fundamental remedies applied in the right way, in the right place and at the right time by officers who are properly equipped both to understand and to implement the social policy involved.

The Poor Law was therefore to be broken up in such a way that the various categories of destitute persons which it handled could be transferred to the aegis of authorities more able to provide specialised services. The Board of Education, through the Local Education Authorities, was to be responsible for both the education and the welfare of all children of sound mind ; the Local Health Authority was to be the sole body in charge of arrangements for maternity and infant welfare, for a domiciliary medical service extending (though not necessarily free of charge) well outside the pauper group, for hospital services provided out of public funds, and for classified Homes for the aged ; Local Pension Committees, already operating under the 1908 Act, were to have power to recommend Local Pensions for those not entitled to National Pensions ; a Local Committee for the Mentally Defective was to watch over all those certified as being of unsound mind and all mental defectives, its duties including the provision both of institutions, including those for epileptics, and of special schools for mentally defective children. Of this clear and logical programme two items only have never come into being. First, Local Pensions were not introduced ; the later trend was towards centrally financed cash payments, and the aged were aided by the insurance pensions provided by the Widows' Orphans' and Old Age Pensions Act of 1925 and, subsequently, by the supplementary pensions payable under the Old Age and Widows' Pensions Act, 1940. Secondly, the Mental Hospitals Committees of Local Authorities did not deal with " special " schools, the Education Committees being the body responsible for all children of school age.

Part II of the *Minority Report* went beyond the Break-up of the Poor Law. It proposed that there should be a Ministry of Labour responsible for organising and linking Employment Exchanges all over the country, for planning the flow and intake of labour both geographically and industrially, and for running training establishments. These latter were analogous in idea to our Rehabilitation Centres except that they were to be for the long-term unemployed and for those who were recurrently difficult to place, rather than for medical cases. The Exchanges were to co-operate with the unemployment insurance schemes of Trade Unions, the receipt of cash carrying the obligation to register with the Exchange. These far-reaching reforms included, as one of their objectives, the removal of the able-bodied from the Poor Law.

The Webbs recognised, of course, that human beings do not always all fit into predetermined categories—that there would be necessitous persons not readily assignable to any of these clear-cut authorities. They also saw that families are not homogeneous and that different members of the same family might become the responsibility of different committees of the Local Authority. For these and other reasons they proposed the appointment of a Registrar of Public Assistance, who should be an officer of the Local Authority. Committees of the Council would have to submit to him all proposals for paying cash allowances, and he, himself, would be responsible for assisting the residual group. His registers would therefore show a complete account, social and financial, for all families receiving any type of public help, whether in cash or in kind. Duplication of assistance would be avoided, and the families would be free from the multiple income declarations and assessments to which many of them were subjected before 1948. Voluntary societies and institutions would be invited to register their cases with the Registrar.

All these services were not necessarily to be free. It would be the duty of the Registrar to assess the payment due from recipients and to recover this amount. However, ability to pay, or, alternatively, proof of poverty, were not to be factors determining whether or not the services, needed on the grounds of health, welfare or improved citizenship, were provided or not. The appropriate department of the Local Authority should have the duty to provide the relevant services and to notify the Registrar that this had been done. It would then be his business to exact payment or to allow the service to be free. Thus the pauper beneficiary would be no longer marked off from the financially solvent ; he would receive the same services provided by the same officers as the relatively prosperous citizen. and these officers would have no means of detecting which subjects were receiving the service free. This plan, we now see, would probably have had the social effect of making public services—e.g., health and education—more respected by the bourgeois classes who, in a mercantile society, tend to think that free service must be bad service. It would also have eliminated the something-for-nothing attitude of those who do not understand that rates and taxes are spread-over payments. This last is a point which continually appears in the *Minority Report*. The Webbs did not propose " free " services ; they wanted people to pay according to their means, and to feel that this was their reciprocal obligation if they accepted the service. They also emphasised the beneficiaries' obligation to co-operate with treatment, whether for sickness or for unemployment, if this were a condition of cash payment. Wherever it was relevant this cash-plus-service plan was to underline the duties of citizenship.

This moral stress is characteristic of the whole *Report*. Each proposal is a synthesis of social, economic and moral considerations. It was included only if it served a definite purpose on each of these three planes, and the moral purpose, the constant strengthening of character, seems to have ranked equally with the other two. But there was a further consideration in the minds of the Webbs ; they continually remembered the need to replace misery by happiness, to comfort the " lonely old women," and to deal with people individually, as differing human beings, within the framework of their plan. Of the long-term unemployed, for example, they wrote, " Maintenance must be merely preliminary to attempting to solve the particular ' Human problem ' that each man represents."[1] This real appreciation of individual human beings as such, of their characters and personal potentialities, gives the *Minority Report* an unexpected warmth ; it was conceived not only as an administrative programme, but as a plan for happiness.

The tools for this mammoth task were mainly to be the officers of the Local Authorities. These were to be trained persons who were inherently suitable for their respective jobs. The Webbs pointed out that the Relieving Officer, however good he might be at one aspect of his work, could hardly be equally efficient throughout ; he was required to select cases and to present them to the Guardians, to undertake whatever case-work was necessary, to keep family records, to estimate liable relatives' ability to contribute, to recover these payments, and to do the necessary book-keeping. The Webbs, strongly " in favour of expert administration in all human affairs,"[2] emphasised that diversity of function calls for diversity of skills. One of the merits of their plan was that specific categories of citizens would be dealt with by those Local Government Departments in which were assembled appropriate staff. They argued that the Education Authority, for example, was more likely to deal efficiently with children, and the Health Authority with the sick, than were unspecialised Boards of Guardians with their too-versatile staffs who suffered from the "lack of any definite standards of professional efficiency."[3]

Public servants were to be reinforced by volunteers :

" It should be a cardinal principle of public administration that the utmost use should, under proper conditions, be made of voluntary agencies and of the personal service of both men and women of good will."[4]

Volunteers (" keeping at bay the mere irresponsible amateur ") were to help in home visiting, provided that they had no contact with assessment or with payment of publicly provided allowances, and that they did not disburse private money as alms ; their function would be to give a " touch of friendly sympathy," and to develop an advisory—and even supervisory—relationship with

[1] *Minority Report*, Vol. II, Chapter V, p. 299.
[2] *Our Partnership*, p. 464.
[3] *Minority Report*, Chapter II, p. 56.
[4] *Ibid.*, Chapter XII, p. 547.

those in need of public assistance. Thus the volunteer and the voluntary society were both, as far as domiciliary assistance went, to work as adjuncts of the public service ; the case-work agency, as we know it today, was to become extinct :

> " No encouragement whatever should be given to any distri-bution of money, food, or clothing in the homes of the poor by any private persons or charitable societies whatsoever."[1]

The Webbs have been criticised because they did not emphasise the need for training social workers. They did not, it is true, foresee the development of social work as a profession standing on its own feet and including employees both of the public services and of private agencies ; they wished to eliminate the latter from the social fabric—a very different thing from training them—but they stressed the need for functionally trained officials. In fact all the people they planned to use were to be trained. Even the volunteer home visitor was " to undergo some sort of technical training." They did not discuss training for what we now call the professional social worker because they saw no reason for such persons to exist.

The *Minority Report* draws a distinction between voluntary bodies making philanthropic contact in the homes of the poor, and voluntary institutions. The former it would " discourage," but voluntary institutions, especially of an experimental nature, seemed to the Webbs to be of great value. However, anticipating later Education Acts, they postulated not only inspection by the Local Authority, but also partial control through public represen-tatives on the governing body of any voluntary institution receiving either subsidies or payment-for-services from Local Authorities.

RECORD OF ACHIEVEMENT

This brief outline gives little idea of the strength of the *Minority Report* in which no word is surplus or colourless and no point repeated. Its argument, reinforced with facts, rolls inexorably on. Seen from the distance of forty years, its inevitability seems to have been predestined by its good sense. At the time, however, it did not look like this ; social insurance was being discussed, and the Webbs thought that the country would have to choose between the two concepts, whereas in practice social insurance, which they so

[1]*Minority Report*, Chapter XII, p. 547.

E

much distrusted, has been the principal instrument in achieving their administrative goal. The Webbs did not know that 1948 would see both the last of the Poor Law and the start of a vast new insurance scheme—that the Webb plan and the Lloyd George plan would blossom fully on the same day. Instead of being killed by social insurance, the *Minority Report* has proceeded, uninterrupted, almost as the Webbs predicted :

> " We can even imagine the scheme being applied to one service after another . . . the final abolition of the Destitution Authority being deferred until the last remnant of its duties could be handed over."[1]

A long series of Acts[2] have given effect to the various proposals of the *Report*, sometimes without their sponsors recognising in their work the long finger of this pervasive document. Finally the National Assistance Act, 1946, taking effect from 5th July, 1948, actually abolished the last remnant of the Poor Law. Its duty to relieve destitute persons was passed on to the National Assistance Board, centralism having replaced that Local Authority responsibility which seemed to the Webbs in 1909 to be normal and desirable. The 1946 Act is based partly on the principle, propounded by the Webbs, that responsible officers should implement assistance policy with uniform impartiality, without deference to the variable opinions of a voluntary committee, and without sentiment, personal acquaintance or neighbourliness affecting judgment. It is not certain that the Board's staff would reach, as yet, the Webbs' postulated level of officers " adequately trained for and professionally engaged in the task of hearing and weighing

[1] *Minority Report*, Chapter XII, p. 552.
[2] The following are among the principal Acts which have features in common with the recommendations of the *Minority Report* ;
  1909 Labour Exchange Act
  1913 Mental Deficiency Act
  1915 Notification of Births (Amendment) Act
  1917 Venereal Disease Act
  1920 Blind Persons Act
  1921 Education Act
  1929 Local Government Act
  1934 Unemployment Act
  1940 Old Age and Widows Pensions Act
  1944 Education Act
  1946 National Insurance (Industrial Injuries) Act
  1946 National Health Service Act
  1948 Children Act

evidence,"[1] but its swift and recent progress towards higher standards in this respect is yet another example of the *Minority Report* coming gradually and unobtrusively to late fruition.

The administrative victory of the *Minority Report* is so spectacular that it obscures one major field in which the battle is not yet won. The Webbs' central objection to social insurance was its unconditional nature. They did not feel that the Lloyd George scheme included prevention of poverty. There were no provisions in his Act for averting or curing sickness or for checking moral lassitude. Benefits were linked with contributions and the wording of the Act did not permit of any synthesis between cash payments and preventive and curative services. The moral and philosophical side of cash aid was not implicit in the Lloyd George Act. This criticism can equally be levelled at the National Insurance Act, 1946. There is no room within its administrative framework for stressing the reciprocal obligations of beneficiaries to develop the social, economic and moral qualities of effective citizens. This is the main point of difference between this Act (and those allied with it) and the Beveridge Report; it is one of the main links between the Beveridge Report of 1942, and the *Minority Report* of 1909. Beveridge accepted the idea of social insurance—it was too firmly established in the national mind to be ignored—but he interwove with it the concept of prevention and treatment not only of sickness but of the other roots of poverty. The historic Beveridge Report is a direct descendant of the *Minority Report* with an infusion of new ideas appropriate to its generation and a restatement of the Webbs' ideas so vivid that they, too, seemed new in 1942. It, also, has had its main administrative proposals carried out and its philosophy neglected. In 1948 we find ourselves without that spiritual core to our social administration which would give citizens a sense of moral co-responsibility for furthering the basic purpose of the scheme; we have not even worked out an efficient method of educating citizens to see and understand the basic purpose. The 1946 Act has been publicised almost entirely in terms of the cash benefits to which people have a right in return for contributions paid. Implicit in the *Minority Report* is the lesson, still unlearnt, that spiritual—or moral—purpose is equally important with the economic and humanitarian content of any social programme.

[1] *Minority Report*, Chapter II, p. 64.

THE WEBBS AS I SAW THEM

by

DESMOND MacCARTHY

VIII

THE WEBBS AS I SAW THEM

by DESMOND MacCARTHY

Since I first began to assemble my recollections of Beatrice Webb, I have read *Our Partnership*, which is the second, and alas, the last volume of her autobiography. It is almost entirely composed of passages from that candid Diary which she kept so diligently for sixty years, and from which more extracts are sure to be published. As a diarist she was a good writer, and what she wrote in it about herself and others she wrote with nature and in the spirit of truth. Such passages, both directly and by implication, convey a better idea of her character than any description of her; yet how she appeared to others is also interesting —perhaps even how she appeared to one like myself who was never among her intimate friends nor concerned with her work. How did the Webbs strike one of a younger generation who had a great respect for them, but disagreed with them about many matters of importance ? It is, I cannot help guessing, to provide at any rate one answer to that particular question that I have been asked to contribute to this book.

My acquaintance with the Webbs, though it extended over nearly forty years, would have soon faded out after it began had not the *New Statesman* been founded by them in 1913 with the backing of Shaw and others—and had not I been made its dramatic critic from the start. (Later on I was to become also its Literary Editor.) This kept me intermittently in touch with them : I could go when I liked to their *New Statesman* luncheons at their house in Grosvenor Road, overlooking the Thames, together with Clifford Sharp, the Editor, and other members of the staff ; and occasionally the Webbs would also ask me to dine to meet, say, Sir Horace Plunkett, in the hope I might conceivably contribute to a discussion of Irish affairs, or Arthur Balfour, because I was intelligent and agreeable. They usually had a definite reason for inviting people on particular occasions, although I like to think it was sometimes vague in my case when later on they would ask me to spend a week-end at Passfield Corner, or to join one of those gatherings of " young people " (most of them, by the way, well in their thirties) at some country hotel, each paying his or her expenses, but with the Webbs as hosts making all arrangements.

Although I have nothing but friendliness on their part to remember, I am certain they would have soon ignored me, had it not been for this connection with the *New Statesman* : they must have seen in early days that I was " no use." Capable now and then of political passion, and vaguely on the side of the " have nots," I took no active interest in politics and had little knowledge of social questions or economics. I was, however, thankful there were others ready to devote themselves to discovering remedies for social evils. I did not believe that the poor " must be always with us " ; translated into " there must always be slums and paupers " such a statement was absurd. But precisely what changes in the body politic would be necessary to abolish poverty, and which of them could be achieved at once, or what sacrifice of desirable life in other directions still further changes might entail— of such questions I felt I was no judge ; while to qualify myself to become one would have meant changing the focus of my interests. These were centred rather on " ends " than on " means " ; on deciding and feeling what things in life were good in themselves and not on how they could be disseminated. I had once a short talk with Webb about that (all our talks together were brief, consisting of a remark or two on either side) ; he said, in his quiet lisping way, " We are interested in the drains and stopping dry-rot in the house ; you in its decoration." I demurred to my share of the metaphor, but I was glad he had spoken like that for it showed he did not expect me to take to plumbing.

I met Beatrice Webb three years or so after coming down from Cambridge. There I had come to believe that the most important things in life were personal relations (love and friendship), aesthetic emotions and the pursuit of truth. After persuading my parents to take me away from Eton I had gone to the University at the age of seventeen, expecting that politics would be my chief interest, and hoping to cut a figure as a speaker in " The Union " debates. In my second year I discovered that I cared far more

about philosophy and literature, and that those of my contemporaries who were similarly interested were superior in intellect and
nature to those who argued about political questions and were
prominent in Union debates. If a Cambridge branch of the Fabian
Society had been then in existence perhaps I might possibly have
been attracted by the discusions at its meetings and have thought
of myself (who knows ?) as a " Socialist, " instead of as a Radical-
Liberal.

I mention these facts so that others may gather through what
kind of a pair of eyes the young man, who was once myself, first
saw the Webbs.

Of course I had often heard of them and of their behind-the-
scenes political influence, especially in the Conservative party—
" the Haldane myth " as Beatrice calls it in her Diaries. It was
through Haldane's friendship that they had originally made the
acquaintance of many who at the time had their hands upon the
gear of the world. Beatrice and Arthur Balfour got on particularly
well together. It is clear from her Diary that he fascinated her and
that he found her company very agreeable. She told him once
that the great difference between him and the Liberal leaders was
that his attitude towards proposals of social reform could be
expressed by " why not ? " theirs by a grudging " Why ? "
From the Liberal point of view the Webbs were not sound on the
Free Trade versus Protection controversy, nor had they been in
the eyes of many Liberals about the Boer War. Nevertheless, it
was said that several young Liberals of promise had come under
their influence, the names of Herbert Samuel and Charles
Trevelyan being mentioned. What is relevant, however, to my
own attempt to describe the Webbs at this time is that the " myth "
—if anything so near the mark can be so described—was largely
their own creation ; the " Beware of those wire-pullers " attitude
towards them had been intensified by their habit of talking about
their success in making others further their own plans.

When, however, I met Beatrice Webb (was it 1904 ?) and sat
opposite her one day at a luncheon, the fame of the Webbs was not
in my mind ; I just thought her a fascinating woman. With her
pale emphatic face, her dark-silver hair, aquiline features, fine
eyebrows and bright brown eyes, she looked rather like a benevolent hawk, if you can imagine such a bird. Her voice also was

E*

extremely agreeable to my ear ; and what impressed me still more
was that she said straight out what she thought. Our host on that
occasion was evidently, perhaps in consequence, far from being at
his ease with her, and he was even rather surprised when I said
how much I should enjoy getting to know her better.

I thought her beautiful : I was to notice afterwards that Beatrice
like most women enjoyed being admired, although she was as much
on her guard against allowing anybody's admiration to influence
her in his favour as she was against being biased in her judgments
by what she used to describe as the " gracious deference of
aristocratic manners." Such manners she thoroughly appreciated,
and she envied them on behalf of those whom she respected far
more, whenever she noticed that their social habits were liable to
wound unintentionally the self-esteem of those they were with.

Hardly anything, not even fundamental economic injustices,
roused her indignation more than the bad manners of the rich towards the poor, of those who gave orders towards those who took
them. If she ever gave an impression of being filled with class-
hatred it was usually when her attention had been drawn to any
instance of "insolence "—a word of violent abhorrence in her
vocabulary—on the part of members of the upper classes. She
struck me as overlooking examples of it among people far lower
in the social scale towards their inferiors. As far as my observation
went the gentry proper and the aristocracy seemed on the whole
rather freer from that odious fault—certainly towards those in their
own employment. She would, however, lend a ready ear to stories,
even when exaggerated or ill-founded, if they smacked of the insolence of privilege. I remember her once asserting with indignation that Lord Hugh Cecil when he went to Wagner festivals at
Bayreuth, was in the habit of taking two seats, one for himself and
the other for his hat, stick and coat. Afterwards, when I had become acquainted with him, I happened to ask if he were going that
summer to hear " The Ring." He seemed rather surprised at the
question. " But you are a frequenter of Bayreuth, aren't you ? "
I asked : " I've never been there in my life."

Beatrice Webb, like Mrs. Bernard Shaw who, if I remember
right, left a large sum of money for founding a school of social
behaviour, set much store by good manners. (How they can be
taught pedagogically I can't imagine, the secret of them—apart

from mere etiquette—lying in a sensitive respect for the self-respect of others.) I suspect Beatrice might not have been always very tactful in pointing out to others their shortcomings in such directions; her parties for the wives of Labour Members were apparently not a success.

As people often do, who examine themselves rigorously, she was apt to take for granted a greater self-detachment in others than is at all common in human nature, and therefore to exaggerate their capacity for accepting criticism in the spirit in which it was intended. There were, too, occasions when her own manner was distinctly reminiscent of a *grande dame* at a haughty moment : an amusing passage in Margaret Cole's *Beatrice Webb* recalled her to me vividly, seated on a low stool before the fire, one thin white hand stretched out towards it, and declaring in a tone of almost bored finality that somebody or other was " a quite impossible person." I don't say this would necessarily be a social verdict— more probably a moral one ; but a similar calm unshakable confidence told at such moments in her voice and expression. She was a skilful hostess, never fussy, and she did not allow her greater intimacy with some of her guests to make the other ones feel out of it. It was pleasant to stay with the Webbs as well as interesting. You could share or keep aloof as you liked from plans of the day, and it may suggest something deeper if I recall that once waking up at the end of a visit to them with a violent sore throat and shivers which might have prognosticated anything, I found myself reflecting that, at any rate, if I should be destined to become an immovable nuisance in the house with a disinfectant sheet in front of my door, few of my friends would remember it so little against me as my host and hostess.

The other source of some misjudgments concerning average human nature to which both the Webbs struck me as liable, sprang from the difficulty which all remarkably steady, single-minded people usually have in understanding the temptations of others, or the contribution which obedience to impulse may make to the happiness of their lives. By all means arrange things so that it becomes easy for everybody to be steady and more difficult to be foolish, but if human beings are so hedged about that to be erratic becomes well-nigh impossible, they will tend to grow low-spirited and tame, however healthy. The upshot would be a social order the citizens of which instead of moving themselves, haunted " the movies," and though sober in their external lives boozed perpetually on day-dreams of outrageous silly adventure—a relief from monotony. An even life for all with a minimum of risks and much direction might well lead to that. In the Webbs' response to human nature there was something that roused in me such critical misgivings about their " ends," although when I remembered their sense of justice and their devotion to the remedying of obvious evils, I felt humble. They had achieved such solid happiness for themselves by living according to plan, that they tended to think a planned life was the secret of happiness for everybody. I remember going with Beatrice to the first of a series of lectures given by Bertrand Russell during the war of 1914 (afterwards published under the title *Principles of Social Reconstruction*), the theme of which lecture was the part played by freedom to obey impulse in personal happiness. I thought the lecture illuminating, but she was emphatically of the opinion that it was not.

Like many women she could not sometimes refrain from planning suitable matches between young men and women in whom she was interested and of whom she approved, thinking how likely a marriage between them would be to increase the efficiency of both. I remember one Sunday at Passfield walking over the heath beside Sidney Webb while Beatrice and a young man were striding along some way ahead, the wind now and then blowing a word or two of their conversation over their shoulders towards us. Sidney turned to me with a smile and said, " I know what Beatrice is saying : she is explaining that marriage is the waste-paper-basket of the emotions." That would be far indeed from describing their marriage, which as everybody knew was a singularly perfect one. Everything they did and almost everything they said seemed to come from both at the same time. No married pair knew better the charm and happiness of being together and belonging to each other in the midst of the world and their work in it. The deepest and surest marriages are based on both involuntary and deliberate choice. In theirs, on his side, both elements had been present and from the first, but on hers, as we have learnt from her Autobiography, the last alone had been decisive. She had chosen him, judging—and how correctly !—that henceforward freedom and common occupation would be one and the same thing in both their lives. This happy result of deliberate decision tended to make her overlook the importance of instinctive attraction in the lives of others. She was a puritan and so was he; and her puritanism, so repulsive to such natures, for instance, as that of H. G. Wells, was intensified by her regarding " love " as a disturbing element in people's lives, destroying their efficiency ; hence that metaphor of marriage as the waste-paper-basket of the emotions. There are few entries in the Diary more arresting than the one where she records her unromantic Sidney stopping in their joint work to say quietly, " I'm frightened at my own happiness." She came to admire him more and more ; he seemed so blessedly and imperturbably immune from temptations from which she herself was not.

" Sidney is simply unconscious of all the little meanness which turns social intercourse sour : he is sometimes tired, occasionally bored, but never unkindly or anxious to shine, or be admired, and wholly unaware of the absence of, or presence of, social consideration. I verily believe that if he were thrown, by chance, into a company of persons all of whom wanted to snub him, he would take up the first book and become absorbed in it, with a sort of feeling that they were good-natured enough not to claim his attention, or that they did not perceive that he was reading on the sly. And the greater personages they happened to be, the more fully satisfied he would be at the arrangement ; since it would relieve him of any haunting fear that he was neglecting his social duty and making others uncomfortable. On the other hand, whether in his own house or in another's, if some person is neglected or out of it, Sidney will quite unconsciously drift to them and be seen eagerly talking to them."

Then speaking of herself she wrote with characteristic candour :

" How any sane mortal with resources of their own and a few intelligent friends can exert themselves to get into ' society ' passes my comprehension. And yet I have just expended twenty-one guineas on an evening dress ! I hasten to add that it is four years since I paid the same amount for my present evening garment. Still I might have done without it—if I had been quite single-minded in my indifference to social glamour. The cold-drawn truth is that though I am honestly indifferent as to whether or not I see the great world, when I do enter it I like to do credit to my reputation—an unworthy desire I own— unworthy of an ascetic student and a collectivist reformer ! "

The years during which I saw most of the Webbs were those of their widest unpopularity. True, they had succeeded in maintaining their hold over the Fabian Society itself in spite of H. G. Wells' attempt to dislodge them from the control of its policy. In some degree I think that attempted rebellion within, and perhaps the rather mocking impatience of young Syndicalists later on towards them, were in part protests against Webbian cut-and-dried planning. But I found when I got to know them that the Webbs were less unfair to others, though they might be decidedly firm about them, than others were apt to be about the Webbs. When they were accused of being intolerably self-satisfied, I used sometimes to remind my friends that considering how consistently the Webbs, year in, year out, had lived up to their own ideals, the marvel was they were not even more imperturbably sure of themselves !

Before the war of 1914 a small Socialist monthly called *The Crusade*, in which they had been interested, came to an end. The other papers with a Socialist outlook like the *Labour Leader* and *Justice* were not suitable for Socialist propaganda among enlightened readers, while Orage's *New Age* was definitely a Guild Socialist organ ; the Webbs therefore resolved to found a new Socialist weekly. I was rather surprised to find that in *Our Partnership* the *New Statesman* was, however, rarely mentioned ; there were only a few extracts from her Diary about its inception. And yet this journalistic venture was certainly one of the Webbs' successes, although as time went on they must have often disagreed with the line taken by the Fabian, Clifford Sharp, whom they had appointed editor, giving him a free hand.

They were in the habit of jokingly dividing those they knew into two categories, the A's and the B's. The first included those who for one reason or another could be described as either anarchistic, aristocratic or artistic (these came second in their estimation), and those who were bourgeois, bureaucratic, or benevolent and were more reliable. I was one of the A's and to some extent always a fish out of water, or shall we say, for I never felt uncomfortable in their company, and was often interested, a fish in a strange pool. Their talk of course frequently took for granted knowledge I did not possess, and their references to institutions or public bodies by their initials often bewildered me. I remember once asking at luncheon what the " L.G.B." was, and the note in Sidney Webb's voice—I will not call it impatient or contemptuous, for such notes were absent from it—nevertheless fixed for ever the information in my mind. Here I am interrupted by reverie : a scene rises before me—a parlour in an hotel. It is the year 1913, and I am staying with the Webbs at Beachy Head. Shaw is there, and several of the future staff of the *New Statesman* which will be coming out on 12th April ; Jack Squire, who will be its literary editor and of course Clifford Sharp himself and others, but I seem to miss Robert Lynd.

We all of us of course remembered how mercilessly H. G. Wells had guyed the Webbs in *The New Machiavelli* which had been published in 1911, and recently another story of his had appeared. I remember Beatrice Webb saying cheerfully, " I'm in this one, too ; I'm the woman whose voice is described as a strangulated contralto ; but you're not in it, Sidney." " Oh, yes, I am," said Webb, speaking from a sofa on which his legs and feet looked absurdly small in comparison with his broad brow and head, " Oh, yes, I am, I'm the man who is described as one of those supplementary males often found among the lower crustacea." This smiling serenity made me feel that I was in high and good company. Everyone who has written about the Webbs has commented on what may be called their practical magnanimity. As soon as any one who had attacked them was ready to forward an end they had in view the past, as far as he was personally concerned, would be forgotten, or at any rate, completely ignored.

I never discussed literature with Beatrice Webb, let alone with Sidney, nor do I remember ever asking either of them if any article of mine in the *New Statesman* had interested them, not even when the subject of it was a play by Shaw. Nevertheless, I used to like listening to Beatrice discussing human nature, because, however much I might differ from her conclusions, her analysis of people was invariably detached and often acute—apart from her moral judgments of them, which were, of course, largely determined by their political or social attitudes. No one can read her impressions of people in her Diary without being struck by their detachment, even when she is describing those to whom she was closely attached. No one has recorded with greater aloofness the unimpressive appearance and deportment of her beloved Sidney. I was once told by an intimate friend of hers that the only passage in her Diary which she had never shown him was that in which she had recorded her first impression. It may not be true ; but certainly the verbal portrait of Sidney in *Our Partnership* could hardly be more matter-of-factly precise had she been describing someone to whom she was indifferent.

She was convinced that poetry was a dumb note on her piano. I think she may have been encouraged in supposing that she was incapable of responding to beauty conveyed through words by her early association with Herbert Spencer, who saw no difference between poetry and prose except that in the former the lines did not run across the page. If she had taken the trouble, or thought it worth while to do so, she could have developed the necessary sensibility, just as she did towards music in her old age, just as she fostered in herself states of mind she identified with prayer, once she had been convinced of the value of religion. I remember telling " H. G. " that she had spoken to me about this, adding " she is convinced that she shares the experience of mystics." He was sceptical : " There's no more mysticism in Beatrice than in a steam engine." But I think he was so far wrong, that although she was predominantly rationalistic, she sought, and valued more as time went on, moments of contemplation.

My last contact with her is rather melancholy to recall. It was after the Webbs' visit to U.S.S.R. They had for many years seen no essential difference between Russian and German totalitarianism ; but, as all the world knows, they came back convinced that " the inevitability of gradualness " was a myth, and that in spite of the O.G.P.U., enforced labour, suppression of free speech, Russian Communism had already established, in the most important respects, that kind of civilisation towards which they had been striving themselves. I met Beatrice at luncheon with the Shaws. The subject of Russia had not come up, but on a remark from me on something remote, she suddenly flew at me with a violence that drew from Shaw, who hates hearing people belaboured, some deprecating murmurs. Her new faith was fanatical.

THE *NEW STATESMAN*

by

S. K. RATCLIFFE

IX

THE *NEW STATESMAN*

by S. K. RATCLIFFE

Early in 1911 the Webbs resolved to make a tour of India and the Far East. At that time they could not have failed to realise that a decisive point in their joint career had been reached. A long chapter of work and extraordinary concentration was about to close. It was becoming clear that their own vital interests, together with the state of public affairs, made a revision of plans and a new direction most desirable. Moreover, for the sake of Beatrice's health and peace of mind one thing was imperative—a long rest and complete change of scene.

The remarkable campaign carried through by the National Committee for the Prevention of Destitution culminated in a London conference and a strikingly successful Albert Hall meeting at Whitsuntide. The Webbs were convinced that there was nothing more to be done along the lines that had been followed during five years of unremitting and, latterly, exhausting labour. In her Diary Mrs. Webb was saying with emphasis that they were about to " quit the whole business." There was, indeed, no alternative if personal disaster was to be avoided. Nearly twenty years had passed since their marriage, years filled to the limit with tasks that demanded physical and nervous power continually at the stretch. No wedded partners before them could point to a comparable record of public service and intellectual achievement. They were eagerly looking forward to the holiday, " that supreme luxury of the propertied brain-worker." She hoped they had " practically converted England to the obligation of preventing destitution." In any case, she confessed, " I am tired, deep-down tired ; I shall just last out."

The eastern journey was to fill the winter of 1911–2. They would not return before June. Mrs. Webb's analysis of the national situation as they were making their preparations underlined the effect of the general election of December, 1910. The strength

of the Liberal Government was not impaired. On the contrary,
Asquith and Lloyd George were more powerful than before ; their
strategy had been effective. Mrs. Webb noted as significant " the
splendid reception by all parties of Lloyd George's scheme of
sickness insurance." Their opinion of that venture was un-
favourable ; she called it " rotten." The " heroic demagogy of
the man," said she, was shown in his use of the word insurance ;
but the expedient to which he was committing the country " was
not really helpful " to their comprehensive plans of the national
minimum. If the Lloyd George Bill went through Parliament,
they would " have to begin a new kind of propaganda."

Meanwhile, with their lengthy absence from England in mind
they surveyed the ground and looked ahead. They were convinced
that the Fabian Society was in need of a new impetus. Their
appraisal of the wider prospect is indicated in a number of reflec-
tive diary entries. " I am not sure," she writes, " whether the
time has not arrived for a genuine Socialist Party, with a completely worked out philosophy and a very detailed programme."
When they came back from the East they would see how the land
lay, and could then decide whether to throw themselves " into
constructing a new party with a religion and an applied science."
All this, however, was no more than tentative speculation. The
Webbs were only too well aware that England in the second decade
of the century was a long way from even the approach to any such
movement. Nor could the mission of which Beatrice was thinking
fall within the destiny of this unique couple. Twelve months
earlier, when toiling amid the fatigues of the National Committee's
campaign, she had touched upon the misgiving with which they
regarded the possibility of " talking and organising " for the
remainder of their lives. That was not what they wanted to do.
And long before they turned homewards from the East they knew
that the next adventure, whatever it was, must be something
wholly different from the creation of a new political party. They
were then in their early fifties. Webb was at the height of his
powers, but her physical reserves were uncertain. During an
illness at fifty-three she had been given a medical warning : " India
is no place for old people " ! The important decision they arrived
at, before reaching England, was for the launching of a new weekly
paper. The late summer of 1912 was spent in Sussex. By the time

they were installed at Arundel they were beginning to see their way. The outlook did not appear too promising. By editors and managers alike it was taken for granted that the clientèle for a high-class weekly was limited. There were three leading sixpenny reviews in the field. The *Spectator*, directed by J. St. Loe Strachey, was by far the most stable. A few years later, when circulations began to be disclosed, its certified figure was something over 18,000. The paper was financially sound, providing a good income for the owner-editor. The *Saturday Review* had already entered upon its prolonged decline. The *Nation*, under its brilliant and impulsive editor, H. W. Massingham, enjoyed a high reputation among left-wing Liberals and intellectuals generally. Massingham commanded a distinguished team and his net had gathered in a large and varied company of contributors. The Webbs saw that the *Nation* would be their direct competitor ; and by an ironic coincidence its owners were tenants of Mrs. Bernard Shaw. Their office occupied the lower floors of 10 Adelphi Terrace.

Once having made up their minds the Webbs moved fast. The preliminary work was compressed into a crowded half-year. By the end of 1912 their plans " were already cut if not dried." As could easily have been predicted, an original method of publicity was devised. Its salient feature was the recruitment of subscribers in advance by direct appeal. There were no means of estimating the probabilities. Experts in the trade asserted that if their efforts brought in as many as 1,000 the result would be a miracle. They themselves were dreaming of 2,000. Actually the total registered before the appearance of the first number was about 2,500. They found in the card-indexes provided by the Fabian Society, the universities, the National Committee and other bodies, a reinforcement of their own large acquaintance. The circularising was as thorough as detailed attention could make it. A joint personal letter was the principal means of persuasion. The " less promising " possibles were attacked by way of a special manifolded letter from Mrs. Webb.

She records their feeling that this was by far the most risky of the enterprises at that time in hand. The capital available was a mere nest-egg—£5,000. Bernard Shaw contributed £1,000, while a like sum was put in by Edward Whitley of Oxford, by H. D. Harben, and by Ernest (now Lord) Simon.

The inexperience of all concerned was revealed in the notion that these modest resources would suffice to cover the losses of three years ; and to begin with, we are told, there was not much thought of the paper's having a longer life than that. As things turned out, there was never any cause for serious anxiety. Many years later the first editor remarked that nothing surprised him more than the generous flexibility of the backers.

It was assumed that if the paper was to be fairly established some 5,000 prepaid subscriptions would be needed, this figure being looked upon as a maximum objective. A half-serious calculation of personal values made for the circulation manager is rather amusing. G.B.S., it was believed, might be good for 1,000 names, the Webbs for not more than 500, and " Squire, if you please, for 100." This last figure was wide of the mark. Upon any such basis, however, Mrs. Webb feared that failure was almost certain. Perhaps, after all, it was a mad adventure ? Yet at the worst it would mean " more than a run for our hard work and other people's money." She diverted herself by recording the forecasts of candid friends. The paper, they said, would be one-idea'd, since the Webbs knew only the social and economic question. That subject they would always be driving at, " exactly as Belloc and Chesterton hammer at the theme of political corruption in the *New Witness*." How, for instance, could they hope to get a really well-informed article on Persia ? And again : the paper " would be the Webbs, flavoured with a little Shaw and padded with the contributions of a few cleverish but ignorant young men."

In October, 1912, a private company was formed. *The Statesman* was the name suggested by Arthur Balfour and at once adopted. It happened that when I was informed, I called attention to the *Statesman* of Calcutta, the most widely circulated daily in India. It had a weekly mail edition with a small circulation in Britain. Webb did not think this a matter of any consequence, but it tipped the scale in favour of the *New Statesman*, and in a short time the adjective was seen to have its own value.

There was no difficulty or hesitation with regard to the editor. The Webbs had known Clifford Sharp in the early days of the Fabian Nursery. He had been chosen to direct the National Committee and to edit its monthly organ, *The Crusade*. He had served a short apprenticeship to weekly journalism with A. R.

Orage on the *New Age*. Contrary to the forecast made by many who knew the Webbs, Sharp was accorded full editorial responsibility (he would not have accepted the post on any other terms), and he received no instructions concerning the staff. The first members to be appointed were J. C. (later Sir John) Squire, as literary editor, and Desmond MacCarthy as drama critic. Emil Davies was invited to contribute a City article, and this he continued to do, with admirable regularity, through the eighteen years of the first editorship. Hubert Bland wrote an incisive page on new novels for twelve months until his sudden death. Sharp said that from first to last questions of policy were seldom discussed at the board meetings. He was led to wonder whether any young editor ever enjoyed greater freedom.

Although the Webbs were most scrupulous in avoiding everything that might look like interference, they kept in close contact with the office in Great Queen Street. There was a weekly lunch at 41 Grosvenor Road. A long series of articles headed " What is Socialism ? " carried the two names and Webb wrote extensively for the first portion of the paper. Diary entries during the first year reflect an unremitting watchfulness. Beatrice remarks that " Sidney is enjoying this work. Once again he takes the lead. He is a far more accomplished journalist than I. He likes Sharp and works well with him." A few weeks after the start she notes that the *New Statesman* is absorbing them both : there is no time or energy for the Diary. All sorts of criticisms are fast coming in, and luckily they cancel one another out. The subscription lists and the renewals make an unexpected amount of trouble. Evidently the method calls for improvement. " And oh, how tired I am ! "

The first number appeared on 12th May, 1913. It was impressive in more than size. There were thirty-two pages and a substantial literary supplement, which opened with Havelock Ellis's essay on Remy de Gourmont and contained a beautifully written review by Mrs. Webb of three books on Japan.

The leader announced that the *New Statesman* was not an organ of the Labour Party. Its policy was Fabian Socialism. Its independence was genuine and complete. It had no axe to grind and no panacea to advocate. It was without party bias, for the world movement towards Collectivism was beyond and above party. On the other hand, social problems were not susceptible of scientific analysis ; but if they were to be solved, the application of the scientific spirit was necessary. The opening front-page note, on Montenegro and the struggle over Scutari, had a reference to the British public's "abysmal ignorance" of foreign affairs. There were no fewer than eight editorial articles, two of them being brilliant examples in which the Shavian hand was undisguised. They were on the Marconi scandal and the forcible feeding of suffragettes in prison.

The Editor and the Webbs suffered a severe initial blow from Bernard Shaw, who announced that he would not sign articles. This was altogether unexpected, for in their publicity the Webbs had stated that Mr. Shaw intended to make the *New Statesman* his main channel of communication through the Press. Sharp notified him that anonymity would involve editorial supervision and unavoidable changes of expression. The reply, not a little surprising, was that this would not be objected to ; but Sharp was immediately disillusioned. His own hand in dealing with editorial copy was by no means light, and of course G.B.S. rebelled. As a leader-writer he was clearly imposssible, for, although he said he enjoyed the privilege of using the editorial We, nothing could induce him to write in harmony with the paper's policy or to respect its rules. There were some brisk outbursts against Sharp, although G.B.S. never challenged the editor's right to the last word. His most characteristic contribution in the first year was a signed article of seven columns, " The Case against Chesterton." It led, naturally, to an exchange of volleys between the champions. Thereafter Mr. Shaw was a very infrequent contributor.

The first World War began almost before the *New Statesman* had got into its stride. During this interval of fifteen months the contents of the paper tell their own story. The predictions of those who looked for an over-weight of Webbian topics were to some extent justified. " What is Socialism ? " held the central position for many weeks. National insurance and trade-unionism were prominent. The discussion of women's suffrage and kindred movements was almost continuous. Ireland, inevitably, was a clamorous subject, with the prosecution of James Larkin of Dublin as a special irritant. Relatively little space was allotted to European and world affairs. It was not without significance that Sharp had appointed a regular correspondent in one capital alone, Berlin.

Dudley Ward wrote thence largely on German industry and administration, touching hardly at all on international or military policy until he left the country in August, 1914. The editor, who had a fancy for unreal initials, signed these articles B–H.

The war of 1914–18, needless to say, was a severe testing time for the *New Statesman*. Clifford Sharp was assured and imperturbable. As early as the first week of September, after a month of shattering news, he wrote a leader headed " Grounds of Confidence " in which the only thing wrong was an over-optimistic view of the Imperial Russian Army. Throughout the four years his line was held straight. Victory over the Central Powers had to be complete and unmistakable, and it must be followed by a genuine European peace. In 1916, the paper published an outline of peace terms. It included the principle of no indemnities and restricted reparations. With that exception it was not far from the terms towards which the British Government was to strive in Paris. The *New Statesman* also had the credit of printing the first detailed design for a League of Nations. It was prepared by Leonard Woolf. The arguments against compulsory service were upheld until Parliament accepted the change. The paper was distrustful of Lloyd George, as the Webbs had always been, and from 1916 onwards it was markedly friendly to Asquith.

When the Cabinet crisis occurred in December, Sharp displayed the peculiar shrewdness which seldom failed him at an awkward moment. He was busy writing a leader when Lloyd George was ready to strike down the Prime Minister. The heading was " Had Zimri Peace ? " (who slew his master). It was left unfinished, with more than a column blank. A brief note explained that, as Lloyd George had been called upon to form a government, it was " undesirable that the matters dealt with in the latter part of the article should be publicly discussed." The trick was highly effective. Everybody inferred that Sharp, having provoked the censor, had preferred cancellation to recasting. But the censor had nothing to do with it. The *New Statesman* was never hampered by the Press Bureau. During the whole period one article alone was submitted. That was an outside contribution which the editor wanted to return but, for a particular reason, without the odium of rejecting it himself.

Meanwhile the paper was being established, with a circulation that increased from the start. Progress, to be sure, was at first very slow, but the manager was able, year by year, to affirm that there was never a month when the sales-sheet showed a decline. During 1917–18 Clifford Sharp was on military service, his place being taken by the literary editor. This gave Squire an opportunity of proving his remarkable value. As a colleague he was unexcelled, and Sharp paid tribute to his brilliant versatility. He could write any part of the paper at the shortest notice. His political articles were fully up to standard, while his oversight of the literary pages suffered no diminution. His astonishing gift of parody in prose and verse was limited only by a desire not to forego the composition of serious poetry. He was the most rapid and accurate of proof-readers.

When Sharp returned to the paper early in 1919 he found its standing improved, although its financial position was anything but satisfactory. Under the conditions then prevailing a high-grade weekly could not pay a dividend. There was a weekly loss of about £120, and for a short time the annual deficit varied alarmingly between £4,000 and £6,500. The original backers, however, did not falter and new supporters came in, one of them being Arnold Bennett who, until his death in 1931, was invariably helpful and optimistic. A word of special acknowledgment is due to the memory of two stalwarts, Glynne Williams and Edward Whitley, who lived on into the 1940's. They were alike in stead-fastness and generosity. The management of the paper in the hands of John Roberts was skilful and economical to a note-worthy degree, so that by 1923 the annual loss was brought down below £1,000. Two years later the books showed a minute profit ; but this good fortune was not repeated until after 1930 when the merger with the *Nation* was arranged.

No account of the making of the *New Statesman*, however brief, would be a tolerable summary without a few words con-cerning the Supplements. They appeared frequently. Each one was carefully planned, and they comprise a series no less remarkable for variety than for timeliness and competence. Special supplements were an integral part of the Webbs' original design, and they began at the birth of the paper. The literary supplement was an ample half-yearly undertaking, dependent upon the publishing seasons. For seven years, until 1920 when he left in order to found the *London Mercury*, J. C. Squire was in charge of it. He was succeeded by Desmond MacCarthy, whose term as literary editor lasted until 1927. Mrs. Webb was responsible for an early venture, on the widening activities of women, and the work of the Fabian Research group (see next chapter) produced a large number of supplements full of meat and facts. Other supplements of the first period dealt with the theatre, the medical profession, teachers, insurance, and Ireland.

In this department a place of special interest belongs to the monthly *Blue Book Supplement*. This was a pioneer enterprise, and emphatically a product of the Webb mind and purpose. They thought it out fully in advance, and decided that the first *B.B.S.* should be produced while the paper was being talked about as a newcomer. Better perhaps than anyone in the country they knew the province of official publications. The National Government had become the largest of publishers. Official Papers were undergoing a significant development in scope and style, although their generally forbidding appearance disguised this important fact. Blue Books and White Papers were rich in the basic material of public education. Very many of them were examples of first-rate social study, while not a few contained good and attractive English writing.

The *Blue Book Supplement* contained reviews of all important official documents and a classified list of the month's Government publications. The editing was entrusted to myself, with Frederick Keeling as chief reviewer. I gave way to him at the end of 1914 when, unhappily, his short career was very near its end. (He joined the Duke of Cornwall's Light Infantry as a private, made a distinctive reputation in his Division, and was killed on the Somme.) Keeling's knowledge and industry, his energy and speed of working, were extraordinary. He was the ideal editor of the *B.B.S.*, which was an early casualty of the war. When Clifford Sharp in 1934 summed up the events and successes of his editorship, he wrote that the *B.B.S.* was worth indirectly more than all the cost of its publication (the income from advertisements was, necessarily, almost nothing) : " It won for the paper a certain solid authority and prestige in official circles which it never lost."

There was one supplement which, by the nature of the case,

eclipsed all others in *réclame* and in the violence of the controversy
it aroused. In the early autumn of 1914 Bernard Shaw wrote
" Common Sense About the War " and offered it to the *New
Statesman*. The editor and he were by that time at loggerheads ;
there was hardly a single subject on which they agreed. G.B.S.
had ceased to write for the paper and left the Board. To the tone
and argument of " Common Sense " Clifford Sharp was of
necessity hostile ; but he could not be indifferent to a pamphlet of
supreme brilliance and audacity, good for any amount of advertisement and the breaking of heads. He accepted it without hesitation, but doggedly refused to allow the author to follow it up.
There was a second blast soon ready. It had to be laid aside, since
Sharp did not need to be told that here was a *succès de scandale*
that could not be repeated. G.B.S. had long since given him up
and was denouncing him in fiery notes as incorrigible. A fortnight
after the launching of " Common Sense " he was writing :

" You are a Tory in grain. You have no patience or principle
when a war is on, and very little when a war is off. Your simple
business is to contrive that there shall be a political crisis every
week. Forgive my perpetual cavilling, but somebody must
complain ; it is for the good of your soul."

The sensation was terrific. Objurgations from all sides were
hurled at the writer of " Common Sense." The problem of filling
the correspondence columns, never an easy matter for this particular editor, gave him no trouble for many weeks. Sharp was in
no way perturbed, and there was no loss of circulation. The sales,
indeed, attested the steadiness of the subscribers and a quiet
incoming of new readers.

Sidney Webb remained a member of the Board until 1924 when
he entered the MacDonald Cabinet. It was then obviously advisable that he should sever his formal connection. His place was
taken by Bernard Shaw who, despite the encounters with Sharp,
had remained altogether friendly to the paper. On this occasion
he came unhesitatingly to the rescue.

Clifford Sharp added to his editorial authority through the
1920s ; he was never lacking either in decisiveness or in candour.
The collapse of the first MacDonald Government stirred him to
the writing of a scornful leader headed " This Absurd Crisis," and
two years later the *New Statesman* scored a notable little triumph

by coming out, with all its regular features, in the middle of the General Strike. When every other weekly was shut down, the manager, John Roberts, discovered in South London a press that was ready to oblige. The five years of the Baldwin Government seemed to Sharp an interlude of stifling dullness in politics. Partly, no doubt, in consequence of this atmosphere he was tempted to mark time. He made no change in the pattern of the paper, and continued to rely for the most part upon a rather small number of regular contributors. Of his close associates in long service, three were possessed of extraordinary gifts.

Charles Mostyn Lloyd returned from the war and the Paris Conference with large resources of knowledge. He became deputy editor and chief leader-writer on international affairs. This post he held throughout the two decades between the wars, retiring in 1939. He was a devoted and indispensable colleague of the two editors in succession.

G. D. H. Cole, although never a member of the office staff, rendered services that were altogether unique. He was the paper's central authority on economic and industrial problems, on unemployment, trade unionism and kindred subjects. He was always at the editor's call : a journalist of unsurpassed range and competence, endowed with a speed and sureness of working that none of us had ever known to be surpassed. During a period of not less than ten years he contributed a weekly average of four columns—leaders and editorial notes, book reviews, special articles. His association with the paper is still maintained ; it has never been interrupted.

Nor has that of Desmond MacCarthy, who fourteen years ago wrote a revealing article on what the *New Statesman* had meant to him. Drama criticism during the entire period under review has been the best-known portion of his work for the paper, but it is no more than a portion. The high and varied quality of his writing is displayed in the several volumes of his reprinted essays. He relinquished the literary editorship in 1927, when he was chosen to succeed Sir Edmund Gosse as leading reviewer of the *Sunday Times*. Thereafter his contributions became of necessity less frequent. There is no contemporary critic with a finer gift of appreciation, a richer intelligence, an equipment more truly humane.

For the twenty-first anniversary number, in 1934, Clifford Sharp recalled the incidents of the foundation and summed up his own stewardship. In this narrative, an example of his direct and pungent style, he discussed several questions of special interest, among them his view of the paper's major purpose and his positive stand on the matter of anonymity. He explained that the *New Statesman* had been markedly detached from the emotional concerns of the old Radicals and earlier Socialists. All such, in his opinion, could very well be left outside the orbit of a Fabian review, and he admitted that on this account not a little criticism had come from otherwise friendly quarters. " Coherence and continuity of policy " had been his aim ; and, for all his independence, he was confessedly influenced from first to last by the attitude and temper of the Webbs in the early days. It pleased him to learn that J. A. Spender of the *Westminster Gazette*, an editorial craftsman whom he greatly admired, had singled out for the highest praise two leaders which he assumed could have come only from the editor's pen. As they were both the work of colleagues, Sharp could cite this judgment as good evidence of the multiple personality that an editorial group ought to attain.

He was immovable on the principle of anonymity. His preference would have been for a paper with virtually no exceptions. Journalistic practice was then changing fast, but he decided to admit as few signatures as possible. As time went on and reputations were being made, contributors were given to protest. Sharp would repeat with emphasis that he did not care a farthing for their names. Good journalists, he said, normally wrote their best under cover, when they were proud of the paper they served ; and as a matter of fact, no writer for the *New Statesman* was ever in danger of having his individuality diminished. In this connection two important contributors came under frequent discussion. That talented Syrian, Dr. C. W. Saleeby, untiring as eugenist and missioner of public health, wrote constantly from the first year, barely disguised as Lens. Demands for the printing of his name were without avail. He was told that his pseudonym was worth more to the paper, and besides, that Lens was a more interesting writer than Saleeby.

A second instance to the point was Robert Lynd, whose middle essay achieved a record unapproached in the weekly press for

length of years, regularity, and sustained distinction. After a spell
of anonymity it was signed Y.Y., the double initial being useful
as allowing the essayist to adopt the first person singular. Reviews
of books in the early years were nearly all anonymous. The
personal page of Books-in-General bore a succession of synonyms :
Solomon Eagle (J. C. Squire), Affable Hawk (Desmond Mac-
Carthy), and Richard Sunne (R. Ellis Roberts).

In the retrospect of thirty-five years nothing is more noticeable
than the contrast between the inexperience, not to say *naiveté*, of
the founders and the air of success and assured stability with which
they faced the future after the trial stage of the first World War.
The lifetime of the *New Statesman* is strewn with the wrecks of
weekly journalism. Old and reputable papers have gone down.
New ventures by the dozen have died at birth or, after a struggle,
have failed to make the grade. The Webbs began with little more
than the hope of a brief run, perhaps for a lustrum ; and Mrs.
Webb's confession implies that an early failure would not have
broken their hearts. Nevertheless their skill and persistence were
amply rewarded. It is true, undoubtedly, that the main and governing movement of the time was in their favour ; but even so, the
enterprise could never have struck the road to success if the
essential supports had not been there. The disciplined purpose of
the Webbs was the first essential. To that was added the confidence
of the moneyed partners, and the singularly fortunate harmony of
the editor and his staff.

As regards circulation and financial return, the record divides
into three stages. The first period ended with the sales standing
at, roughly, 12,000. The junction with the *Nation* did not bring
a doubling of this figure, but for a short time a settling down to
about 15,000. Then soon after 1934, when the *Week-End Review*
with its modest figure came in, there began the ascending movement which carried the circulation to a higher total than has
ever been reached by a weekly paper of this character in any
English-speaking country. It has now passed the 85,000 mark.
There is no mystery in this remarkable and gratifying success.
Since 1939 the public to which a paper such as the *New Statesman*
can appeal has undergone a great expansion. That public may or
may not be of positive or permanent leftward tendency. But
beyond all question it is in favour of the freest possible discussion

of all public questions, and is of ever-widening curiosity in the realms of art and thought and literary expression.

The conduct of a journal of opinion demands the closest possible co-operation between the editorial room and the management ; and in this respect, during the current period of popularity, the *New Statesman* has enjoyed the right kind of relationship without friction of any kind. The boundary is never overstepped from either side ; and the management throughout has been marked by the wisdom that never cares to seize an immediate gain to the detriment of a considered long-distance policy.

By 1948 the two editorships had become of almost exactly equal length, eighteen years. Since 1931 the *New Statesman* has been directed by Kingsley Martin, who was appointed after several years with the *Manchester Guardian*. He bears no resemblance to his predecessor. In training as in temperament, in attitude and method, no two editors could well present a sharper contrast of personality. Clifford Sharp and Kingsley Martin may be described as differing types of the publicist and the journalist-crusader. The proof of the pudding is in the eating, and the digestion in Socialism. In the hands of its present editor, the *New Statesman* is vigorous, many-sided, and amazingly prosperous.

LABOUR RESEARCH

by

MARGARET COLE

X

LABOUR RESEARCH

by MARGARET COLE

This chapter is concerned with a particular period—possibly the word should be " episode "—in the career of the Webbs; and to a certain extent with the history of the principal institution founded during that period, after the Webbs had ceased to have any share in its direction. Its especial interest, as far as concerns the Webbs, lies in two facts : the first, that it coincides with the period of their greatest unpopularity, acknowledged by Beatrice in her Diaries. The era of permeation was over ; all that could be achieved by that method had been achieved ; and the only result of trying to carry it further was to alienate the sympathy of those of the ruling powers among whom they had moved and dined. The upper-class circles of the " Souls " and their friends thought the Webbs dangerous and unpleasant doctrinaires ; on the other hand Radicals and Socialists thought them dogmatic, overbearing and narrow-minded. Those were the days of *The New Machiavelli*, in which Wells satirised their Grosvenor Road " political-factory " so sharply as " the horrid little house " of Oscar and Altiora Bailey, and of the Guild Socialists and other opponents referred to in later pages. John Burns, still believed by many to be a Socialist, was openly hostile, and as a Cabinet Minister took delight in " dishing the Webbs " ; the I.L.P. was suspicious of their aims and methods, and the young Labour Party hardly counted in their eyes. They had a very difficult personal period to live through.

The second fact is that in connection with " Labour research " they lost the immediate battle. They created a new organisation only to see it captured by a brand of Socialism which, temporarily at all events, felt itself to be in strong opposition to what they stood for, and at moments was very anxious to push them out of any participation in it. This did not happen ; the processes by which

it failed to happen, the reasons why it failed, and the development
of the new organisation, notwithstanding all the sound and fury,
along lines that were basically Fabian, provides one of the most
revealing historical chapters in the lives of the Webbs and of
British Socialism.

The subject of the chapter is the Webbs and Labour research.
The words " Labour research," both to the Webbs and to others,
can bear two meanings. They can connote either " research into
subjects of importance to the Labour movement," that is to say,
in effect, most of what we now call sociology, or " research designed to establish conclusions in accordance with the general
tenets of the Labour movement." These two interpretations of
course tend to overlap at times, since it is almost impossible to
work on sociological subjects without any bias whatever or any
advance idea of the conclusions which you are likely to reach.
Nevertheless, there is a pretty clear difference between " pure "
research, of the kind which the Webbs pursued in their ten great
volumes on English local government, and the " tendencious "
research embodied in the informatory tracts and pamphlets of the
Fabian Society ; and there is an equally clear difference between
" tendencious " research and propaganda. Straight propaganda,
such as the Webbs, in common with other Socialists, undertook
from time to time for specific purposes on specific occasions, such
as General Elections, the campaign for the break-up of the Poor
Law, or the 1919 railway strike, is essentially a weapon of war.
The business of the propagandist is to collect and publish the
facts which support his case, and those facts only. It is no duty of
his to publish facts making the other way ; his business is so far
as possible to suppress them altogether.

The tendencious research worker, however, is in a different
position. He may be seeking to convert others to a thesis in which
he strongly believes ; but he is not entitled to suppress the
evidence. Naturally, he will select, and give prominence to, those
facts which he considers of greatest importance, which will probably be those tending to support his own conclusions ; but he
must accord weight to those which do not, and he must give the
evidence from which his own conclusions and his rejection of the
conclusions of others can be checked. (Marx, whose name has
often been taken in vain by the most unscrupulous of propagan-

dists in the narrow sense, was himself extremely scrupulous in both giving and verifying his references.)

The point is important, because it has been sometimes alleged against the Webbs and other Fabians that all their research work was " propaganda " ; this is not true. Of " tendencious research " they did a very great deal ; the Fabian belief was that by *proper presentation* of the actual verifiable facts capitalism could be convicted so to speak out of its own mouth, and the necessity of Socialism established. They knew quite well that a very great deal turned on the proper presentation of the right facts, as Sidney amusingly revealed during the Sankey Coal Commission when the mine-owners presented a series of statistics which he did not like the look of, and he snapped, " What are these ? Mere arithmetical calculations ! " But even in the Webbs' most tendencious work of reference, *Soviet Communism* (most tendencious because in it their emotions were most strongly engaged), the material for checking their statements is fully present. They may disagree with W. H. Chamberlin's view of what happened in the Ukraine in 1932, but they do not ignore him ; they argue with him in a footnote of colossal size. Nor do they hide what they do not approve of in the Soviet Union, such as " the disease of (Marxist) orthodoxy " or the secret police ; they criticise it. (Many of those who have attacked this particular book of theirs as a deliberately falsified picture do not appear in fact to have read it through.) The worst that they can be accused of is that when a fact turned up which seemed to make against the conclusions they were reaching they looked at it with suspicion, meditated whether it were not a misleading fact to which too much attention ought not to be paid, and looked around to see whether there were not some other facts which contradicted it ; but there are few research workers with opinions of their own who have not done likewise.

The Webbs engaged in both types of Labour research. The first, however, which led them to follow up their studies of Trade Unionism and industrial democracy by the foundation of the London School of Economics, lies outside the scope of this chapter, which is concerned with " Labour research " in its second and more restricted meaning. It is also mainly concerned with " Labour research " over a brief period, the years between

1911, when the Webbs realised that the agitation to destroy the Poor Law had failed of its principal objective, and 1919, when the research organisation which they had set up within the Fabian Society finally shook itself free of any connection with its parent body, and having changed its name sought a new physical home in the offices of the Labour Party. The idea of Labour research, however, had presented itself to the minds of the Webbs a great many years before.

To Sidney, indeed, long before he was married. The famous Tract Five of the Fabian Society, *Facts for Socialists*, which was his idea and almost entirely produced by him—it came out first in 1887, and has been constantly revised, either by him or by his successors, down to the present day—was a perfect example of tendencious research. Beatrice Potter's early text-book on the Co-operative Movement was more like pure research, so far as it went. So was the first work of the partnership, the *History of Trade Unionism*, at least in its pristine form, for though the revised edition of 1920 does bear some unscholarly traces of their controversies with Syndicalists and other theorists with whom they disagreed, to see in the first edition, as some have done, an apologia for a Labour Party that was not born for another six years, is to be really perverse. As a result, however, of the Trade Union connections which they had made in the course of writing the *History* they found themselves for a while in the position of acting as counsellors to some of the Trade Union leaders, drafting, for example, for the Royal Commission on Trade Unions, a minority report to be signed by persons of such widely-differing political opinions as Henry Broadhurst, spokesman of conservative craft unionism, and Tom Mann, the fiery young orator of the Left. As Beatrice's Diary shows, she was encouraged by these experiences to have visions of their becoming " clerks (in the medieval sense) to Labour "; that they did not do so for many a long year was due in great measure to the attitude of John Burns, then without question the most prominent among Labour leaders, who made it quite clear that he had no intention of being tutored by the Webbs or by anyone else—but also partly to the fact that before the end of the last century they had, for the time being, exhausted their interest in the working-class movement, Trade Union and Co-operative alike, and were turning their attention to local government research on the one hand, and on the other to political and social " permeation " of governing-class circles.

Sidney did not, during the subsequent years, altogether give up Labour research ; in his capacity as executive committee-member of the Fabian Society he was responsible, directly or indirectly, for a fair number of informative pamphlets and special inquiries ; but Beatrice played very little part in the Fabian Society of those days, and her Diaries show much more concern with personages like Balfour, Haldane, and the Progressive leaders of the London County Council than with specifically Labour issues or Labour men.

This period of permeation lasted right through the reign of Edward VII, until after Sidney had written out in his own fair round hand Beatrice's *Minority Report to the Poor Law Commission*. During the four long years of that Commission's sittings, Beatrice gradually discovered that " peaceful permeation " was not going to succeed in converting Sir James Davy, Lord George Hamilton, and the representatives of the Charity Organisation Society to a semi-Socialist remedy for the problem of destitution ; in the next two years she made the further discovery that a mass propaganda assault through a large all-party organisation (the National Com-mittee for the Prevention of Destitution) was not going to be any more successful—was in fact going to result in nothing but a contributory insurance scheme on a very niggardly scale. If that were so, if one could neither bore from within nor shake from without, she concluded that the only possible course was for a Socialist body to work out afresh, by careful and detailed study, plans for the transformation of Britain into a Socialist country— plans which would in due course be implemented by a Socialist Government. The body which was to formulate these plans was the Fabian Society ; it is interesting to observe, as an indication of the low estimation in which the official working-class leaders were held by the intelligentsia of Edwardian days, that the Webbs apparently never thought of making use of the official Labour Party with which Sidney was to be so closely associated only a few years later—and that nobody else suggested it either.

Mrs. Webb had not paid much attention to the Fabian Society in the years immediately preceding ; it was Sidney's spare-time occupation rather than hers. In 1907 her Diary notes rather patronisingly that "the little boom in the Fabian Society continues"—the boom being, of course, part of the great Radical uprising which produced the huge Liberal majority and Campbell-Bannerman's Government ; and she was annoyed at the apparent insubordinateness of the new membership—it rushed to elect that stormy petrel H. G. Wells to the Executive Committee, and took to forming Groups and Committees which tried to force the old hands (the Old Gang, as Pease called them in his *History of the Fabian Society*) to alter their time-honoured procedure. Nevertheless, her visit to the 1909 Fabian Summer School impressed her with the possibilities of Socialist education through concentrated group study. She was equally impressed with the abilities of the young men and women who came in to help with the Poor Law campaign, and in 1910, on her initiative,[1] a week of the Summer School was definitely assigned to discussions of Socialists from the universities. She had already written with appreciation of some of them, particularly the young Cambridge Socialists, among whom was Hugh Dalton.

By the end of 1912—the gap in time was due to the Webbs' world tour—the nucleus of the Fabian Research Department was already in existence, in the form of a vast " Control of Industry Committee," presided over by Beatrice and including, besides some eighty members of the Fabian Society, " sixty-six consultative members drawn mainly from the Co-operative and Trade Union movements " (Fabian Society Annual Report, 1913) ; and a " Land Problems and Rural Development Committee," which pursued its own separate inquiries. The latter need not detain us ; it kept an even tenor and eventually published a book. The former, which was much the more important and excited all the controversy, soon gave birth to the Fabian Research Department, a regularly constituted group with its own controlling committee ; its first secretary was Julius West, the historian of Chartism, who on his translation to the young *New Statesman* was succeeded by William Mellor, Guild Socialist, conscientious objector during the war, and afterwards editor of the *Daily Herald*.

The name Control of Industry Committee and the name of

[1]Possibly on Sidney's also ; it is very difficult to assign separate responsibility for any particular bit of work of the *Partnership*. But the impression I gain is that Beatrice's " fresh eye " saw opportunities which Sidney would not have thought of if he had been alone.

William Mellor give the clue both to the Webbs' first thoughts about Fabian research and to the difficulties they found in implementing them. They wanted to harness and to use the abilities of the young men from the universities. How were they to do so ? Clearly, the best way would be to set them to intense study and encourage them to produce reports and memoranda on some or other of the most important and burning questions of the moment, in which they might reasonably be supposed to be interested. The subject selected, a subject on which the Webbs felt that an authoritative report ought to be produced as soon as possible, was the methods by which, in a Socialist or semi-Socialist State, industry should be controlled and administered—and it was urgent. Let Sidney speak for himself—for though the following passage occurs in the anonymous Fabian Report already quoted, the phrasing (and the capital letters !) are unmistakably his :—

" The subject chosen—the Control of Industry—was suggested by the ferment of Syndicalism in the Socialist and Labour movements on the one hand and on the other by the dangerous proposals of the Liberal Government and the Conservative Opposition to give legislative encouragement to Compulsory Arbitration or Profit-sharing schemes. On both sides the Socialist proposal to control industry by the elected representatives of the people was challenged : reactionary proposals to the right of us, and a good deal of anarchic and disruptive sentiment to the left of us. Hence it seemed desirable that the Society should make up its mind to definite, concrete proposals for the Control of Industry.

" The Committee (on the Control of Industry)," the Report continues, " has divided itself into four sub-committees, dealing with Associations of Wage Earners, Associations of Producers, Associations of Consumers, and Public Services respectively . . . Reports have been or are about to be drawn up on the following subjects : the extent and character of the Syndicalist movement in England ; the relative advantages of federation and amalgamation for the Unions in any given industry ; the organisation of German Trade Unionism ; the gradual transformation of the Co-operative ideal of the Self-governing Workshop into schemes of Industrial Partnership between the Capitalist, the Consumers' Society, and the Workshop Employees, either individually or through the Trade Unions : the relative success of Municipal and Private Management

F*

of Electricity ; and the organisation of the productive departments in one branch of the Government . . . The final
report of the committee will, it is hoped, be written during
the winter and published early in 1914. It will probably
constitute a book, rather than a pamphlet."

A year later it seemed that the result was to be " a library rather
than a book." Much had happened meantime.

This opening statement is extremely illuminating. The report
is to be finished and issued quickly ; the directions in which research is to proceed are firmly laid down ; and the conclusion to
be reached—the superiority of "pure" Collectivism to any other
form of industrial organisation—is also pretty clearly indicated.
The initial success of the proposal was gratifying ; the young
Fabians flocked in to do the research work. But, much to the
Webbs' surprise and annoyance, on certain important points they
entirely failed to come to the correct conclusions.

The great majority of the projects announced in 1913, it should
be emphasised, proceeded tranquilly and effectively towards their
goals. Reports were in due course produced on German Trade
Unions, on State and Municipal Enterprise, on Producers' Co-
operation, and on various other subjects—some being published
as Supplements to the *New Statesman*. All contained a great deal
of valuable information and suggestions. In due course, the Webbs
set up another inquiry, into industrial insurance, with the purpose
of throwing a fierce light upon the workings of that great capitalist
interest which had played so large a part not merely in the defeat
of Beatrice's own Poor Law proposals, but in the negotiations over
Lloyd George's Act ; they also in the early stages of the first
World War initiated a new and fruitful experiment by making a
grant to Leonard Woolf to enable him to write a report on means
of achieving a world political system. The result of his labours,
published under the title *International Government*, was one of
the earliest blue-prints for a League of Nations. All this was
success ; one of the groups, however, that described in the 1913
Report in the innocent-sounding phrase, " Committee on Associations of Wage Earners," almost immediately put the cat among
the pigeons.

As Webb had made clear, the task laid down for this Committee
was to produce an unequivocal denunciation of Syndicalism, In-

dustrial Unionism, and all the variant demands for "workers' control" which were reaching their height in the first years of the new reign. It is a matter of history that the Labour unrest which accompanied a slow but steady rise in prices and the apparent inability of the Liberal Government and its Labour tail to do anything effectively to raise the status of the working classes, and which broke out in the most formidable and spectacular strikes seen since the London dockers won their "tanner" more than twenty years before, were largely inspired if not caused by propaganda of Syndicalist type. The Webbs—Sidney in particular, who was not at that time prepared to make any concessions whatever in the pure milk of Collectivist Socialism—regarded Syndicalism in all its forms as pernicious anarchistic nonsense which might make—was in fact making—a dangerous appeal to the more feather-headed among the manual workers. They did not realise, however, that the ideal of Syndicalism and the General Strike had a strong appeal to many Socialists outside the manual ranks, Socialists who like the Suffragettes and the left-wing Irish Nationalists were exasperated beyond measure at the inefficiency and apparent double-dealing of parliamentary governments and were not at all disposed to accept the view that turning the whole of Britain's economic life over to "State and Municipal Enterprise" would bring about anything remotely resembling a Socialist Society. The form in which the virus of Syndicalism (or "functional representation") attacked the Fabian Society was the Guild Socialism preached first by Arthur Penty, S. G. Hobson, A. R. Orage and the *New Age ;* its chief protagonists within the Society were the Oxford University Fabians, led by G. D. H. Cole and William Mellor. When, therefore, the Webbs asked the Fabian Society to give its close attention to Socialist research, they found that the keenest and ablest of the new recruits were fully at one with them on the need for research, but were determined that so far as industry was concerned the conclusions reached should be Guild Socialist, "functionalist" conclusions ; and that the new opposition within the Society, which from 1912 to 1915 produced such stormy sessions, was not merely anxious to make changes in the constitution of the Society but was also attacking some of its traditionally-established opinions. It was extremely annoying for Mrs. Webb, just when the agitations connected with Wells and with the " Fabian Reform Committee " appeared to have been happily disposed of, to be confronted with a much more serious, hardworking, effective and sharp-tongued opposition which proposed to let her form her Research Department and then run away with it. At first neither she nor Sidney grasped what was happening, or that they had to deal on this occasion with a real clash of principle.

The difference of principle was real, even if both sides seem in retrospect to have been rather Utopian in their propagandist arguments, the Webbs displaying extravagant faith in the abilities and imaginativeness of "enlightened civil servants " and the Guild Socialists similarly advertising shop stewards and mining checkweighmen. But in my own view, the view of one who in the later days of the conflict served as a ranker on the Guild Socialist side, the difference of principle was much accentuated by differences of temperament and intellectual upbringing. The Fabian Guild Socialists—at least, the most prominent of them—were university-trained. Neither Beatrice nor Sidney—nor Bernard Shaw—had ever been to a university ; the Webbs' training before their marriage had been almost entirely executive, his in the Colonial Civil Service, hers as head of a household and confidential secretary to an important businessman. They had thus no experience either of prolonged and eager discussion of doctrine— throughout their lives, they were both impatient of time spent in " philosophic talk ; " they wanted quickly to find an acceptable doctrine and then get on with the job—or with the irrepressible ragging and abusive controversy of serious-minded university youth. The elder Fabians were staid creatures by contrast ; what Shaw called " our invaluable habit of freely laughing at ourselves " did not extend to horse-play ; and even in her first experience of a University week at the Fabian Summer School, Beatrice noted with some pain that the young men were very easily bored with inferior speakers and made no effort to hide this, and that they seemed to think that " house rules " were made for them to break. After 1914, differences of opinion about the war added something to the tension. The Webbs were not emotional anti-Prussian fire-eaters, and were hardly concerned at all with issues of foreign policy—nor were the Fabians as a body, as G.B.S. has time and again pointed out. But once war had been declared and was clearly being supported by the vast majority of the nation, they accepted it and its consequences as a fact, like the existence of the monarchy ; whereas the Fabian Researchers tended to be against the war, on pacifist or anti-capitalist grounds, and in later years C.O.s on the run were often to be found in the offices in Tothill Street.

War-differences, however, were less sundering among Socialists between 1914 and 1918 than the present generation would believe —Ramsay MacDonald, the pacifist, remained Treasurer of the Labour Party throughout the war ; and those differences were less important than the difference in temperament and outlook to which I have already referred. It would have been quite unthinkable, for the young ones among us who came into the movement during the years of the Fabian Research Department, to have ranged ourselves on the Webb side. All the enthusiasm, all the *fun* of playing games with press-cuttings, of knowing by heart the initials of Trade Unions and their ramifications, of meeting with rebellious local leaders of industry whom the war-time industrial truce had brought into positions of prominence and importance, all the organisation of Parliamentary questions, resolutions, and other methods of embarrassing and annoying the Government and promoting the cause of workers' control, were to be found in the opposition camp ; and in that camp we were happy to serve, in office hours and outside. Meanwhile Sidney, though up till 1919 he co-operated to some extent in the work of the Research Department, was giving more and more time to that of the War Workers' Emergency National Committee[1] and through it to the 1918 reorganisation of the Labour Party.

These reflections have taken me a little ahead of events, which must now be briefly traced. For a while it seemed that the Guild Socialists might succeed in capturing the Fabian Society to the extent of inducing it to sever connections with any political party and devote itself to research—a resolution to that effect, moved by G. D. H. Cole in March, 1914, was lost by one vote only. In the following year, however, a Guild Socialist manifesto, presented under the title of *The Right Moment*—in allusion to the sentence in the Fabian Society's motto which ran " when *the right moment comes* you must strike hard, as Fabius did, or your waiting will be

[1]See Chapter XI.

useless "—was rejected by the Annual Meeting in a session of considerable turmoil, during which a member of the Society was heard to complain " I've been a member of the Fabian Society for forty years, and now these young men make me come *all the way from Streatham* to vote against them ! " Cole and some others then resigned ; but a good few of the Guild Socialists, including Mellor and Page Arnot, stayed on in order to get on with the work of the Research Department, which already had about 250 " members and subscribers."

Beatrice was not at all anxious to see the work of the Research Department come to an end owing to the conflict ; and she actively supported its continuance. At the beginning of 1916 she proposed and carried a resolution opening its membership to persons who were not members of the Fabian Society—which enabled the dissidents to return to it ; and she raised no objection when a year later it dropped the word Fabian and called itself Labour Research Department ; she was a frequent visitor to its premises, and she consulted and discussed with its officers, not merely upon research, but on general questions of Government policy on social affairs and in particular upon the old problem of the Poor Law, with which she was again engaged as a member of the Maclean Committee on the reform of local government.

It was during this period that I first met the Webbs, and it is curious to recollect how very different was the impression I then formed from that given in most of the other chapters of this book. I must emphasise that, as a very junior and enthusiastic recruit to the staff of the Guild Socialist F.R.D., I had been well-conditioned to regard them as reactionaries before ever I set eyes on either of them. I *knew* that they were wilfully wicked opponents of the legitimate aspirations of the working class, supporters of the Government in an imperialist war—my brother was a conscientious objector—and in general old obscurantists who wanted to bully and hamstring the high-souled workers and voluntary helpers in our office. Apart from the differences of policy which I have mentioned earlier, this extremely biased picture—not to say caricature !—did derive a certain measure of validity from two facts. First, that the Webbs did display parsimony in the payment of salaries to Fabian employees. This was a curious trait in people who had written so much and so strongly about the need for collective bargaining and national minima ; and I can only account for it (inadequately) by suggesting 1. that their idea of national minima were scales negotiated by a strong Trade Union—and we Fabian workers had no Union ; and 2. that they were unconsciously influenced by the immense amount of unpaid work which members of the pre-war Fabian Executive—and of the Fabian Society itself—managed to put in. Whatever the explanation, we Fabian research workers did find it exceedingly difficult to wring salary increases out of the Webbs ; and the fact hardly tended to make us feel more kindly to them.

Secondly, as far as I myself was concerned, I resented a little the lack of interest shown by the Webbs in young women in comparison with young men. Sidney, as we know from his wife's authority, liked hardly any woman save herself ; Beatrice had been an anti-suffragist in her earlier days, and, though she had recanted before the war, she never, in all the long years that I knew her, displayed towards the young women of the Socialist movement anything like the avid curiosity which she evinced towards the " coming " young men. Fundamentally, I believe, she thought that the women in the movement, with very few exceptions, were either socially unpresentable wives of Trade Union leaders, whom she tried with very limited success to groom for their future rôle in that odd experiment of the 'twenties, the Half-Circle Club—or potentially dangerous sirens who might deflect the young men's attention from their proper pursuits. I do know that when she first saw me in the Fabian office she warned its chief against allowing the men there to fall in love with me.

This second point is not, of course, a very important one, though, as the Fabian research workers were almost all feminists as well as Socialists, it had its influence ; and it certainly helped to fix my own attitude to the Webbs. I regarded Sidney as a contemptuous little man in a hurry who bullied committees—this was an unfair judgment, mainly based on a single incident when, during the course of a long argumentative committee, he heard another member open his mouth with the word " but," and impatiently rapped out, " That's the same point over again ! " (In fact, it was ; and no doubt the whole business was very irritating to him.) When I first saw Beatrice in Tothill Street, I thought she looked infinitely frail and infinitely old—she was thirty years older than

I was, which when one is a little over twenty is an enormous gap; and my only concern was how I could get out of the room, without either being sacked on the spot by the formidable lady in the hideous hat, or doing anything violent—such as sneezing, for example—which might cause her to disintegrate on the spot. I had no idea, nor had any of my junior colleagues, of how much we really had in common with her, or how deeply I should come to appreciate and admire her in later years.

For although I have stressed—because it was a fact—the continual and vociferous opposition of the Guild Socialist Fabian researchers to what *Punch* called " Sidneywebbicalism," I must also emphasise that it was a rollicking rather than a bitter opposition —something which those trained in the later language of Communism can hardly be expected to understand. We did not call the Webbs *vipers*, or *hyenas*, or even *social traitors*—our abuse ran rather to such simple undergraduate rhymes as :

> O that Beatrice and Sidney
> Would get in their kidney
> A loathsome disease—
> —Also Pease.

—which hardly anyone could have taken very seriously. I know as a fact that Beatrice had no idea of the extent to which we had decked out her and Sidney as political Guy Fawkeses ; and, as I said in a previous paragraph, there was continuous co-operation and discussion between them and the Guild Socialists throughout the war, and neither party was really trying to double-cross the other.

There was, however, some fundamental difference ; and on the first darling project, the Report on " Associations of Wage-Earners," no agreement was possible. The Webbs' draft report was torn to pieces by the opposition and never saw the light ; counter-drafts made by their opponents came equally to grief and were refused publication in the *New Statesman*. A division was therefore inevitable ; the Webbs worked through the Labour Party ; the Guild Socialists issued their fundamental policy proposals through their own propaganda organisation, the National Guilds League ; and the L.R.D., under Guild Socialist guidance, came to occupy itself with intensive studies of existing Trade Unionism and gradually added to its functions those of an extensive inquiry bureau serving Trade Unions, Trades Councils, and other Labour bodies. It soon had a long list of such organisations affiliated directly to it ; and Beatrice, far from opposing, signified her approval of this development by accepting the chairmanship of the Trade Union Survey—the name given to the group of affiliated Trade Unions—and at a later stage by using the machinery of the Labour Research Department for the purpose of selling throughout the Labour movement the cheap edition of their revised *History of Trade Unionism*. Just previously, during the 1919 railway strike, when the L.R.D. ran a big and successful publicity campaign paid for by the National Union of Railwaymen, Sidney had returned to it to play an active part on the committee which ran the propaganda ; the connection was far from being severed.

All this while, the L.R.D. was expanding faster and faster and taking on new lines of inquiry. In 1917, it began to issue, under the title of the *Monthly Circular*, a journal of Labour *information*, the only one of its kind in Britain, which is still published to this day ; it set up a regular inquiry into the doings of employers' associations and capitalist firms, a subject which the Webbs had left alone ; it added a Local Government Section and an International Section ; and in the days when adequate research machinery in Trade Union offices was still in a very embryonic stage—when the *total salary bill*, for example, of the Trades Union Congress central office was £400 a year, covering the general secretary, C. W. Bowerman, and his assistant !—it frequently undertook the preparation of long and detailed briefs for Trade Union secretaries engaged in wage negotiations. It did not issue *Fabian Tracts*, for that name was copyright ; but it produced, under other titles, what were virtually Tracts of its own—printed and Memoranda, for example, full of facts on such subjects as Wages and Prices during the war, Legal Regulation of Hours, Facts from the (Sankey) Coal Commission, short studies of the history and organisation of labour and capital in various industries, later on penny *Labour White Papers* briefly summarising facts or proposals on immediate questions of the day, and a series of Study Syllabuses for adult education classes—all these being eagerly snapped up, at least until the post-war slump, by Labour organisations all over the country.

Throughout, whatever the political opinions expressed or the conclusions reached, the tradition of *Facts for Socialists* and Fabian research was faithfully observed. The office in Tothill Street, when I worked in it, was a stiff school of accuracy and adequate knowledge. You were expected to have mastered your subject before you wrote about it and to get your facts right ; no one of the officers was inclined to be merciful to slovenly work or wish-thinking where it was obvious—though of course wish-thinking cannot be altogether eliminated from the work of any group of persons with strong emotional political convictions. (It must also be admitted that the day-to-day scramble of an inquiry bureau occasionally resulted in some window-dressing by junior members of staff unexpectedly confronted by the personal visit of a large important Trade Union Secretary asking a question of whose meaning they were entirely ignorant—to say nothing of the answer to it !) But the staff were expected to " verify their references," to find out the answer to the Trade Unionist's question and to make sure that the answer was correct and would stand up to cross-examination. The L.R.D. was financed very largely out of subscriptions, affiliation fees, and " payment-by-results " from Labour organisations with scanty funds ; it would not have succeeded in collecting these monies had it not been able to establish the confidence that the information services it provided were copper-bottomed and could be fully relied on. This was the tradition established, and it endured. Many years afterwards, when the L.R.D. was admittedly under Communist influence and Transport House endeavoured to ban it, along with other " sub-versive organisations " to loyal supporters of Labour, a large number of its affiliated societies defied the ban ; they had found its services too useful and too reliable. But that stage in its history falls outside the scope of this chapter.

The Webbs' connection with the L.R.D. became gradually fainter and fainter. Formal connection, as I said, ended when Sidney left the executive and the L.R.D. found a temporary home with the Labour Party in Eccleston Square ; and long before the final capture of the L.R.D. by Communists in the mid-'twenties—since when, one would imagine, it would regard any suggestion of Fabian inspiration as a mortal insult—the Webbs had ceased to have anything whatever to do with it, or to feel any interest in its fortunes. But up to that point, its history provides an extremely interesting specimen of the Webbs' methods and of the standards they set themselves. Its start was their idea, eagerly taken up by their juniors ; it turned very rapidly into something very different, not merely in opinion, but in organisation and purpose, from what they had imagined—and very much bigger, it may be said, than their vision of a tidily sectionalised Control of Industry Committee. But it owed a very great deal to them ; and however much they disliked it, they never at any time either repudiated it or tried to effect a recapture ; granted that such an attempt would have had no hope of success, there have been many Socialist politicians, with less practical realism and self-restraint than the Webbs, who under such circumstances would have tried either to discipline or to destroy their self-willed offspring. They did not ; they remained on good terms with those who had been their most vigorous opponents, and long afterwards, when some of those same opponents revived in the New Fabian Research Bureau and the reconstructed Fabian Society[1] the tradition of fact-finding and policy-making on a basis of facts, they gave the venture their blessing. *Mutatis mutandis*, the story of the Webbs' relations with Labour Research has something in common with that of their attitude to other institutions founded by them, such as the *New Statesman ;* its particular interest lies in the fact that there, and there alone, they had to adjust themselves to an organised opposition within the ranks of what they had believed to be their " own " movement ; nobody will deny that the course of events did very great credit to their own public spirit, the strength of the ideal of Labour Research, and the energy and ability of those who took over from them.

[1]See Chapter XV

WEBB AND THE LABOUR PARTY

by

J. S. MIDDLETON

XI

WEBB AND THE LABOUR PARTY

by J. S. MIDDLETON

It was not until the outbreak of the first Great War in 1914 that Sidney Webb's immediate and personal impact upon the Labour Party really began. For nearly thirty years previously his contribution to the moulding of Socialist and Labour opinion and the ultimate creation of the Party had been as constant as it had been notable. He joined the Fabian Society in 1885—three years before the historic bye-election in Mid-Lanark in which Keir Hardie's defeat led to the formation of the Scottish Labour Party. In 1892 the Fabians had inspired the " Newcastle Programme " and had forced its list of constructive social reforms upon the Liberal Party with the reluctant consent of Mr. Gladstone. Keir Hardie's election for South-West Ham in the General Election of that same year and his isolated stand for the Socialist gospel in the House of Commons was the rallying point for the forces south of the Border to follow the Scottish example and inaugurate the I.L.P. at Bradford in 1893. That, too, was the year when Robert Blatchford wrote *Merrie England* and proposed that the Trade Unions should form a Party of their own, independent of the existing Parties and financed by themselves, with organisations in the constituencies to return men of their own choice to Parliament. It was also in November, 1893, that the *Fortnightly Review* published the historic Manifesto, " To your Tents, O Israel " (afterwards issued as " A Plan of Campaign for Labour ") which was mainly the joint effort of Sidney Webb and Bernard Shaw. That, too, proposed that the working classes should abandon their support of Liberalism—as the Fabians had then decided to do—form a Party of their own, and raise £30,000 to finance fifty candidates for Parliament.

Six more years of ardent propaganda and education among the masses, to which the Fabian Society and the I.L.P., with a few Socialists among the more prominent Trade Union leaders of the time contributed incessantly, brought the Trades Union Congress to take the initiative in an attempt to federate the Unions and the Socialist organisations for the promotion of Independent Labour Representation. In February, 1900, the Labour Representation Committee was formed and henceforth its National Executive became the common meeting ground for representatives of the Unions, the I.L.P., and the Fabians. Edward Pease, in his *History of the Fabian Society*, has related some of the outstanding events of the early days of the L.R.C., and in innumerable biographies the effect of the General Election of 1906, when the L.R.C. actually ran fifty candidates and secured the return of twenty-nine of them, has been commented upon from various points of view. Pease was active in the preparation of L.R.C. Conference resolutions and the terms of its Constitution, and from 1900 to 1914 brought to the Executive his own particular gifts of criticism and draughtsmanship. It was not the way of the early Fabians to work as " lone hands," and it was accepted that on the greater issues which had to be considered by the Party, Sidney and Beatrice Webb and Bernard Shaw, along with Pease, were pursuing the traditional Fabian policy of Socialist permeation which had failed to rouse the Liberal Party to face the immense social problems which then demanded fundamental remedies.

The stream of Fabian Tracts, apart from the continuous influence of *Fabian Essays*, provided scholarly education for the more serious minds of that generation and gave solid substance to the never-ending platform propaganda of the I.L.P. In particular, Webb's first Fabian pamphlet, *Facts for Socialists* (Tract 5), published 1887 and revised time and time again, gave logical point to the Socialist crusade against the prevailing poverty in the midst of Victorian opulence. The influence of the Fabians upon the growing Labour Groups in City and Municipal Councils cannot be measured. In this field, Webb, from his vantage point as a member of the newly-created London County Council, Shaw as member of the St. Pancras Vestry, in addition to other specialists in different phases of municipal activity were informed and inspiring guides to many lonely little coteries who blazed the trail for the later Labour majorities.

When war seemed imminent at the end of July, 1914, the Joint Board of the Labour Party, the Trades Union Congress, and the

General Federation of Trade Unions, had hurriedly convened a conference of the chief working-class organisations with a view to the setting up of a Peace Emergency Committee to prevent the outbreak of hostilities. War was declared on Monday, 4th August, but by the time the Conference met in the Grand Committee Room of the House of Commons on 6th August, it was too late to move effectively for peace, for the armies and navies of the combatant nations were under battle orders. In these circumstances the Conference initiated the War Emergency : Workers' National Committee, the most representative body the British Labour Movement has ever created and one which was the most fruitful in its efforts to protect the working class in time both of war and of peace. The Committee was composed of representatives of the following bodies : the Trades Union Congress, the Labour Party, the General Federation of Trade Unions, the Miners' Federation, the National Union of Railwaymen, the Women's Labour League, the Women's Trade Union League, the British Socialist Party, the Independent Labour Party, the Fabian Society, the Co-operative Union, the Co-operative Wholesale Society, the Women's Co-operative Guild, the Textile Factory Workers' Association, the Transport Workers' Federation, the National Union of Teachers, and the London Trades Council. Arthur Henderson, who had succeeded Ramsay MacDonald as Leader of the Parliamentary Party, was chairman of the Committee until he entered the Asquith Coalition Government, when Robert Smillie took his place. The present writer, then Assistant Secretary of the Party, was appointed Secretary, chiefly because it was necessary to use the machinery of the Party to conduct the continuous and varied work that awaited the Movement under the direction of the new body.

It was through this Committee that Sidney Webb, representing the Fabian Society, became intimate with the Party leaders over a very wide field, upon which he found the fullest scope for his amazing fertility of ideas, his unrivalled mastery of detail, and his special genius for draftsmanship.

Within a week from the start Webb had prepared a thirty-two-page pamphlet, *The War and the Workers,* giving clear advice and guidance to local organisations throughout the country, urging the institution of local committees similar in scope to the National

Committee to co-ordinate local Labour opinion and influence Municipal and similar authorities to prevent unemployment consequent upon the dislocation created by the war by the provision of local schemes of work, instead of merely seeking to relieve distress financially. The institution of comprehensive Citizens' Committees was also urged as the duty of local authorities to cope with the special war problems which were rapidly developing as the armed forces increased in numbers, and upon which the National Committee, under Webb's stimulus, began to formulate immediate policy. In all fields of social necessity, excluding all matters affecting military or naval action, the National Committee was constantly engaged in promoting specific measures, legislative and administrative, and urging them by deputations to Ministers, through the Parliamentary Labour Party, by steady press propaganda, by Regional Conferences, Demonstrations, and platform campaigns, and the regular circulation of the informative minutes of the Committee's weekly meetings to a wide network of national and local organisations and individuals. It was an outstanding achievement to secure the continual co-operation of national leaders holding conflicting views upon actual war policy in the discussion, decision, and direction of a mass of miscellaneous problems which required prompt action by the Government. In its early days the Committee demanded the regulation of food prices and subsequently the rationing of staple necessities, including coal. Working class rents began to rise to an extortionate level as increased separation allowances for serving men were granted, and a joint consultation between representatives of small property owners, building societies, and ratepayers' organisations, and of the National Committee was arranged. Within an hour Webb had produced a basis, upon which agreement was reached by all parties concerned, by providing for the restriction of the levels of rents and mortgage interest to that of August, 1914. This was the beginning of the many measures which successive governments have promoted during the ensuing years.

The Committee's campaigns for improved separation allowances for the families of servicemen, increased payments for the relief of distress where necessary, and later its programme for adequate pensions for disablement, were not the least successful of its many achievements. Undesirable practices in connection

with war contracts including various instances of the substitution
of shoddy for genuine material required for service needs were
publicly exposed. The position of Belgian refugees, old age pen-
sioners, unmarried mothers, the distressed relatives of prisoners
of war were all subject to publicity and pressure upon the Government ; and the hardships inflicted upon the community by
excessive shipping freights and the extortions of food profiteers
were examined in detail and given wide advertisement.

The Committee was composed of men and women with special
knowledge in many fields of industry and public service and
worked with an unexcelled enthusiasm throughout its existence.
That so fine an example of unity of purpose and effort should
have been allowed to dissolve was one of the gravest misfortunes
to the working class movement in Britain.

Edward Pease, writing from long and intimate association, has
recorded his conviction that " whenever Webb is on a Committee
it may be assumed in default of positive evidence to the contrary
that its report is his work." Certainly during the period of the
war in the Workers' National Committee Webb found an instrument specially devised for the exercise of his unique gifts and
conducted at a tempo which evoked the enthusiasm of his colleagues and established his position in the larger movement in a
manner which could not have been possible otherwise.

The war was also responsible for giving Webb a place on the
National Executive Committee of the Labour Party in place of
William Sanders, who in 1913 had succeeded Pease as Secretary
of the Fabian Society and had enlisted in the forces in 1915.
This was a position of immense advantage to Webb. Differences
with Ramsay MacDonald during the South African War had led
to estrangement, though they had worked together for the promotion of technical education in London. Upon Arthur
Henderson's accession to the Party Secretaryship in 1911, however,
opportunities for friendlier and more intimate relations with the
Party were seized and side by side with his work on the Workers'
National Committee from 1914 Webb cultivated cordial co-
operation with the Party Office. Thus he was able to bring to
successful issue three great policies each of which had an immense
and lasting effect upon the fortunes of the Party, and the nation.

From 1900 to 1918 the Party had been a Federation of Trade

Unions, Socialist Societies, and local organisations (originally Trades Councils and afterwards local Parties formed on the same federal basis as the National Party). In only a few instances were there opportunities for men and women to join the Party as individual supporters : they were affiiliated either through their respective Trade Unions, or through the I.L.P. or the Fabian Society. The situation created by the war and notably the extension of the franchise on an adult basis and the inclusion of women for the first time, necessitated a complete reorganisation of the Party machine. In this, Webb's inspiration and practical assistance were prominent in the devising of the new Constitution of 1918. Emphasis was given to the aim of the Party " to secure for the producers by hand or by brain the full fruits of their industry " and steps were taken to place the Party upon a firm national foundation. A team of men and women regional organisers were appointed to assist the National Agent of the Party and a newly-appointed Chief Woman Officer to institute Constituency Parties, and Local Parties embracing individual members and functioning through Ward Committees. In addition, the absorption of the Women's Labour League, which had met the needs of Labour women since 1906, and the institution of Women's Sections eligible for affiliation with Local and Divisional Parties, was an innovation which history has more than amply justified. The inclusion of women members on the National Executive has also brought to the Party the services of many gifted women, and with the establishment of the Standing Joint Committee of Industrial Women's Organisations, comprising representatives of women in the Socialist, Trade Union, Labour, and Co-operative Movements, the Party has at its call a magnificent loyalty that is unrivalled anywhere in the world.

As the war ran to its close and the downfall of Tsarism led to the triumph of the Bolshevik Revolution in Russia, there was a growing sense throughout the Labour Movement that the circumstances demanded the formulation of specific war aims. Preliminary discussions took place at joint meetings of the National Executive of the Party and the Parliamentary Committee of the Trades Union Congress (reconstituted as the General Council in 1921). Upon the preparation of the document which afterwards formed the basis of Committee and Conference

decisions, Webb, Henderson, and MacDonald collaborated with
Camille Huysmans, the Secretary of the Second International,
who had taken up residence in London early in the war and who
had succeeded in keeping contact with the Allied Socialists as well
as those of the Central Powers, not without raising the hasty and
ungrounded suspicions of the extreme Right on either side of the
battle-line. The "War Aims" were approved by a special conference, representing the industrial and the political sections of
the Movement, held at Westminster on 28th December, 1917.
They stressed the common interest of the peoples of Europe in
bringing the conflict to an issue in a secure and lasting peace for
the world ; that the world should be made safe for democracy ;
and an effective method be found for the prevention of war. As a
means to that end the "War Aims" statement urged the complete
democratisation of all countries and the frank abandonment of
Imperialism, the suppression of secret diplomacy ; concerted
effort for the universal abolition of conscription ; the limitation of
armaments and the entire abolition of profit-making armament
firms. It also emphasised the establishment of a super-national
authority, or League of Nations, which in turn should inaugurate
an International High Court, appropriate machinery for mediation
between States ; and an International Legislature for the gradual
development of international legislation agreed to and binding
upon the several States ; and for a solemn agreement and pledge
by all States that all issues between any two or more of them
should be submitted for peaceful settlement, and for all to make
common cause against any State failing to adhere to the agreement.
Thus was the British Labour Movement committed to the popular
doctrine of Collective Security which inspired all phases of its
Foreign Policy thereafter.

"War Aims" repudiated the conversion of the struggle into a
war of conquest, whether of territory or of wealth, although it
recognised that reparations and restoration by territorial adjust-
ments were required, if causes of conflict were to be removed for
the future ; such readjustments should be achieved by the means
of self-determination of the peoples concerned. It therefore
made elaborate and detailed proposals to cope with all the territorial problems arising immediately out of the war, such as the
position of Belgium, the problem of Alsace-Lorraine, of the

countries liberated by the break-up of the Austro-Hungarian and Turkish Empires, of the future of Palestine, and of " reparations." A further section dealt with tropical Africa, and suggested the administration and development of the entire area under League of Nations auspices.

The section on the economic future of the world deprecated the possible development of economic warfare by protective tariffs and capitalist monopolies ; it urged that the immediate world shortage of foodstuffs, raw materials, and merchant shipping should be combated by international co-operative action and strong Governmental control acting upon the principle " no cake until all have bread " ; within the several countries it asked Labour Parties to press upon their own Governments the need for establishing adequate standards of living (by factory acts, anti-sweating regulation and the like) and further for promoting what is now called Full Employment by means of regular and orderly demobilisation, and a public works programme which would maintain year by year a steady demand for labour.

On what may be called the punitive aspect, " War Aims " suggested (1) that funds for reparations and compensation for war damage should be allocated on an equitable basis by an International Commission, (2) that there should be " a full and free investigation " into all alleged acts of cruelty, theft, or oppression, and (3) that an International Court of Claims should be set up, to which Governments should bring the claims of their respective nationals.

The publication of this long and elaborate document by the British Labour Movement created sensation far beyond Great Britain. In addition to the full text appearing in some of the London and provincial press, and summaries elsewhere, the New Republic, of New York, published the whole of it as a special supplement. So it secured considerable attention in the United States and helped to prepare public opinion for President Wilson's " Fourteen Points," which so greatly influenced the termination of hostilities.

The document immediately became the subject of discussion with representatives of the Labour and Socialist organisations of the allied nations, including at a later stage the American Federation of Labor. There were various modifications of detail, but in fundamentals the " War Aims " remained unaffected in principle ; and it may truly be affirmed that to the extent that its proposals were neglected the Peace declared at Versailles was a failure.

It would be too much to claim that Sidney Webb was the sole author of this historic Party document, the principles of which are still the subject of world-wide discussion, but it is right that his great contribution to its production should be placed on record.

The upheavals in social life created by the war and the impact of the Russian Revolution of 1917 upon the organised workers of Britain marked the coming of a new epoch. The need for Reconstruction in many phases of national administration was obvious to reformers everywhere. In a great many cases the idea was a new one. To Sidney Webb the idea was old, but the opportunity seemed to be heaven-sent. His whole career had been devoted to the problems of social reorganisation and his mind was teeming with practical possibilities.

No sooner were the " War Aims " promulgated than Webb seized the moment to lead the Labour Movement, through the Party, to co-ordinate its miscellaneous decisions on Home Policy into a definite programme, compact with idealism and practical sense, and, as more recent events have so amply demonstrated, perfectly feasible once the national will found expression in a Parliamentary majority.

Labour and the New Social Order was ostensibly the Report of a special committee of the National Executive, but, with the exception of one or two paragraphs it is, as the following quotations will show, unmistakably the work of Webb.

It begins with the postulate that :

" What this war is consuming is not merely the security, the homes, the livelihood and the lives of millions of innocent families, and an enormous proportion of all the accumulated wealth of the world, but also the very basis of the peculiar social order in which it has arisen. The individualist system of capitalist production has received a death-blow. With it must go the political system and ideas in which it naturally found expression. We of the Labour Party . . . must ensure that what is presently to be built up is a new social order, based not on fighting but on fraternity—not on the competitive struggle for the means of bare life, but on a deliberately planned co-operation in production and distribution for the benefit of all who participate by hand or by brain—

not on the utmost possible inequality of riches, but on a systematic approach towards a healthy equality of material circumstances for every person born into the world—not on an enforced dominion over subject nations, subject races, subject colonies, subject classes, or a subject sex, but, in industry as well as in government, on that equal freedom, that general consciousness of consent, and that widest possible participation in power, both economic and political, which is characteristic of Democracy.

The members of the Labour Party themselves actually working by hand or by brain, in close contact with the facts, have perhaps at all times a more accurate appreciation of what is practicable, in industry as in politics, than those who depend solely on academic instruction or are biased by great possessions. But today no man dares to say that anything is impracticable . . . What we now promulgate as our policy, whether for opposition or for office, is not merely this or that specific reform, but a deliberately thought out, systematic, and comprehensive plan for that immediate social rebuilding which any Ministry, whether or not it desires to grapple with the problem, will be driven to undertake. The Four Pillars of the House that we propose to erect, resting upon the common foundation of the Democratic control of society in all its activities, may be termed, respectively :—

(a) The Universal Enforcement of the National Minimum ;
(b) The Democratic Control of Industry ;
(c) The Revolution in National Finance ; and
(d) The Surplus Wealth for the Common Good."

Webb then proceeds to elaborate his four principles.

(a) *The universal enforcement of a national minimum.*

" The first principle of the Labour Party is the securing to every member of the community, in good times and bad alike (and not only to the strong and able, the well-born or the fortunate), of all the requisites of healthy life and worthy citizenship . . . The Labour Party today stands for the universal application of the Policy of the National Minimum, to which (as embodied in the successive elaborations of the Factory, Mines, Railways, Shops, Merchant Shipping, and Truck Acts, the Public Health, Housing and Education Acts and the Minimum Wage Act—all of them aiming at the enforcement of at least the prescribed Minimum of Leisure, Health, Education, and Subsistence) the spokesmen of Labour have already gained the support of the enlightened statesmen and economists of the world.

. . . The Labour Party insists—as no other political party has thought fit to do—that the obligation to find suitable employment in

"TOUT PEUT SE RÉTABLIR"

" Urgent Conclave of Doctrinaire Socialists to decide on some means of inducing the Lower Orders to regard them once more as Visionaries merely "

Those depicted include H. M. Hyndman, H. G. Wells, G. B. S., John Galsworthy, Sidney Webb and R. B. Cunninghame Graham

Cartoon by Max Beerbohm, 1920

THE WEBB OF DESTINY

" Mr. Sidney Webb : ' I am waving this red flag not provocatively, but to signalise what I have so happily called the "Inevitability of Gradualness" which marks our roller's advance. '

This refers to Webb's 1923 Presidential Address to the Labour Party Conference which included the phrase " the inevitability of gradualness."

Cartoon by Frank Reynolds in Punch, 4 *July,* 1923

productive work for all these men and women rests upon the Government for the time being. To the Labour Party it will seem the supreme concern of the Government of the day to see to it that there shall be, as a result of the gigantic [post-war] ' General Post ' which it will itself have deliberately set going, nowhere any Degradation of the Standard of Life." . . . We claim that it should be a cardinal point of Government policy to make it plain to every capitalist employer that any attempt to reduce the customary rates of wages when peace comes, or to take advantage of the dislocation of demobilisation to worsen the conditions of employment in any grade whatsoever, will certainly lead to embittered industrial strife, which will be in the highest degree detrimental to the national interests ; and that the Government of the day will not hesitate to take all necessary steps to avert such a calamity . . . It is [further] the duty of the Government to adopt a policy of deliberately and systematically preventing the occurrence of unemployment . . . and to make all necessary preparations for putting instantly in hand, directly or through the Local Authorities, such urgently needed public works as the rehousing of the population alike in rural districts, mining villages, and town slums . . . the immediate making-good of the shortage of schools, training colleges, technical colleges, etc. . . . new roads ; light railways ; the unification and reorganisation of the railway and canal system ; afforestation ; the reclamation of land ; the development and better equipment of our ports and harbours ; the opening up of access to land by co-operative small holdings and in other practicable ways. Moreover, in order to relieve any pressure of an overstocked labour market, the opportunity should be taken . . . immediately to raise the school-leaving age to sixteen ; greatly to increase the number of scholarships and bursaries for Secondary and Higher Education; and substantially to shorten the hours of labour of all young persons . . . Finally, wherever practicable, the hours of adult labour should be reduced to not more than forty-eight per week, without reduction of the Standard Rates of Wages."

(b) The democratic control of industry.

" What marks off this [Labour] Party most distinctively from any of the other political parties is its demand for the full and genuine adoption of the principle of Democracy. The first condition of Democracy is effective personal freedom . . . But individual freedom is of little use without complete political rights . . . The Labour Party stands, as heretofore, for complete Adult Suffrage, with not more than a three months' residential qualification, for effective provision for absent

---

[1] This phase recurs continually throughout the Report.

G

electors to vote, for absolutely equal rights for both sexes, for the same freedom to exercise civic rights for the 'common soldier' as for the officer, for Shorter Parliaments, for the complete Abolition of the House of Lords, and for a most strenuous opposition to any new Second Chamber, whether elected or not, having in it any element of Heredity or Privilege, or of the control of the House of Commons by any Party or Class. But unlike the Conservative and Liberal Parties, the Labour Party insists on Democracy in industry as well as in government. . . . What the Party looks to is a genuinely scientific reorganisation of the nation's industry, no longer deflected by individual profiteering, on the basis of the Common Ownership of the Means of Production ; the equitable sharing of the proceeds among all who participate in any capacity and only among these, and the adoption, in particular services and occupations, of those systems and methods of administration and control that may be found, in practice, best to promote, not profiteering, but the public interest.

" It stands not merely for the principle of the Common Ownership of the nation's land, to be applied as suitable opportunities occur, but also, specifically, for the immediate Nationalisation of Railways, Mines, and the production of Electrical Power . . . for the National Ownership and Administration of the Railways and Canals, and their union, along with Harbours and Roads, and the Posts and Telegraphs—not to say also the great lines of steamers which could at once be owned, if not immediately directly managed in detail, by the Government—in a united national service of Communication and Transport . . . The Labour Party demands the immediate Nationalisation of Mines, the extraction of coal and iron being worked as a public service . . . and the whole business of the retail distribution of household coal being undertaken, as a local public service, by the elected Municipal or County Councils. There is no reason why coal should fluctuate in price any more than railway fares, or why the consumer should be made to pay more in winter than in summer, or in one town than another. What the Labour Party would aim at is, for household coal of standard quality, a fixed and uniform price for the whole kingdom, payable by rich and poor alike, as unalterable as the penny postage-stamp."

The paragraphs immediately following demand the elimination of private profit-making from Industrial Assurance, the drink trade and various services of "common utility," and the maintenance of the war-time controls of other various commodities and industries

(c) On the third Pillar, *A revolution in national finance*, the Report declares that :

" In taxation, also, the interests of the professional and house-keeping classes are at one with those of the manual workers . . . The Labour Party stands for such a system of taxation as will yield all the necessary revenue to the Government without encroaching on the prescribed National Minimum Standard of Life, of any family whatsoever ; without hampering production or discouraging any useful personal effort and with the nearest possible approximation to equality of sacrifice."

To that end, it repudiates protective tariffs, taxes on food, indirect taxation on anything but luxuries ; and for the raising of revenue it looks to " the direct taxation of the incomes above the necessary cost of family maintenance . . . to the direct taxation of private fortunes both during life and at death " ; and a special Capital Levy to pay off the whole or the greater part of the National Debt. " In this matter " [of paying the cost of the war] " the Labour Party claims the support of four-fifths of the whole nation, for the interests of the clerk, the teacher, the doctor, the minister of religion, the average retail shopkeeper and trader, and all the mass of those living on small incomes are identical with those of the artisan."

(d) Finally, under the heading *The surplus for the common good*, the Report explains that the House of the Labour Party, of which the Four Pillars have been described, must stand in the Street of Tomorrow, where imperialism and colonial exploitation are repudiated and international relations are strengthened by means of a League of Nations. (These paragraphs are in effect a summarising of the proposals in *Labour's War Aims*.) It ends with a characteristic passage calling for light as well as warmth in political affairs, of which these are the concluding words :

" What the Labour Party stands for in all fields of life is, essentially, Democratic Co-operation ; and Co-operation involves a common purpose which can be agreed to ; a common plan which can be explained and discussed, and such a measure of success in the adaptation of means to ends as will ensure a common satisfaction. An autocratic Sultan may govern without science if his whim is law. A Plutocratic Party may choose to ignore science, if it is heedless whether its pretended solutions of social problems that may win political triumphs ultimately succeed or fail. But no Labour Party can hope to maintain its position unless its proposals are, in fact, the outcome of the best Political Science of its time ; or to fulfil its purpose unless that science is continually wresting new fields from human ignorance. Hence, although the Purpose of the Labour Party must, by the law of its being, remain for all time unchanged, its Policy and its Programme will, we hope, undergo a perpetual development, as knowledge grows, and as new phases of the social problem present themselves, in a continually finer adjustment of our measures to our ends. If Law is the Mother of Freedom, Science, to the Labour Party, must be the Parent of Law."

The reception of this document, published as a 2d. pamphlet, was amazing. A review by Webb himself in the *Observer* led to many thousands of individual inquiries and it aroused public attention both at home and abroad. The *New Republic* as in the case of the " War Aims " reprinted it as a special supplement, and there were various other editions issued throughout the United States.

There have been other documents outlining the Party's policy on similarly comprehensive lines, notably *Labour and the Nation* in 1928, and *Let Us Face the Future* in 1945, but *Labour and the New Social Order* was unique in its time and marked a new departure in popular political propaganda well adapted to the growing intelligence of the masses of the people consequent upon their wider educational opportunities. Its terms were condensed into a series of twenty-seven Resolutions on Reconstruction approved by a special Party Conference on 26th June, 1918, and the remainder of that year was given up to its propaganda prior to the General Election in December. The Party ran 361 candidates (compared with seventy-eight in 1910) and polled 2,244,945 votes. It was evident that although only fifty-seven Members were returned, and the Lloyd George Coalition had a sweeping success, the Labour Party was now to be counted as a nation-wide organisation deliberately aiming at the ultimate capture of Government. Webb contested London University unsuccessfully, polling 2,141 votes in a five-cornered election, 669 behind Sir Philip Magnus, the successful Coalition Unionist.

It is impossible within the limits here imposed to give any adequate conception of the continual effort to promote the Party's influence that Webb stimulated by his own example, pursued as always with a steady purpose and a modest helpfulness that won for him an unrivalled reputation and the sincere regard and affection of all sections of the Movement. In all this work, of course, it was recognised that Beatrice Webb was ever the good companion and constant partner.

On the administrative side of the Party's activities, one of the most useful and fruitful of Webb's schemes was the institution of a series of Advisory Committees to work out in greater detail the various aspects of Party policy to which Conference decisions had committed it, and also to serve as informed consultants on both long and short term policy confronting the Parliamentary Party from time to time. At the outset these comprised Army, Navy, and Pensions Problems; Education, Finance and Commerce; Home Office and the Mines Department; Industrial Affairs covered by the Board of Trade, the Ministry of Labour, and the Factory Department; International Affairs, covering the Foreign and Colonial Office, the India Office, and the Irish Problem; the Legal System and Administration of Justice; Local Government; Machinery of Government; and Public Health. As the years have passed the range of the Advisory Committees has been extended and the Party has had at its service expert advisers on almost every phase of national and international politics. The steady stream of memoranda, reports, pamphlets, and brochures in which its policy has been expounded forms a contribution to political thought unsurpassed by any Democratic party throughout the world.

In the year 1922-23, Webb was the Chairman of the National Executive Committee of the Party and was able to report to the Annual Conference in London an affiliated membership of about 4 million, the Party being at once the poorest and the largest political party in the country, and having polled some 4,250,000 votes at the General Election in November, 1922, only a million or so fewer than the victorious Conservatives. Its 142 Members were now recognised as the Official Opposition. Webb had been elected for Seaham Harbour, his adoption by this mining division being an acknowledgement of his magnificent services to the mining community as a member of the Sankey Commission. His presidential address to the Conference in June, 1923, was a characteristic review of the Party's achievements and prospects, one phrase of which has passed into popular political parlance.

" Let me insist," he said, " on what our opponents habitually ignore, and indeed, what they seem intellectually incapable of understanding, namely, *the inevitable gradualness of our scheme of change.* The very fact that Socialists have both principles and a programme appears to confuse nearly all their critics. If we state our principles, we are told ".That is not practicable.' When we recite our programme, the objection is ' That is not Socialism.' But why, because we are idealists, should we be supposed to be idiots ? For the Labour Party, it must be plain, Socialism is rooted in political Democracy ; which necessarily compels us to recognise that every step towards our goal is dependent on gaining the assent and support of at least a numerical majority of the whole people.

" The success of the Labour Party in this country depends, more than upon anything else, upon the spirit in which we hold our faith, the spirit in which we present our proposals, the spirit in which we meet our opponents in debate, the spirit in which we fulfil our own obligations, the spirit in which, with inevitable backslidings, we live our own lives."

Emphasising the gospel of William Morris, he concluded : " We shall not achieve much—whatever changes we can bring about, unless what we do is done in the spirit of fellowship."

When in 1924 the Labour Party, as the largest Party, took office as a Minority Government with Ramsay MacDonald as Prime Minister, Webb was President of the Board of Trade and was elated with the attainments of the Party he had served so faithfully and well. Unspoilt by success, he continued his career of useful-ness in Cabinet and in Council, in Parliament and in the Ministry, in his constituency and among his familiars of the Fabian Society and the London School of Economics, adding to his own know-ledge and ever seeking to expand the intellectual bounds of his fellows.

He resigned from the National Executive in 1924, giving place to Miss Susan Lawrence as the Fabian nominee, a very worthy successor in every way.

Webb did not contest any constituency at the General Election of 1929. He was sixty-three when he entered the House of Commons in 1922 and he had looked upon his Parliamentary work only as an episode in his life. However, when the Party was again returned as the largest in the House with 288 Members representing over 8 million voters, and it was decided to assume the responsibilities of Government, although again in a minority, he accepted a Peerage as Lord Passfield and served as Dominions and Colonial Minister.[1]

When the Labour Government fell in the summer of 1931, Webb followed Henderson and the overwhelming majority of the Party into opposition; and after the ensuing General Election, when the Parliamentary Party was reduced to forty-six members, with George Lansbury, Clement Attlee and Stafford Cripps as the only surviving Ministers (although its poll still exceeded 6 million), he withdrew from the Parliamentary scene. His cool summing up of that catastrophe may be read in an article appearing in the *Political Quarterly* in the following January, which ended :

" Meanwhile the shock that the Labour Party has received by the magnitude of its defeat may be expected to do it good. The Party is still only a quarter-of-a-century old, and its growth in that time to nearly one-third of the nation is little short of marvellous. But its representatives in Parliament have been, as we can now see, injuriously affected by what were only accidental successes. In being called as a minority to ministerial office in 1924, and again in 1929, merely through disunion among its opponents, the Labour Party was, as its members now realise, prematurely born into governmental life. It had never come near comprising a majority of the nation. At no election, not even at that of 1929, did it obtain the support at the polls of a majority of the wage-earning voters. Most of its parliamentary representatives have found it difficult, in their inexperience, to rid themselves of the mental habits of a lifelong opposition to the powers that be, whilst some of them have seemed almost to regret the chance that has put them, for a time, among those powers. Nor can the Labour Party, in this generation of mediocrities, be said to have yet found, any more than its Liberal and Conservative opponents, the high statesmanship, or even the amount of governmental talent, required to cope with the recurring crises of the present century. The Labour Party has now the opportunity, during the next few years, of (1) applying itself continuously to the ubiquitous educational propaganda by which alone it can double the number of its adherents ; (2) of quietly working out in greater detail its constructive programme, without prematurely committing itself as a Party to any but general principles ; (3) of steadily accustoming the public to one item after another in that programme by

[1] See Chapter XIII.

the publication of an incessant stream, not only of popular pamphlets, but also of books, lectures and articles in the weeklies and monthlies by individual members ; and last but not least, (4) of seeking to develop, within the Party itself, much more of that friendly social intercourse among fellow-workers in a common cause which so effectively promotes its success."

Other pens will tell of Webb's life and work in other fields, but to those who were intimate with him during the years of his actual Labour Party activities, he will always be remembered for his patient skill, his untiring industry, and as one who cared not who got the credit so long as the work got done.

THE DISCOVERY OF SIDNEY WEBB

by

JACK LAWSON

XII

THE DISCOVERY OF SIDNEY WEBB

by *JACK LAWSON*

The work two thousand feet below ground did not much trouble us; indeed, we were not a little vain of our craftsmanship. Naked, balled up between a pony and a small truck, which sometimes weighed a ton when filled with coal, we raced along narrow, dark roadways. Now and then the truck struck a joint in the rail : over she went, coal smashing over you, often leaving marks for the rest of your life.

Or, as a coal hewer at the face, we doubled ourselves up in very low places, sweating, squirming, wielding the pick, coal getting. There was no Minimum Wage. If you were lucky and the place was good, the grocer and butcher was paid—there were no vegetarians down there.

The writer neither smoked nor drank, his only luxury was a rare new book, but it was hard come by.

We didn't mind the conditions ; we didn't mind the contorting, sweaty, dangerous work ; it was the demand for Reductions of Wages that made us angry.

The Miners' Federation was little more than a name. We were organised in Districts *and one was played off against the other.* So we rebelled, fought our long battles and were usually driven back, sullenly to accept that against which we had fought.

Only bitter, unforgettable days were left as a memory. Those strikes !

A certain Richard Fynes had written a history of the miners of Northumberland and Durham. He had " lifted " some of it from various books, like *Sykes's Local Records* and Hugh Miller's *My Schools and Schoolmasters*, but he had also seen things for himself and he told a dramatic, stirring story for students of Mining History.

That *was* a find !

A steady, thoughtful, elderly miner said he thought a man called

Sidney Webb had written a *History of Trade Unionism*. There was not one to be found in the colliery, so it was ordered off a bookseller in Newcastle.

That was how the writer *discovered Sidney Webb*. The book held him spellbound as the tale of the efforts of workers to organise was unfolded. It was a new thing altogether, in that year 1900, to learn that other workers in other trades and crafts struggled to organise in order to maintain or improve their conditions and that others fought long strikes as well as miners.

That linked us in the pits with other workers, gave a sense of oneness with all men and women in industry and unconsciously gave the young reader a sense of heritage—a heritage born of the Industrial Revolution.

Of general history, that young reader—which was me—was not ignorant, neither did he lack pride in the achievements of his nation, but Sidney Webb told another story which was not in history books. He explained much that needed explanation, answered many questions—some only half-formed—and prompted others. Above all was the sense of oneness with all those who laboured. True, the book was written in a different language and style to that of Fynes, but it told the same story on a larger scale. It was objective—though the reader would not have understood that word at the time.

It was obviously the work of a scholarly man and there was not a little pride in the knowledge that a real scholar, capable of great detachment, was taking this matter of industrial workers seriously. So, we were really somebody after all !

Who was Sidney Webb ?

Local Trade Union leaders like John Wilson and Tom Burt were household names, Keir Hardie was a firebrand, alternately praised and blamed. Tom Mann we had heard in our Miners' Hall, Ben Tillett was a great union orator—these were familiar names—but who was Sidney Webb ?

There was no *Who's Who* to consult and anyhow we had never heard of it. The colliery wise one who had guided the would-be student to his *History* said he was a Fabian who lived in London : and London in those far off days of isolated communities might as well have been in another world. What was a Fabian ? Standing

there in a colliery street that elderly Socialist miner explained what
a Fabian was. His explanation was probably simple and accurate,
but his listener was as wise as ever !

*   *   *   *   *

Such was the frame of mind of the young student of the pits,
factories, workshops and workers on the land at that time. We
were among the first fruits of the old Board Schools and had gone
to work, mostly at twelve years of age : but we *had* learned to
read. Now the thoughts of Sidney Webb were reaching and
shaping us. Little did we guess that we were the subjects of
Fabianism. Thus did Sidney Webb take the crude inquirers who
were asking the why and wherefore of this Industrial Age, supply
them with information, analyse its organisation and point the way
to solutions of its problems. Webb wrote for the student, but
probably none would have been more surprised than himself had
he seen the kind of pupils he taught in the towns and villlages of
Great Britain. When his pupils had completed their education
under him, the battle between the Old Unionism and the New
was old news ; and his constructive work had helped to make an
end of the bitter controversies that raged among the working class
politicians of that day.

*   *   *   *   *

This is a true picture, as far as Webb and the Fabians were
concerned and talks with many Trade Unionists and Labour men
shows it to be a common experience, varying a little according to
personality and environment. We did learn later who this Sidney
Webb was, as well as the policy and objects of the Fabian Society,
and though few of us joined that body we purchased and used its
pamphlets for propaganda purposes through the Independent
Labour Party.

SIDNEY WEBB'S PUPILS

It will be noted that the *History of Trade Unionism* has been
mentioned as though it was written by Sidney Webb alone. Of
course, that is not the case. Every student of Trade Unionism
knows it was the joint work of himself and his famous wife. But,
the husband's name came first and it is a fact that it was always
given Sidney Webb's name—which was rough on that able
collaborator, Beatrice Webb. The same thing is true of the

companion volume, *Industrial Democracy*—" a scientific analysis of Trade Unionism in the United Kingdom," as the authors put it in the original preface to that book.

To have the structure, methods and aims of Trade Unionism analysed scientifically was something new and not only gave it an important place in our Social and Economic life, but also set the younger man in industry thinking along new and larger lines. It also increased the sense of responsibility. There is no doubt whatever that these two books gave a new status to the Trade Union Movement and profoundly influenced the political life of Britain.

The sense of unity and the new status of Trade Unionism, as well as the new outlook, given to the younger, studious, industrial workers was no small factor in bringing large numbers of them into the Independent Labour Party. The place that Movement held in Britain in the first quarter of the twentieth century is impossible to understand by the present generation. Indeed, it is almost incredible that a movement which swept the country like a religious revival should have sprung up and practically passed away within living memory.

Led by able, eloquent men, it gripped the imagination of thousands of young unknown idealists, who preached Socialism in every town and village in Great Britain from crude platforms in the open air.

It was this which gave direction and voice to the awakening thoughts of the industrial masses and laid the foundations for the Labour Party of today ; and Sidney Webb and his wife played a notable part in shaping the minds of those propagandists.

It is true that the outstanding figure in that Movement was Keir Hardie and the fact that he was a miner undoubtedly influenced many miners, who joined and often spoke for that Movement.

But, it was Webb, who, by his *History* and *Industrial Democracy*, gave that sense of unity and purpose to the young leaders and potential leaders, which enabled them to wean the industrial masses from the two great political parties that had long held their eyes.

Long before, of course, Marx had urged the workers of the world to unite, but it was from the I.L.P. platforms, manned mainly by industrial speakers, that the British masses first heard it. Perhaps that is one reason why Marx has had such little influence on

Britain and her workers. When they did hear the slogan it was old news. It had been patented by political leaders like Hardie, the sense of it given by Sidney Webb and driven in from a thousand platform speakers of the Independent Labour Party.

It would be true to say—and the writer speaks with some knowledge of the personnel of the I.L.P. speakers—that most of the propagandists of that Movement in the early years of the twentieth century, were young workers in industry and many of them had been brought up on Sidney Webb. As he was a Fabian they were also diligent readers of the pamphlets put out by that organisation. In other words, they had been " permeated."

By 1908 another figure stood out clear on the industrial horizon —that was Robert Smillie. He had long been a member of the I.L.P., an advocate of eight hours for miners, and a friend of Webb. He was not yet President of the Miners' Federation, but he was its chief as far as the miners were concerned, and the victory of less hours was a victory for Smillie. This, too, had been Webb's policy.

There was a snag in this as far as the miners of the north were concerned. The method of work, the low seams and the relentless pressure of the work had long ago compelled the owners in Northumberland and Durham to reduce the coal hewers' hours to seven. Things were so arranged that two shifts of seven hours at the coal face were linked with ten hours for boys and men responsible for the transport of coal, and young, strong men who were called putters—as well as all surface workers.

The cry went up that coal hewers would be compelled to work eight hours. Those who had worked the ten hours, as well as the seven hour shift, were ready to take the consequences, whatever they were : ten hours for boys was too much : we knew that by experience.

When the eight hours did become legal, then the trouble began, as we well knew it would.

The coal-owners' attitude was that we had asked for it and we would get it. We did. They laid down conditions which were vile in their effect, in the mine, in the home and in the community. The result was a boomerang. The miners of the north joined the Federation and the owners could no longer dictate terms to districts fighting alone.

At last the miners throughout Britain stood as one man for a common policy.

*   *   *   *   *

The Eight Hours Act was only the beginning. Under Smillie's leadership, in 1912, the demand was made for a Minimum Wage, which was almost revolutionary compared with the claims of British miners when they were divided.

The owners and the Government had to yield, and the Minimum Wage Act was passed. Webb had trained his pupils well !

Worse still for the owners of mines in Britain, was the revelation of the dangerous nature of the occupation by a series of great disasters when human life was destroyed on a scale and with a suddenness almost unparalleled in the history of British mining.

The tale of disaster in British mining was bad enough before these explosions, but the British people thought those tragedies of the bad old days were left behind. Then, suddenly, the name of one previously unknown colliery after another became familiar to everyone in the land.

In 1908, the Maypole Pit in Lancashire fired with a loss of seventy-six lives and the number was almost magnified by the grim story of the conditions under which those men had been working.

In 1909, West Stanley Pit exploded with a loss of 168 lives. In 1910, Hulton fired with a loss of 344 lives. In the same year, Whitehaven, with a loss of 136 lives : 1912, Cadeby Main, Yorkshire, with a loss of eighty-eight lives : 1913, Senghenydd, Wales, with a loss of 440 lives.

*   *   *   *   *

The disasters of those years made a deep impression on the miners and increased the influence of the Miners' Federation, drawing the men closer together.

But, the effect upon the public was also very great and was a factor of considerable weight in future legislation affecting the miners.

The writer was a miner at that time and will never forget the emotion that swept pitmen and public alike. The time was ripe for large scale action as far as the mines and miners of Great Britain were concerned. That was emphasised by the growing power of the low-paid railwaymen and transport workers. The workers, generally, in these industries had very low wages and a low standard of life. So they combined with the miners to form a " Triple Alliance " to enforce higher wages and better conditions.

There were only about forty Labour Members in the House of Commons and little could be done there. The stage was set for large scale industrial trouble, when war broke out in 1914. Calculating that this situation, combined with the troubles in Ireland, ruled Britain out as far as war was concerned, the Emperor of Germany thought it the moment to strike. He made a mistake.

Of all men in Britain, it was the miners who enlisted in such large numbers that the Government had to stop them. Indeed, thousands had to be brought back from the fighting front to the mines.

For the time being industrial trouble was adjourned, but only adjourned, as events proved immediately the war ended.

THE SANKEY COMMISSION

To a generation which takes for granted the control of prices in the time of war—and in the troubled years which follow—the conditions prevailing in the war of 1914–18 are a closed book. Even for those who lived through the period it requires a great mental effort to recreate the world of that time. It is almost incredible today that until late in the first great war unrestricted profit-making operated in all its glory. " Business as usual " was the cry —and it was so. There had been bad times, so now for the good time. War was the good time for profit-making.

Prices of food, clothes and all other necessaries of life simply rocketed. By 1917 indignation had so mounted that something had to be done about it. The threat of the organised workers to take industrial action about this matter finally compelled the Government to set up a Ministry of Food with power to control prices. It was too late. The profiteer had cashed in.

When the war ended and a Government Committee had reported on their investigations into super-profits made during the war, it was found that these amounted to 2,000 million. Not profits, but super-profits. A million of our men had been killed and masses wounded and broken for life.

That was the background of the Peace of 1914–18 !

As for the industrial workers, and, not least, the miners, something like a revolution had taken place in their attitude to politics
and social affairs generally. Masses of men called to the Forces
had been rejected as C.3 men. The limelight had been turned on
the living conditions of the workers. " Never again " was the cry
heard on every hand.

*   *   *   *   *

To none did this apply more than to the miners. They had
leaped out of the trenches below ground to rush to the trenches at
the front—until the Government was compelled to stop them and
bring large numbers back to the pits. Ill-paid, ill-housed—they
had forgotten old evils in the face of the common enemy, but, now
he was destroyed, the reckoning day had come. Requests of yes-
terday became the imperatives of today. The Government was
faced with no mere claim for higher wages and better conditions.
That was part of it ; but only a small part. Nothing less than that
the mines should become the property of the Nation would satisfy
them. The claim of the miners for the Nationalisation of the
Mines of Britain was no longer theory ; it was a menacing fact.

" Early in 1919 the Miners' Federation determined on a strike
to secure 1. the transfer of the mines to National Ownership ;
2. an advance of wages of 30 per cent ; and 3. a reduction of hours
by 25 per cent. In February, 1919, the whole Federation Membership voted determinedly for enforcing the demand by a National
Strike." (Webb, *The Story of the Durham Miners.*)

The Government answered by proposing to appoint a Statutory
Commission to examine these claims. The miners were loath to
accept this proposal but finally accepted it on the condition that
the Federation was allowed not only to nominate three of its own
members, but also three out of the six members to be appointed
who were not connected with the industry. So three miners would
face three coal-owners and three of the six Government nominees
would be theirs. The Government finally accepted the proposal.
Smillie, Frank Hodges and Herbert Smith were chosen by the
miners along with three nominees from the Fabian Society.
These were Sidney Webb, R. H. Tawney and Sir Leo Chiozza
Money.

After an investigation lasting a fortnight, an " Interim Report " was made public. The six Federation Representatives reported in favour of the Nationalisation of the Mines and granted the claims of the men. The Coal-owners' Representatives, in the old pre-war spirit, offered slight concessions in wages and hours but resisted any change in the organisation of the industry.

* * * * *

At last the tide had turned. The Chairman, Mr. Justice Sankey, had his own report in which three disinterested Capitalists joined. They awarded an increase of 20 per cent, a reduction of one hour working time, and suggested extensive improvements in housing conditions. More important still, they said :

" Even upon the evidence already given, the present system of ownership and working in the coal industry stands condemned, and some other system must be substituted for it— either Nationalisation or a method of unification by national purchase and, or, by joint control."

There was much more to it than that, but at last Nationalisation was the central fact in the politics of the day. In a further report, Sankey stood firm for Nationalisation. Mr. Bonar Law, speaking for the Government, promised to accept Mr. Justice Sankey's report " in the letter and in the spirit " if strike notices were withdrawn. That promise was not kept and the result upon the mining industry was tragic in the years that followed.

* * * * *

What happened in the inner circles among the members of the Commission the writer is not able to say. But it is on record in the Report that Sidney Webb, the Commissioner, volunteered to give evidence on the claim for Nationalisation. He submitted a reasoned memorandum such as Webb alone could prepare and defended it in the witness box.

* * * * *

The writer was at that time working at the mine and can testify to the effect of Webb's evidence. Smillie, with his demand for the credentials of land-owners who claimed Royalty Rents, held the eyes of all miners. Sankey, with his obvious sympathy for the miners' lot, became a household name. Webb, unemotional, practical and factual, won their respect. He got no headlines but he won the esteem of those who had long been conscious of their need of such a man to state their case. The miners as a whole had at last discovered Sidney Webb.

*   *   *   *   *

WEBB AS A CANDIDATE

During that time, every miner devoured the Press reports of the Sankey Commission. At mass meetings the proceedings supplied texts and sermons. Every coalfield was in ferment : the miners' representatives on the Commission were almost demigods. Seaham wanted a candidate, so they sent for Sidney Webb. He consented, went to Seaham, addressed the Divisional Labour Party and was adopted. At the first public meeting he addressed he was received with the enthusiasm befitting one who had played a notable part in the Sankey Commission. But Webb was neither a Demigod nor a Demagogue. He was at home in a Royal Commission, but a crowded miners' meeting was another thing. Mass meetings were not in his line. His figure was not striking to say the least of it ; neither was his style of speech, as far as popular crowds were concerned. A renowned master of research, who could order his material and present it was one thing ; gripping the mass mind was another. Webb was conscious of his shortcomings in this respect and said so.

*   *   *   *   *

There was another fact about Seaham Division. It is a constituency in the County of Durham and that is one of the oldest coalfields. A century of mining, with the way of life of such a community, its daily toll of accident, and sometimes disaster, has produced a strong communal sense in which emotion is not lacking. Religion has also played a great part in the life of that community. Webb was not only facing a new kind of audience, he was facing a new experience. Those who have read his *History of Trade Unionism* will see the effect of this if they compare it with his *Story of the Durham Miners*. One is detached, the other is warm and certainly not detached. Here, in Seaham, he was meeting, perhaps for the first time, the average man and woman in a warm-hearted community, and their influence on him was marked.

*   *   *   *   *

It was also in Seaham that he heard much of a story that is familiar to the Durham miner. It is the story told by Richard

Fynes in his *History of the Durham and Northumberland Miners*. That is a dramatic story and Fynes had plenty of material and first-hand experience for his drama. There is no detachment about that *History* for the writer had been part of it. The book is so gripping with its facts that it was, and is, a kind of Bible to the average northern miner.

The Methodist Revival also had a powerful effect upon the un-lettered masses who swarmed into the expanding coalfield of Durham in the early nineteenth century. It is true that it was in some measure a conservative influence, but it is simple fact that the men who led the battle for Trade Unionism, for the destruction of bad old conditions and for better wages, were products of that religious revival. Webb says, as Fynes said, that those who suffered and made great sacrifices for the miners' cause were in the main " Ranter " preachers. As was the case further south with the Tolpuddle martyrs.

It is a fact that in time Webb " got " his audiences, in his own quiet way, but it is also true that his audiences in time also " got " him. It is also worth noting that he brought Bernard Shaw north to share his experience.

But there was one thing certain, and it was that Mrs. Webb gripped the women much more than ever he did. There was the real stuff of the north when she addressed meetings and she left a memory which will never be forgotten by those now living.

* * * * *

Sidney Webb was elected for Seaham in 1922 and the writer had many opportunities of seeing and hearing him as a private Member of Parliament, as a Minister and in Party meetings. His speeches have left no impression, but his activities in Party Meetings have left vivid memories. When a Party is in a minority it scraps, and if not carefully and firmly guided it will soon be in splinters. The Labour Party had lively and even gay times in those days. When the inevitable crisis arrived Webb was always there, not with a speech but with a resolution. The " scrappers " did not like him because he never failed to produce his resolution, uniting dissident members who did not want to be united. While speeches were being made, of the independent, determined, no-surrender type, Webb was busy with his pencil. It was fascinating to watch, for we came to look for him, and at him, while red-hot speeches were being made. It was not the speaker who had the stage, but Webb sitting near the platform, silent, detached—as ever. We knew the sincere, enraged dissident was wasting his time, for we had got used to Webb, and after long experience we were certain he would reconcile the irreconcilable even if he did not bring all-round satisfaction. For industry, mental agility and seeing the flaws, as well as the strength, of a case, he had no equal. But his authority, born of long years of service to the British worker, was unchallenged. And were we not all, in one way or another, his pupils ? Despite his distant, diffident ways, despite his lack of personal impact upon us, we were all " permeated " by him. He was not so much a person as a Mind : and few minds have rendered such great service to the working classes of Great Britain as that of Sidney Webb.

THE MAN

As far as public life was concerned Sidney Webb as a personality was concealed from all men; at home, of course, it was a different matter. In *Our Partnership* (edited by Barbara Drake and Margaret Cole) there is on record a beautiful tribute paid to Sidney Webb by his wife, that would be difficult to parallel in the whole range of English literature. But in public he was as impassive as a sphinx. For most of us our motives lie open to be read of all men. Ambition, money-getting, idealism, all these and more, often jumbled together.

That was not the case with Sidney Webb, for his real self lay too deep to plumb as far as the average person was concerned. But in Seaham he was himself " permeated " by the warmth of the people, unconsciously searched and known by them : the real spirit of the man seen, known, and understood. The workers there, won to a knowledge of him by instinct where the most acute observers had failed. They knew that all Sidney Webb's work had behind it a deep sympathy for the masses, a passionate desire to make an end of evil conditions, wrong and injustice.

Not all *public* men, in their latter years, have the satisfaction of knowing that their labours in life have been worth while, and that they are understood, but Webb knew it among the people of Seaham. They discovered the real man through an instinctive sympathy : and it may be that in this understanding, Sidney Webb discovered himself.

SIDNEY WEBB AS A MINISTER

by

SIR DRUMMOND SHIELS

XIII

SIDNEY WEBB AS A MINISTER

by SIR DRUMMOND SHIELS

Sidney Webb was President of the Board of Trade from January to November, 1924, in the first minority Labour Government, under Ramsay MacDonald as Prime Minister. In the second Labour Government, during the period from June, 1929 to June, 1930, he held office, under the same Prime Minister, as Secretary of State for both Dominion Affairs (now called Commonwealth Relations) and the Colonies. He entered the House of Lords as Lord Passfield at the beginning of this period. Then, the two Ministries being placed under separate Ministers, he held the post of Secretary of State for the Colonies from June, 1930, till the fall of the Government in August, 1931.

AT THE BOARD OF TRADE

There is not a great deal to say about Sidney Webb's Board of Trade days. I had occasional opportunities at that time of seeing and hearing him as he carried through his duties in the House of Commons and it must be admitted that he was not outstandingly successful in that connection, partly because his voice was weak and he was not always well heard, and partly because he was not ready in debate. He gave, however, an impression of calmness and of quiet competence. The period of office of the 1924 Labour Government was short and there were no striking events to differentiate the activities of the Board in any marked degree from those in the non-Socialist Governments which preceded and succeeded it. Mr. A. V. Alexander, who was his Parliamentary Secretary, has said that the President asked him to collect a number of facts about the mercantile marine, whose conditions he rightly thought needed improving. But there was no time to develop that line of investigation.

He was—as always—well thought of by his staff. One of his former senior officials has said: "The first impression he made on us at the Board of Trade was his great personal modesty ; and then, quickly, we learned to respect his gift for analysis and the speed and thoroughness with which he got through a mass of hard work. Once he had made up his mind on any point, he would stick firmly to his guns. A member of Parliament of his own party had written making a criticism of some action or inaction of the Board. The reply was drafted in the department, and after satisfying himself, in his usual thorough way, Webb sent it off. The member replied suggesting that the Minister was being led by the nose by the department. This hurt him ! He sent for the papers—a bulky file going back over several years—and spent an evening studying them and in writing out in his own hand a full reply, running to several pages, which covered the whole ground and was a masterly statement of the position. This reply was despatched in manuscript, a copy being kept for the record. Nothing more was heard from that Member. Much of the more important work of the Board of Trade concerns other departments as well—the Treasury or the external departments, like the Foreign Office. My impression was that he thought it more appropriate for important decisions on their own subjects to be taken by his colleagues in these departments : this may have contributed to criticisms that he was lacking in decisiveness ! "

Another member of the Board of Trade staff tells of Sidney Webb's presiding over an Advisory Council, consisting of representatives of the main Trade Associations, which met monthly. " At the first meeting one could sense an atmosphere of scepticism, not to say of suspicion, on the part of the business men present, but Webb's tact and sweet reasonableness worked to good effect, and soon they were talking almost as readily as to our previous Ministers."

At the Board of Trade, Sidney Webb was dealing largely with facts, figures and statistics. Human factors, and important ones, were no doubt involved, but they were in the background and the nature of the work was well within his competence and experience.

AT THE DOMINIONS AND COLONIAL OFFICES

At the Dominions and Colonial Offices, and particularly at the Colonial Office, the position was somewhat different. There human emotions and psychological factors were all-important and Sidney Webb (or Lord Passfield, as he had now become) did not find it easy to understand why people got so worked up about things and why there was always such a note of urgency in the de mands of outside political or humanitarian organisations. He was very gentle and patient about it all, but it was not an easy sphere for one who had so orderly and methodical a mind and who was more interested in investigating and devising the form and machinery of government and administration than in considering how these should and could be applied to a world-wide variety of human beings by other human beings. Nevertheless, as will be seen later, he did not entirely overlook this aspect.

There was some surprise at his appointment to these Offices. I believe it is true to say that it was a last-minute decision by the Prime Minister, the first choice having been Mr. J. H. Thomas, who had held the same position in the first Labour Government. Sidney Webb had only been in office a few days when the Prime Minister told him he would like him to go to the House of Lords to represent the Government there. This elevation was distinctly distasteful to him. Indeed, he attached so little importance to the titular side of his peerage that it is said he allowed his private secretary to select his title. The Royal College of Heralds asked him to make suggestions for his coat of arms. " I haven't got a coat of arms," he replied " and I do not propose to have one." A message came back to say that he would be the only peer without one. And so he created a precedent, which, I believe, has been several times followed since. It was through no desire on his part to be different from others—it was merely that his innate simplicity of character made these " frills " meaningless to him.

The outstanding feature of Sidney Webb's time as Secretary of State for Dominion Affairs was the carrying into effect of the very important recommendations of the Imperial Conference of 1926 on equality of status in Commonwealth relations. The legal prob- lems were very intricate and a special conference on the Operation of Dominion Legislation was called when experts from the Do- minions, with our home representatives, hammered out the prin- ciples of the Statute of Westminster. (This became law in 1931.) It was a difficult conference, self-government having developed on different lines in the different Dominions. One of the members

present says of it : " We had a series of crises, and my memory
of Webb, as Chairman, is that he showed great impertur-
bability and at all times remained calm. He listened sympathetic-
ally to legal advice and took it." There was some criticism of the
conclusions reached, which were, nevertheless, subsequently
adopted in substance by the Imperial Conference of 1930. As
events have proved, the Conference achieved its aim in the promotion of free co-operation among members of the British Commonwealth, and may be counted as a real stepping-stone on the
way.

SOUTHERN RHODESIA

Another happening during his Dominions Office period may be
mentioned. It was part of his duties to approve or disapprove any
Southern Rhodesian legislation which did or might appear to dis-
criminate against the African inhabitants of that country, which
had Dominion status in most other respects. A long controversy
on the land question had culminated in an Act which passed
through the Southern Rhodesian Legislature making a division
of Southern Rhodesian land between Whites and Africans.
Previously, Natives had been entitled, equally with other subjects
of the Crown, to purchase or lease land in any part of their own
country. Sidney Webb had the unpleasant task of being asked to
agree to a measure which withdrew from the Natives in Southern
Rhodesia this right and which imposed a segregation policy. The
Report of the Southern Rhodesia Land Commission, of which this
Measure was the outcome, suggested that the setting aside of land
for exclusive Native use—and vice versa—was in the interests of
the Natives, as the Whites were buying up all the good land. I do
not know what considerations influenced the Secretary of State
but, in the end, he gave his approval and incurred criticism.

THE OPTIONAL CLAUSE

An important question which also arose during this period was
that of acceptance of the Optional Clause of the Statute of the
Permanent Court of International Justice under which Governments were required to refer to the arbitration of an international
body all disputes of a legal kind arising with other countries. The
Labour Party were pledged to the principle of arbitration of

international disputes, and the Prime Minister was anxious to take action at the earliest possible moment after assuming office. On the other hand, some of the Dominion Governments (like a section of opinion in this country) were strongly opposed to referring to international arbitration all legal disputes and particularly those arising out of action during time of war. In these circumstances there were those who urged that the United Kingdom Government should take action alone, irrespective of what the other governments might do or say. Such a cleavage on an important issue of foreign policy would, however, have had a most unfortunate effect both on relations between the countries of the Commonwealth and upon public opinion whether in this country or in the world outside. In these circumstances, the Secretary of State for Dominion Affairs sought to restrain his more impetuous colleagues from any precipitate step and to ensure that there should be full discussion between all the Commonwealth Governments with a view to united action, if at all possible. In this Webb was successful. The Prime Minister was persuaded to renounce his original intention of announcing acceptance of the Optional Clause at the outset of the Assembly of the League of Nations and to agree to full discussion with the representatives of the Dominions and India in the hope of agreement on a common policy. When this discussion took place, all the Governments accepted the Optional Clause with certain identical reservations (except the Irish Free State which accepted without reservations).

On the personal side, Webb got on well with visitors from the Dominions, who respected his intellectual eminence and were charmed by his characteristic personal kindness and thoughtfulness.

AT THE COLONIAL OFFICE

Whilst Sidney Webb had some quiet satisfaction in knowing that his was the only case of a junior Civil Servant rising to be Minister of the same department, it was in this sphere also, as Secretary of State for the Colonies, that he had his most arduous task, and one which aroused much heat and controversy. He had, among his critics, a small but vigorous band in his own party, particularly concerned with our African Colonies, who made life a little difficult for him at the Colonial Office. The late Charles

Roden Buxton (quiet, courteous, but persistent) was then Chairman of the Imperial Advisory Committee of the Party—with Leonard Woolf as Secretary—and this Committee—active and earnest as it was—was constantly stimulated into greater activity by gallant and public-spirited stalwarts like McGregor Ross, Dr. Norman Leys, Archdeacon Owen, Leonard Barnes and others, who demanded a Labour forward policy, especially in Kenya, in which they were particularly interested.

It may be convenient at this point to consider some of the background factors which, for better or worse, affected Webb's position as a Colonial Minister. It has been asserted that he was dominated by his Civil Servants. This is not accurate, though the effect of the real position may seem to have been somewhat similar. He had spent the first ten years of his career in the Colonial Office and during these impressionable years, he, no doubt, got into a civil service way of looking at things. This was not entirely a disadvantage to him in Ministerial office, more especially in his relations with his staff, but it may have made it difficult for him, sometimes, to regard matters from the more detached position appropriate to a Minister.

Another influence which affected him was his great respect for the individual whom he believed to be an expert. His personal modesty was remarkable, as was his zest for information, and if he wanted to learn about bricklaying or about the work of a Trade Union Secretary, he would sit at the feet of a bricklayer or of a Trade Union Secretary and listen with respect to what they told him. He regarded as experts most, if not all, of the senior men in the Colonial Office and was, perhaps, inclined to accept their judgments without always applying the same critical examination which he gave to other matters. And, in those days—it is different now—quite a few of the senior men had never visited the territories with the administration of which they were concerned.

I had this outlook of his impressed upon me by his calling me —as his Under-Secretary—to his room one morning to warn me that the minutes I was writing might put the heads of the Divisions against me. On my inquiring what was wrong with the minutes, he generously assured me that he entirely agreed with them but cautioned me, in his kindly way, against going too far. What he had in mind, I am sure, was (apart from the effect of my standing and effectiveness in the Office) the same general principle which made him seem sometimes hesitant or even reactionary when faced with demands, for Kenya or other places, by the militant upholders of native rights. I have permission to quote what was to me an illuminating passage in a letter he sent—in April, 1930— to a strong but friendly critic of his attitude to the difficulties in Kenya. "We cannot," he wrote, "get improvements in these places faster than our officials can be persuaded to go! Theirs are the hands that must carry out the reforms; and we have to carry them with us in each successive change, which must be mainly a change of spirit." That was a real old-time Fabian pronouncement and it contains a good deal of worldly wisdom. And there was no lack of courage in saying it—rather the reverse! But I think he did not realise that many of the younger men, at least, in the Colonial field, as well as in the Colonial Office itself, had already got this change of spirit and were expecting a vigorous lead in its application from a Labour Government.

ACHIEVEMENTS OVER A WIDE FIELD

But, although he did not go so fast or so far as many—without his responsibilities—demanded, there is no occasion to apologise for his record in the Colonial Office. It compares very favourably with that of more spectacular occupants. It is, indeed, surprising to see, in retrospect, how much he did do or get done. He had a great capacity for work and his minutes and comments, invariably written in his own bold, flowing and legible hand, were a delight to read. He never gave the impression of having doubts and hesitations, certainly not about factual matters. His directions were clear and straightforward, like the man himself. In the broader and more psychological fields of policy, where human prejudices, communal antagonisms, nationalist aspirations and racial complications were involved, as in Kenya and Palestine, he had more difficulty. He was dealing there, not with intellectual conceptions or factual realities but with feelings and emotions which dictate the attitude and conduct of most of mankind. Kingsley Martin, in one of the most penetrating studies that has yet been written about the Webbs, says: "Sidney was really the man of pure reason." This is certainly the case and it was this characteristic that probably often made things difficult for him;

but he did go on, and he did make decisions, and many of them were good and sound. Moreover, it must be kept in mind that his difficulties in these fields have been experienced alike by his predecessors and by his successors, and that they—like him—have left problems that are still unsolved.

It will be possible to indicate some only of the many matters with which he had to deal as Secretary of State for the Colonies.

On behalf of the Government, he accepted the Report of the Donoughmore Commission on the constitution of Ceylon. This was in many ways a revolutionary document and was not regarded with enthusiasm in Civil Service circles in Ceylon or by some officials in the Colonial Office. It gave adult franchise for the first time in the East, without income, property or educational tests; it began the stage of Ministerial responsibility and set up an arrangement of Executive Committees; it also abolished the pernicious system of Communal representation. Webb was good enough to say: " I had nothing to do with the invention of it (the Constitution) but I jumped to it when I saw it . . . " There will be few to deny that the new Dominion of Ceylon—so gladly welcomed as a full member of the British Commonwealth—is the outcome of the adoption of this Report.

During the preparation of the Order in Council and the other necessary instruments for carrying out the new scheme for Ceylon, an incident occurred which illustrates the Minister's quickness to set right what he saw to be wrong and which showed, too, that he was not dominated by his Civil Servants. Although not able (owing to heavy House of Commons duties) to scrutinise these extensive documents in detail, I did notice two glaring instances in which these ran almost directly counter to the recommendations of the Report. Since the official mainly concerned demurred to my request to have the necessary alterations made, I brought the matter to the notice of the Secretary of State who promptly got the matter put right and so prevented a charge of breach of faith with Ceylon, though some other minor inconsistencies did slip through.

THE KENYA CONTROVERSY

As I have already indicated, East Africa, and especially Kenya, was a source of great controversy during Webb's term of office.

SIDNEY WEBB (PRESIDENT OF THE BOARD OF TRADE) WITH NOEL
BUXTON (MINISTER OF AGRICULTURE) LEAVING THE KING'S LEVÉE ON
THE OCCASION OF THE FIRST LABOUR GOVERNMENT (1924)

SIDNEY WEBB AT WORK, GROSVENOR ROAD

Part of Kenya—the Highlands—is suitable for White settlement and a rather special type of British settler had gone there, including Lord Delamere and other aristocratic people, who became leaders of the European community. Many ex-army officers of the First World War had also gone to Kenya, with the approval and assistance of the United Kingdom Government. There was a Legislative Council with limited powers ; and the Secretary of State for the Colonies exercised, through the Governor, a close and careful control over the affairs of the Colony.

There was an urge to manage their own affairs which always arises in any British community and, as the Kenya group included men with experience in politics and public affairs in Britain, and since they could command a considerable amount of British Parliamentary sympathy and influence, the Parliamentary pressure from their side was substantial and active. The main line of propaganda was to ask for, or to demand, increased powers for the Legislative Council, which had no African members. The great bulk of the settlers were not politically minded, but were busy in farms and plantations and contending with locusts and other pests which constantly menaced their economic welfare. The small and influential nucleus in Nairobi, however, kept the political pot boiling and, when the word went round that "Whitehall" was at it again, the whole community loyally lined up and supported the exposure of the new iniquities of the Home Government.

On the other hand, there was—in the House of Commons and out of it—our little band of earnest and well-informed defenders of the rights of the Africans of Kenya, who pointed out that the European settlers were dependent on the Africans for certain kinds of agricultural work which Europeans could not do in the climate of that country ; and that it would be entirely wrong and be putting too much strain on human nature to allow employers the right, through their power to direct the laws of the country, to impose such wages and working conditions and such discriminations in land allocation, in taxation, in railway subsidies, in education and in transport facilities, as the grant of greater powers to a Legislative Council, without direct African representation, would give to them. A common roll of electors based on a " civilisation " test which should be identical for all was demanded.

The controversy raged ! The Governor had one of the most

H

difficult jobs in the Colonial Empire. The settlers, individually, were delightful people. Together—in a political connection—they were very difficult. To complicate the problem further there was a substantial Indian and Arab population whose representation had also to be considered. Some of Webb's troubles in Kenya can, therefore, be imagined. He did not like to be rushed. But about Kenya there was always rush and excitement.

In June, 1930, Sidney Webb published his notable White Paper—the " Memorandum on Native Policy in East Africa."[1] It emphasised the principle of Trusteeship for all British Colonies and affirmed the main declarations of the Duke of Devonshire's White Paper of 1923, particularly re-emphasising " . . . that the interests of the African Natives must be paramount, and that if, and when, those interests and the interests of the immigrant races should conflict, the former should prevail . . . " Our stalwarts were fairly well satisfied, though they would have liked more constructive proposals, but the Kenya settlers were some-what uneasy, even though the Paper, in its essentials, did not differ materially from the 1923 Paper. Much disputation followed, both in Kenya and in the British Parliament, as to its meaning and prob-able effect. Our pro-African group demanded immediate or early implementation in the Kenya Budget of the principle that there should be no discrimination against the African population in the allocation of funds.

THE JOINT SELECT COMMITTEE ON EAST AFRICA

Ultimately, Webb did a wise and big thing. He carried a motion in the House of Lords for the setting-up of a Joint Committee of both Houses of Parliament to consider the Hilton Young Com-mission's Report, a more recent one by Sir Samuel Wilson, then Permanent Under-Secretary of State for the Colonies, and, also, the White Paper in which the Government had outlined its policy. " The Government ", he said, " had no desire to shirk their re-sponsibility, but they were anxious, before coming to a final decision, to acquaint themselves with all points of view ; and they thought this could best be effected through the medium of a Joint Committee." The proposal was cordially welcomed by—among others—Lord Lugard and the Archbishop of Canterbury.

[1] Cmd. 3573.

The other House agreed and the Joint Committee was duly set up. It contained the Colonial experts of all Parties; it sat from December, 1930, to June, 1931, and produced the most interesting and instructive Colonial discussions I have ever heard. Webb did not, I think, miss a session and showed great interest in the proceedings. By the Secretary of State's direction arrangements had been made and public funds provided for the attendance of Native witnesses from Kenya, Uganda and Tanganyika. The presence of these witnesses made the occasion unique. The chief witness from Uganda, speaking the most fluent English and countering with ease the debating points of the lawyer members of the Joint Committee, gave a fascinating presentation of his case. And there is little doubt that the fears expressed by the witnesses from Uganda and Tanganyika about the possibility of being handed over to the control of Kenya (the Conference was ostensibly on Closer Union of the three territories but the discussions ranged over practically every controversial subject) not only greatly impressed the Joint Committee but also had an effect on the Kenya attitude which seems to have produced—in these later days—some hope of an agreement for closer and more harmonious working between the three territories.

The recommendations of the Joint Committee[1]—if its widely representative character is taken into account—were remarkably progressive and, although the drive and the will to implement some of these were lacking when the Labour Government, very shortly afterwards, went out of office, their influence has been felt in subsequent developments in East Africa. This, in my view, was one of Webb's best achievements, and I believe it was his own idea.

THE COLONIAL GOVERNORS' CONFERENCE

Another good thing he did, which had only been done once before and which I do not think has been done, on a full scale, since, was to have a conference of the Governors of all the Colonies. This took place in June, and July, 1930, most of the meetings taking place in the Foreign Office Dining Room. It was a great occasion and took a lot of arranging. The Report[2] shows the extent of the subjects discussed. The mere list of those present is impres-

[1]Cmd. 3574.
[2]Cmd. 3628-9.

sive. As well as the Governors, and at least one Chief Justice,
observers attended from the Government of India, the Union of
South Africa, Southern Rhodesia and other parts of the Commonwealth. The Colonial Development Fund, communications
and transport, broadcasting, trade questions, and films were all
brought under review and Committees formed to study them and
to report to the main Conference. Senior officials who attended
still refer to it as one of the most useful Colonial Conferences they
have known.

Penal and Prison Reforms

It was brought to Webb's notice that serious abuses were present
in connection with penal arrangements in some, and indeed, in
most Colonies. Savage sentences were being imposed on children,
prison accommodation was bad and warders' pay and conditions
were not conducive to the recruitment of the best type. He at
once set up a Committee with the Parliamentary Under-Secretary
as Chairman, to go into the whole question. We were fortunate in
having on the Committee Mr. (later Sir) Alexander Paterson, of
the Home Office, the great authority on penal questions, and Sir
Alison Russell, who had recently retired as Chief Justice of
Tanganyika. This Committee found so much to justify its existence
that it became a permanent institution and is now (as the Treatment of Offenders Sub-Committee of the Colonial Social Welfare
Advisory Committee) part of the standing advisory machinery of
the Colonial Office, bringing into our Colonies the most humane
and advanced methods of dealing with delinquents. It may be
that this was not the least of Webb's contributions to the full
equipment of the Colonial Office.

Iraq, Malta and Mui-Tsai

During his time of office, the Treaty with Iraq—originally included among the Mandated Territories for which the United
Kingdom was responsible—was carried through, and Iraq's
membership of the League of Nations sponsored. The Constitution of Malta was suspended when a high dignitary of the Catholic
Church intervened in an election campaign. The debates on these
matters were mainly in the Commons and Webb took a normal
official course in regard to them. Considerable and long overdue

improvements in the lot of adopted children—known as Mui-Tsai—in Hong Kong and Malaya were carried out, including registration, which previous Governments had hesitated to impose. Webb was firm about this in spite of considerable local, and some official, opposition.

PALESTINE AND THE WHITE PAPER

Perhaps the greatest anxiety which Webb had throughout his term of office and, certainly the subject which took up more of the time of the Ministers and senior officials than any other in the whole Colonial Empire was Palestine. There was never any relief or escape from it. The representatives of the Zionists in London were constant in their requests for interviews with the Secretary of State, with myself, or with the head of the Palestine Division. Bigger immigration quotas was the main subject but there were others. Vigorous Zionist propaganda was being carried on in the Press and in Parliament.

There was no Arab Agency in London at that time and there was no popular public statement of the Arab case. There were no Arab members in the House of Commons or the House of Lords. On the other hand, every political party had its Jewish (though not always necessarily Zionist) members in both Houses, the Labour Party having perhaps more Jewish members than any other. Only the Zionist side of the Palestine question was heard and pressure was constantly being applied to the Colonial Office by Members of Parliament and others who did not clearly understand what the responsibility of the Colonial Office was.

It was the job of the Office to apply the very difficult terms of the Mandate[1]—to promote the establishment in Palestine of a national home for the Jewish people but at the same time to ensure that the civil and religious rights of existing non-Jewish communities in Palestine were not prejudiced. The Arabs were a large majority of the inhabitants of the country. The Colonial Office simply tried to carry out loyally and impartially the Mandate instructions. It had to act as trustee for all the people of Palestine. The result was that the Colonial Office was sometimes accused,

[1]Owing to the lack of clearness in its terms, the Mandate was a very unhelpful instrument of administration. It was almost impossible to do anything constructive in Palestine without one side or the other, and sometimes both, complaining that the mandate was being broken.

both of being anti-Semitic and of being unduly under Jewish influence. Both accusations were equally untrue.

It can be imagined that Sidney Webb found this subject difficult. It was one in which reasoned argument was often in abeyance. He had frequent interviews with Dr. Weizmann and did his best, as did the rest of us, to meet Jewish requests, so long as these appeared to be within the terms of the Mandate. None of us had any axe to grind or prejudice to overcome, and our interviews were always friendly.

I had on two occasions been before the Mandates Commission at Geneva to answer criticisms of the Labour Government and of the Palestine Administration and, in the autumn of 1930, the Secretary of State sent me to Palestine on an official mission. I visited and spoke in many Jewish agricultural colonies and Arab villages, as well as in the main towns, and was generously entertained by the Jewish Municipal authorities in Tel-Aviv. I met the leaders of both the Jewish and Arab communities and explored possibilities. I was struck by the fact that the Jerusalem and Haifa Town Councils, composed of both Jews and Arabs, seemed to work fairly harmoniously and I had visions of a wide extension of local government in all the different areas, with increased powers of rating, etc., as a road towards the solution of the Palestine problem. But it was not to be.

I returned home to find myself in the midst of a controversy on the White Paper of October, 1930.[1] This White Paper followed the Report of the special Commission under Sir Walter Shaw[2] and the further Report on land settlement, immigration and development by Sir John Hope Simpson.[3]

I need not go into the detail of the Paper. I had not seen it until my return but I entirely agreed with it. It presented, as one would expect in a document for which Sidney Webb was responsible, a fair and balanced statement of the position in Palestine, both the political position and that in respect of land development and cognate matters, and it gave indications—later amplified in the Parliamentary debate—that, in respect of new land made available by irrigation or drainage (£2,500,000 was to be set aside for this), something would be done for the humblest class of rural Arab who had become landless, a number of them having become so

[1]Cmd. 3962. [2]Cmd. 3530. [3]Cmd. 3686.

owing to their land having been bought up for Jewish use. Afterwards, there would be equal distribution between Jews and Arabs. There was nothing extreme or provocative about it, and I have no doubt that no one was more surprised than Webb at the repercussions. The Jewish reaction, however, was hostile and their efficient organisation for world-wide propaganda came into action, demonstrations taking place before British Consulates as far apart as Warsaw and Chicago.

It is not quite clear what happened in the domestic field, or what passed between Webb and the Prime Minister. But Palestine affairs were temporarily taken out of the former's hands and a Committee of Ministers—in which the Foreign Office was prominently represented—took control. It was suggested to Webb by some of his friends and colleagues that the only dignified course was to resign his office, but he refused to do this. He gave as his reason the fact that the Government had few representatives in the House of Lords and that to resign would not be fair. No doubt his feeling that way was part of the reason but, here again, his profound personal modesty, his great loyalty to the team, and a set of values different from that of the ordinary man were, probably, also responsible. But some of those around him felt regret that he did not act otherwise.

The White Paper, in the meantime, had formed the subject of a big debate in the Commons (17th November, 1930) without any effective points being made against it. It had a good effect on the Arabs and promised some improvement in Jewish-Arab relations. Some months later, however, in February, 1931, (presumably as the result of Zionist pressure from various quarters and on the advice of the Committee of Ministers already mentioned) the Prime Minister addressed a letter to Dr. Weizmann explaining away the substance of the White Paper. And so one more effort to bring about better relations in Palestine had failed ; and the belief of the Arabs in the good faith of the United Kingdom Government was shaken.

A Unified Colonial Service

The Corona Club—founded by Mr. Joseph Chamberlain in 1900—is a one-night-a-year dinner club of members and ex-members of the Colonial Office and Colonial Service and of Colonial Ministers and ex-Ministers. On 16th July, 1930, Sidney

Webb presided over the dinner of that year and made the one speech which is permitted. He was in good form and paid the Colonial Service a well-deserved tribute which was greatly appreciated by his large audience. It was at this dinner that he announced his intention of proceeding with the scheme for the unification of the Colonial Service, and said that he had secured the help of Sir Warren Fisher, then Permanent Secretary of the Treasury, in the working out of the plan. There were difficulties because of the different conditions of entry into the Service in different Colonies. The unification of the Colonial Service is another great constructive achievement to Webb's credit. It had been long talked about, but his is the merit of having carried it through. He was personally responsible for it and it has had permanent and beneficial results.

A Democratic Dinner

For one normally orthodox in Civil Service matters, he did on one occasion a rather unexpected thing. He asked for a dinner to be arranged to which the whole of his administrative and clerical staff should be invited. The affair took place in Lyons Corner House in Coventry Street. The seating at the tables was arranged by drawing the names out of a hat and the oldest and youngest members were called upon to make speeches. Such an event would not be considered notable in these later days when seniors and juniors mix on a common footing in the canteens of Government Offices, but in those earlier years it was a novelty, and the notice of it is said to have caused some mild perturbation among the older civil servants.

It is interesting to speculate—especially as she was herself present at the dinner and made a little speech—as to whether this was one of the few occasions or, perhaps, the only one, in which Mrs. Sidney Webb came into the Dominions and Colonial Office picture. It happened soon after Webb came into office and before I was Parliamentary Secretary, and while I am sure he would have given full approval to the idea when it was presented to him, I am doubtful if he would have initiated it, as, in his selflessness and with his democratic outlook, he would not have considered such a social gathering of Minister, senior and junior civil servants particularly significant or called for. One of his former assistant private secretaries told me that one day he said to Webb : " Do you know, Sir, I think it would be a very good idea if you could spare the time to see the junior members of your staff, such as the assistant principals, and talk to them each for a few minutes about their work. They know who you are when they see you, but it would please them very much and I am sure make them take far more interest in their work if they felt that you were taking a personal interest in what they were doing." Webb looked at him in amazement for a moment, and then said, " Do you really think so ? " He replied : " Yes, I most certainly do." The Secretary of State then said, " In that case, please arrange it at once." Which the private secretary did, with the successful results anticipated. Some say that this classless evening dinner went well, while others report a rather strained atmosphere. At any rate, the experiment was never repeated.

SOME CHARACTERISTICS AND CONCLUSIONS

He was considered by his staff and, indeed, by his colleagues to be a somewhat reserved and remote person. Former private secretaries tell me that he seemed to them to be often living in a world of his own. They say that, sometimes, when his day's work on Colonial affairs was done, he would sit silently in his chair, with his finger-tips together, absorbed in reflection.

His relations with myself were always harmonious, but he seldom discussed policy, and even with his senior civil servants he proceeded mainly by minutes. He had never been a junior Minister and knew nothing of the frustrations and humiliations of Parliamentary Under-Secretaries (I believe that, nowadays, they are brought more into consultation): on the other hand, there were many instances of personal kindness and thoughtfulness. And there was, for my wife and myself, the one memorable week-end visit to Passfield Corner, which was on similar lines—including the Sunday morning six-mile walk—to those so well described by Kingsley Martin and others.

This inadequate account of his Ministerial phase, will, I hope, have shown at least that Sidney Webb took his Cabinet and Office duties, as he took other jobs, in his stride, and that he went quietly and calmly ahead, confident in himself, and not without some outstanding achievements to his credit.

H*

As a Minister, however, he had not some of the qualities that make for the greatest success. In the first place, he was too aloof from the political field always to impress his colleagues in the Cabinet with the merits and importance of his proposals. He was an objective thinker rather than a political fighter and tactician and, with so many competing projects from so many Ministries, he allowed himself, sometimes, to be pushed aside. He did not carry the weight in the Cabinet that he should have done and, in some of his best efforts, he did not get the backing he should have got. It may be, however, that this is more a judgment on the ways of Cabinets than on Sidney Webb.

In the second place, although he had courage and was not affected by any personal considerations in his decisions, he lacked a certain potential ruthlessness, which, however unpleasant to produce and apply, has to be within the capacity of those with high responsibilities. A certain Governor—a man of experience and distinction—committed two serious breaches of discipline, one of them openly and the other—more serious in its consequences—only known to a very small circle. These were concerning matters of Government policy. Although it was urged on Webb on each occasion that this very individualistic and almost defiant Governor should be recalled, he refused to do it. The reason was probably a mixed one, in which his respect for the expert, his wide tolerance for a view different from his own, and his personal modesty all played their part.

And so we come back to the man himself—not in fact different from the man as Minister. He impressed his colleagues, as well as his officials—severe critics—as a man without guile, simple, sincere and highly-gifted. His personal character emerged unbesmirched and, indeed, enhanced, from all the chequered days and nights of the second Labour Government.

THE WEBBS AND SOVIET COMMUNISM

by

BARBARA DRAKE

XIV

THE WEBBS AND SOVIET COMMUNISM

by BARBARA DRAKE

Sidney and Beatrice were not by nature revolutionaries. Nor could they, until later years, be counted in any sense as disciples of Marx. That " law is the mother of freedom," " the inevitability of gradualness," were Webbian axioms ; and, before the rise of the Labour Party to political independence, " peaceful permeation " of the party in power—Tory or Liberal— was their chosen line of Socialist advance. Steeped in the traditions of parliamentary government, they were appalled at the horrors of the Russian revolution, accompanied as it was by civil war and foreign invasion, and followed by widespread famine and disease. As members of the British Labour Party, they disliked no less the " splitting tactics " of the Comintern, or the Third International, and its interference in the home affairs of other countries. Nor had they any use for a British Communist Party taking its orders from Moscow. Ten years after the Russian revolution, indeed, in a letter to Sidney's women constituents at Seaham, Beatrice could still describe it as " the greatest misfortune in the history of the Labour Movement," and likely " to keep back the achievement of economic democracy in England for half a century."[1]

The Russian revolution, however, was not the sole work of the Communists, or Bolsheviks. The bourgeois revolution of February, 1917, took place while Lenin was still in exile. In the rural areas, the peasants—at that time three-quarters of the total population—themselves had seen to the liquidation of the hated landlord and his satellites. It was a whole decade, and many changes were to take place, before the Bolsheviks succeeded in their major task—the liquidation of the profit-making capitalist.

Nor were the Webbs favourably impressed by accounts of the early experiments in peasant holdings and " workers' control."

[1] *Beatrice Webb.* Margaret Cole, p. 161.

While the Bolsheviks had, what most governments lack, a fixed purpose of social change, and the creation of a new " classless state," they had no definite ideas of how the changes could be made, but proceeded slowly and painfully by the process of trial and error. The break-up of the great landed estates, the primitive conditions of Russian peasant farming and the extreme individualism of the small holder, together with war devastation, had brought a catastrophic fall in food production. Something had to be done to relieve the famine of 1921. As an emergency measure, concessions were made to the peasant-owner to sell in the free market, and to develop his holding on a profit-making basis— even at the expense of his poorer neighbour. As an immediate result, the kulak, or well-to-do farmer, was soon found to be climbing into a new capitalist class, while the army of landless peasants was rapidly growing. Nor did the return in agriculture to private enterprise succeed in its main object, or meet the needs of the steadily rising urban population. After three years of endless meetings and discussion, it was finally decreed in 1928 by the Sovnarkom, or Central Government—a move not out of keeping with Webbian philosophy—summarily to amalgamate the innumerable scattered strips and tiny holdings in the U.S.S.R. into some 225,000 collective farms, and to bring these under state direction as part of an overall plan.[1] Bitter opposition came from the kulak who had prospered in the emergency period. Land was left uncultivated, stocks of grain and cattle were destroyed rather than deliver them to the collective farms, thus aggravating the two bad harvests of 1931 and 1932, and leading in many areas to acute famine. The kulak had come, meanwhile, to his fate in his own ruthless liquidation.

First experiments in " workers' control "—a subject, unlike agriculture, to which the Webbs had given much time and thought—were even more short-lived. The conception of " the self-governing workshop " they had always rejected as the dream

[1]According to Sir Bernard Pares, collective farming, in one form or another, was an ancient practice in Russia, and he records that, as late as 1910, a meeting of peasants decided for the first time to divide up the village holding for the purpose of hay-making (*Russia and the Peace*). On the other hand, as Sir John Maynard has pointed out, there still remains today a large element of individualism in the collective farm, particularly in respect of cattle, and this has played a leading part in the reconciliation of the peasant to the change (*The Russian Peasant and other Studies*, Chapter XVII).

of syndicalists and anarchists. Not merely did they take the view that a committee elected by factory operatives had seldom the necessary knowledge and skills for the quite different tasks of direction and management—defects which might in time be remedied—but they also insisted that " workers' control " was foredoomed to failure by the fact that, deprived of the checks of supply and demand in a free market, each factory must inevitably determine its policy, not by what was wanted by the community as a whole, but by its own wishes and preferences. This weakness, indeed, was recognised by Lenin himself and, as early as June, 1918, the Sovnarkom decreed that each individual enterprise must be controlled by a manager appointed by, and responsible to, the Central Government. A " step backwards " was taken and, under the New Economic Policy of 1921, substantial concessions were made to private enterprise in industry both at home and abroad, but only, as Lenin remarked, in order to take later " two steps forward." Nor did these concessions touch " the commanding heights of Socialism." The entire banking system, the whole of international commerce, communication and transport, practically all urban land and buildings, mineral resources, every kind of fuel and power, and the heavy industries, remained under state control. A first State Planning Authority, or Gosplan, was appointed in 1923, while the steady expansion of state and co-operative undertakings, and the preferential treatment given to them, tended to undermine the foundations of private enterprise. The New Economic Policy came finally to its close with the first Five-Year Plan of 1928.

The Webbs, at first, were sceptical as to the working of a " central plan." After listening, at a Fabian gathering, to an elaborate exposition by Leonid Krassin of new Soviet ideas of state planning, Beatrice writes in her diary (August, 1920)[1] : " One is tempted to wonder whether this creed does not consist almost entirely in an insistent demand for the subordination of each individual to the ' working plan ' of the scientifically trained mind of the expert." At one time, indeed, and not without misgiving, Beatrice foretold a new kind of religious order—a " creed-autocracy," dogmatic and infallible—but based on Marxian ideology as interpreted by its own High Priests. It was, neverthe-

[1] *Soviet Communism.* S. and B. Webb, p. 617.

less, the departure from " workers' control " and the substitution
of " planned production for community consumption," that more
than anything else roused in the Webbs a new interest in Soviet
Communism and induced them later, despite the disqualification
of old age, to see for themselves what was happening in the
U.S.S.R.

Some years, however, were to elapse before the " plan " took
final shape. The difficulties in the way were greater than was at
first anticipated, and many amendments had to be made to the
original draft. It was not, as we have seen, until 1929 that the
first Five-Year Plan came into actual operation, or that news began
to penetrate into the British press and to excite among Socialists
considerable interest. Sidney was at that time a member of the
second Labour Government. He was absorbed in parliamentary
duties, and had little or no time or thought to give to outside
affairs. Beatrice had greater leisure. She began seriously to study
Soviet events and to collect Soviet documents, while she made
friends with the Soviet Ambassador, who himself suggested a
visit to Russia. After the fall of the Labour Government in 1931,
Sidney joined her in research. The rising power of " monopoly
capitalism " and its part in the birth of the Fascist movement,
the weakness and final collapse of the Labour Government in the
face of hostile financial interests, had caused the Webbs, meanwhile, somewhat to reconsider their views. At this point, they
were even heard to declare " the inevitability of gradualness is
dead." Sidney tried to learn the Russian language but decided
almost at once that a little learning is a dangerous thing, and they
engaged instead a Russian-speaking secretary. In May, 1932, they
travelled by boat to Leningrad, where they received a royal
reception. For in Soviet Russia Sidney and Beatrice were already
notable personages. Had not Lenin himself come under their
influence, and even translated into Russian the *History of Trade
Unionism* ? They soon moved from Leningrad to Moscow, where
they were housed in the Foreign Office Guest House. Stalin was
away on holiday, but they were able to interview highly-placed
ministers and officials. They were given the services of a Foreign
Office interpreter, and also a pass to visit public institutions,
collective farms and industrial undertakings, and to attend
official meetings—except, apparently, those of the Central

Executive of the Communist Party.[1] Afterwards they journeyed to Nishninovgorod ; visited the Autostroy Motor Plant and the Stalingrad Tractor Plant, recording failure in the one case and success in the other; they passed on to Rostov, where they were sumptuously entertained by soviets, co-operatives and trade unions, while they discovered to their surprise, in the best room of the hotel, a young " production specialist," sentenced as a " wrecker " to imprisonment, but returned at once to his job because " his services were too valuable to lose ! " Beatrice at this stage was taken ill, and Sidney continued his tour alone to the Ukraine, to Kharkov and Dnieprostroy. The stay was only a short one (May–August), but they returned home ladened with an immense body of Soviet documents of every description, to be translated later for their use by Professor S. P. Turin and his wife—Russian residents in London attached to the staff of the London School of Economics—and it was these documents which formed the main body of material for their great book—*Soviet Communism : a New Civilization.*

Their earlier doubts had been completely dispelled. Not merely were they able to record the prior discussion of new plans by the worker, at the highest to the lowest level, on all matters directly concerning himself or his job, and the awakened interest of the ordinary citizen in public affairs—the draft constitution of 1936, Beatrice tells later, was discussed at no less than 527,000 meetings attended by 36,500,000 persons[2]—but they also observed that, released from the fear of exploitation and unemployment, the worker had developed a new civic conscience and sense of social responsibility. The function of the trade union itself had changed. " An agreement made by Soviet workers," the Webbs quote from a pamphlet by a trade union official (L. Kaufman, 1932[3]), " is in reality a promise they make to themselves and their fellow-workers to fulfil certain self-determined conditions. . . In capitalist countries collective agreements are the armistice terms of two hostile forces. Here there is no enemy. No one tries to give as little as he can for as much as he can." In a document privately circulated on her return from Russia (August, 1932)

---

[1] *Beatrice Webb.* Margaret Cole, p. 172.
[2] *The Truth about Soviet Russia,* (1942), B. Webb. p. 24.
[3] *Soviet Communism,* p. 189.

Beatrice writes. "And finally, and most emphatically, I think that the moral uplift, to use a horrid expression, and the intellectual advancement of the Russian people is today far more pronounced and obvious than the increase in their material wealth and comfort. This is good for the future but bad for the immediate influence of Soviet Russia. The average sensual man in other countries, and it is he who will be the arbiter, will judge success more by the cubic space of house room per person, the amount and variety of available food and the widespread possession of motor cars and wireless sets, than by any reformation of manners and morals, or advancement of literacy and learning." The emphasis on personal hygiene, self-control and parental responsibility made a special appeal to her; " there is no spooning in the Parks of Recreation and Rest," and she relates a warning, said to be given by Stalin, to a high-placed Commissar : " I do not want to inquire into your private affairs, but if there is any more nonsense about women, you go to a place where there are no women." To quote again from the same document : " If I had to pick out any one institution of Soviet Russia as the most striking in its hopefulness, it would be the Comsomols, with their attendant Pioneers. The combination, in this organisation of Communist youth (which is a preparation for party membership), of the passion for self-improvement and self-discipline, with the passion for social service, and the consequent growth in the young generation of personal initiative and personal responsibility, is one of the finest disciplines the world has ever seen, so far as man as a producer and consumer of goods and services, for himself, and the community, is concerned. In describing later what she called the " scientific humanism " of the U.S.S.R., she writes[1] : " The ancient axiom, ' Love your neighbour as yourself ' is embodied, not in the economic, but in the utilitarian calculus, namely, the valuation of what conduces to the permanent well-being of the human race."

The Webbs were no less impressed by the new " cult of science," and the persistent testing of the order of ideas by the order of things. They had always held that, while aims and ends, or the purpose of life, belonged to the sphere of religion or conscience and were the concern of the great mass of citizens

[1] *The Truth about Soviet Russia*, p. 43.

speaking through their elected representatives, it was the part of the expert or scientist, each at work in his particular field, to devise ways and means of carrying out the common purpose. " Unlike," they write,[1] " the groups of landed proprietors, lawyers, merchants, bureaucrats, soldiers and journalists in command of most other states, administrators in the Moscow Kremlin believe in their professed faith. And this professed faith is science." Sidney visited Russia again in 1934, when I had the privilege of accompanying him. The stay was an even shorter one (September–October) and confined to Moscow and Leningrad. It was before the Kirov murder, when suspicions of foreign intervention were temporarily lulled ; when a new era of political tolerance, to be embodied in the Constitution of 1936, seemed already on its way ; when peasants and workers were elated by the success of the first Five-Year Plan ; when new goods were appearing in the shops and bread-rationing was about to be abolished ; when Stalin was soon to announce : " Life has grown better, life has grown merrier." As we inspected factories, farms, co-operative stores, schools, hospitals, maternity homes, reformatories, community centres, parks of recreation and rest, visited crowded theatres and opera houses, seated in the state box or side-by-side with rough-handed peasants and workers, attended trade union meetings or industrial courts, or watched, at work or at play, healthy and happy-looking peasants and workers, young mothers and children, Sidney would whisper to me, with the relish of the scientist whose theoretic proposition has stood the test of practical experiment : " See, see, it works, it works."

The Webbs fell in love with Soviet Russia. They saw in it the emergence of a new civilisation—the realisation of Socialist dreams. Full employment and the prospect of a new freedom from want ; the urge of the worker to raise the level, not of wages, but of production ; women's enfranchisement in the economic no less than in the political field ; the phenomenal growth and success of the health and education services ; the new thirst for knowledge, and popular appreciation of classical literature, of music and drama ; all made on the Webbs a profound impression. While the temporal power of the churches—until the second great war a main stronghold of reaction—had been broken, and

[1] *Soviet Communism*, p. 1132–3.

religious propaganda, together with religious instruction in the schools had been definitely banned, they found no interference with "freedom of worship."[1] "From each according to his faculty, to each according to his needs" or, indeed, as interpreted later by Soviet philosophy, "to each according to his contribution to the common good,"[2] seemed to them a nearer approach than "the profit-making motive" to the historic Christian idea. Even more were the Webbs impressed, in a country of traditional pogroms and racial intolerance, and at a time when the Central European states had lamentably failed to solve the problem of their national minorities, by the complete absence in Russia of race discrimination; and they compared favourably the successful treatment, throughout the vast Soviet territories, of racial minorities with the treatment of natives in our own Colonies, or of the negro in the U.S.A.

"The U.S.S.R.," the Webbs tell us,[3] "does not consist of a government and a people confronting each other as all other great societies have hitherto been. It is a highly-integrated organisation, in which each individual man, woman or youth, is expected to participate in three separate capacities; as a citizen, as a producer and as a consumer." Leadership belonged to the Communist Party, of which Stalin was General Secretary—a teaching order, or "vocation of leadership," rather than a political party, but democratic in its internal structure—whose function it was to inspire with the passion of community service a multiform democracy, in which soviets, trade unions, co-operative societies and voluntary associations provided for the personal participation

---

[1] According to Sir Bernard Pares, Russia remains the most religious country in Europe. As the French Ambassador to the last Tsar remarked: "This people is more religious than the Church." Sir Bernard estimates that one-half of the town population and two-thirds of the peasants are believers (*Russia and the Peace*, 1944. Chapter, III). After the early Bolshevik attack on the Church, the anti-God campaign soon came to a natural end. "It has always been less dangerous," Rudolph Schlesinger writes, "to profess religious beliefs in any place in the U.S.S.R. than Rationalism in an American small town." *The Spirit of Post-War Russia*, 1917–1946. Rudolph Schlesinger, pp. 52, 162.

[2] Piece-rates or differential payment, according to output or type of work or to the qualifications of the worker, together with certain privileges, have been accepted by Soviet authorities as necessary incentives both to production and to recruitment to certain trades, and also as in keeping with the "functional" needs of the worker, e.g., privacy, study, social intercourse, etc., at the professional and higher administrative or managerial level.

[3] *Soviet Communism*, p. 450.

of an unprecedented proportion of the adult population.[1] Stalin,
Beatrice insisted, unlike Hitler or Mussolini, was not a dictator.
As presiding member of the Sovnarkom, and later as Prime
Minister, he had nothing like the autocratic powers of the President
of the U.S.A. She even doubted " whether Stalin would have
offered, as Churchill did, to amalgamate the U.S.S.R. on terms
of equality, with another great power without consulting the
Presidium of which he was a member."[2] Without agreement,
moreover, on the fundamentals of social and economic structure,
the Webbs saw no alternative to a " one-party " system—*vide* the
collapse in Europe, in the last twenty years, of the political democracies to be superseded by dictatorship in one form or another."
" It is obvious," Beatrice writes,[3] " that when there is civil war
within a country, or international war between sovereign states,
the ' one party ' system, with its suppression of incipient revolt
or Fifth Column treachery, will and must prevail." Nor did she
see any reason, once the class conflict had ceased to trouble
humanity, for the survival of political parties, one, two or many,
seeking to dominate the whole life of the country. " I foresee,"
she concludes,[4] " a rise of infinite varieties in the grouping of men
and women for different but not inconsistent purposes ; " and
she adds, " so called ' free thought and free expression by word
and by writ ' mocks human progress, unless the common people
are taught to think, and inspired to use this knowledge, in the
interests of their Commonwealth . . . It is this widespread
knowledge, and devotion to the public welfare, that is the keynote
of Soviet Democracy."

That the exclusive and overwhelming influence of the Communist Party would be out of place in a mature democracy and
tend to " wither away," or that it could be, and had been, used
for ill as well as for good, the Webbs did not dispute. In the
" disease of orthodoxy," in the activities of the secret police, in
political intolerance and the ruthless suppression of all organised
opposition to, or propaganda against, the Communist régime,
in the disregard of individual rights or human suffering where the

[1] It is estimated by Rudolf Schlesinger that in Russia, ten million citizens take
an active part in political life. *The Spirit of Post-War Russia*, 1917–1946, p. 90.
[2] *The Truth about Soviet Russia*, p. 15.
[3] *The Truth about Soviet Russia*, p. 30–1.
[4] *Soviet Communism*, p. 596.

security of the state was concerned, they saw the dark side of the picture. " It was the fate of Russia," the Webbs point out, " to have its religious, its industrial and its political revolutions, not separately, but almost simultaneously . . . No one can compute the sum of human suffering caused by the Triple Revolution, over so vast an area, in so brief a time, amid the most embittered civil war, supported by half a dozen foreign armies actually invading Soviet territory. But, equally, no one can compute the sum of human suffering, even unto death, caused in England by the Protestant Reformation, the Industrial Revolution and the triumph of democratic parliamentarianism, the whole drawn out over four centuries, with only the mildest of civil wars, and with next to no foreign invasion." Beatrice once said to me, " Is Christianity a sham because brutal deeds have been done by the Christian churches in its name ? "

Nor did the Webbs change their minds in the light of subsequent events. The much advertised " treason trials " of the " Old Bolsheviks," or " Internationalists," and of the Generals, they believed to be justified by intrigue with the German army against the Stalinist régime. Nor had they any liking for the Trotsky plan to create " world revolution," but they welcomed instead Stalin's announcement to concentrate, as an alternative, on the building up of Socialism within his own vast country. They contrasted the intervention by the Western Democracies in Russia's own revolution with their non-intervention policy in the case of Spain, resulting in the overthrow of the Spanish Republic with the aid of two Fascist powers. They deplored the foreign policy of the Chamberlain Government, its scare at the threat of the " Bolshevik bogy," the appeasement of Fascist dictators and the sacrifice of Czechoslovakia. After reading Ambassador Dodd's Diary, Beatrice writes,[1] " There is documentary evidence that the Governments of Great Britain and the U.S.A. were, through their diplomatic representatives, official and unofficial, trying to turn Hitler's aggressive ' intuitions ' away from their sea-bound frontiers towards the common enemy of Hitler's Germany, and of the capitalist democracies of the U.S.A. and the British Commonwealth of Nations—the Soviet Union." The Russo-German pact of 1939 came as a shock to them. But

[1] *The Truth about Soviet Russia*, p. 53.

they accepted it later as a justifiable measure of defence against German attack when the Red Army was unready to meet it, and no help could be expected from the West.[1] They interpreted, in similar manner, the Russian attack on Finland and occupation of Polish and other neighbouring territories, whose Governments were less hostile to Hitler than to Soviet Communism. Nor were they among those who questioned the loyalty of the Russian people to the Soviet Government, or underrated the strength of the Red Army, when Hitler made at length his attack.

To the question : " Will Communism spread ? " the Webbs' answer was emphatic—" Yes, it will ! "[2] Even before the second World War, they foretold that the two great powers of the future were the U.S.A. and the U.S.S.R. ; and they foresaw, sooner or later, a trial of strength between them—or between American Capitalism and Soviet Communism—but they did not doubt the final issue. In describing their latter-day conversion to the Marxian theory of history and the eventual passing of " free enterprise " into " trustified imperialist capitalism," Beatrice writes : " In the years before the [first] Great War and for some time afterwards, we did not foresee the collapse of Western civilisation : that is of the strange and mutually destructive trilogy of the Christian religion, profit-making capitalism and political democracy." For, in America as elsewhere, the rule of the profit-making capitalist seemed to them inconsistent, not only with Christian teaching, but also with political democracy ; and in this hopeless contradiction between the political power of the many and the economic power of the few, they could see no permanence of social peace. Nor did they believe that the struggle would be changed in its course by the ugly growth of Fascism or Nazism, with its idolisation of a God-like and infallible leader, its glorification of race and force, and its gospel of hate.[3] In spite of superficial

[1]Ambassador Joseph E. Davies writes in his Diary (October, 1941) ; " The real question which is vital now is, ' Will we force Stalin to make peace with Hitler again ? ' We, or rather the European Democracies, forced Stalin into Hitler's arms in August of 1939." *Mission to Moscow* (1942), p. 325.

[2]*Soviet Communism*, p. 1143.

[3]In comparing Communism and Nazism, Ambassador Joseph E. Davies writes : " The point is that the Christian religion could be imposed upon communistic principles without doing violence to its economic and political purposes, the primary one of which is based upon ' the brotherhood of men ' . . . The principles of the Christian religion cannot be imposed upon the Nazi philosophy without destroying the political base of the state." *Mission to Moscow*, (1942), p. 311.

resemblances to Soviet Communism, the Webbs could find in it no evidence of a social creed, or of any change in economic structure, but saw only a new brand of "opium of the people," serving to obscure the real issue, and appealing, in a defeated or disorganised country, at a time of acute economic depression, to a disillusioned generation, while winning everywhere, as an anti-dote to Soviet Communism, the passive, if not active, support of threatened capitalist interests and political reactionaries. Between Democratic Socialism and Soviet Communism, on the other hand, the Webbs were conscious of no fundamental contradiction, but were convinced that the divergences, important as these were, arose from the accident of history or circumstance. For political democracy can only plant its roots in times of peace and security, and does not grow over-night in an inexperienced and immature people. Civil war and foreign invasion leave invariably an after-math of fear and hate. Where the safety of the state itself is threatened, the individual counts inevitably for less. The Webbs strove, therefore, to the last for mutual understanding and goodwill between the British Socialist Movement and the Soviet Union, and the sympathy of an elder and wiser for a raw and difficult but sound-hearted and powerful younger brother. In the post-war period, Sidney was critical to the end of Anglo-American foreign policy, its anti-communist bias and the favouring of reactionary elements, first in Italy, then in Greece, Persia, Turkey, China. He regretted no less the revival of Soviet suspicions, not necessarily justified, of the Western Democracies, the formation in conse-quence of the Cominform, and a return to earlier tactics in the determination to resist "dollar diplomacy" and "American expansion" in Europe and Asia, and to create, if not world revolution, a *cordon sanitaire* of friendly states on the Soviet borders. The Webbs did not shut their eyes to the "infantile diseases" of Soviet Communism, but they remained nevertheless convinced that its social and economic system, or "planned production for community consumption," in one form or another, must survive and spread. "How, when, where, with what modifi-cations, and whether through violent revolution, or by peaceful permeation, or even by conscious imitation,"[1] they left the answer to posterity.

[1]*Soviet Communism*, p. 1143.

THE FABIAN SOCIETY AND THE NEW FABIAN RESEARCH BUREAU

by

JOHN PARKER

XV

THE FABIAN SOCIETY AND THE NEW FABIAN RESEARCH BUREAU

by JOHN PARKER

Preceding chapters have made it clear that at an early date Sidney and Beatrice Webb realised the desirability of recruiting for " Fabian Socialism " among the coming men in the Civil Service and in other walks of life. As has been described by Beatrice Webb in *Our Partnership*—and from a less favourable angle by H. G. Wells in *The New Machiavelli*—they found considerable satisfaction in making their home in Grosvenor Road a centre both of political discussion and what is more commonly termed wire-pulling. There, though their main concern was with contemporaries, they also gave careful attention to attracting successive generations of young men and young women. Whereas of the original Fabian group comparatively few had received a university education, of Fabians in the new century a considerable and talented proportion came from the universities. A local Fabian Society had been formed at Cambridge University as early as 1894, and by 1899 there were small groups in the universities of Aberystwyth, Edinburgh, Glasgow and Oxford. Fabian membership in universities, however, did not reach any sizable figure until the general expansion of the Society which followed the 1906 Liberal victory, and which was marked by the revolts against the " Old Gang " leadership promoted first by H. G. Wells and later by the Guild Socialists.[1]

These revolts were all defeated ; largely as a result of them young Socialists during the First World War and immediately afterwards, even where they were not directly associated with " subversive " movements, ceased to draw inspiration from the Fabian Society or from the Webbs insofar as they were identified with that body. The local Fabian Societies which had bulked so large in the conflicts of 1911–4 faded away—many of their most

[1]See Chapter X.

active members being absorbed into the Forces; the Webbs (Sidney in particular) turned their attention to the establishment of a new Labour Party as a real political rival to the Tory and Liberal organisations; and after the war was over the majority of those young Socialists who might have been potential Fabian recruits either turned to the Independent Labour Party or set themselves to working for the Divisional Labour Parties set up under the new constitution of 1918. (The Westminster Labour Party, in particular, had an almost entirely Fabian membership.) The Webbs themselves—although Sidney maintained his member-ship of the Fabian Executive Committee—transferred the major part of their political energies to the services of the Labour Party which became in 1918 His Majesty's Official Opposition and thereafter for two short periods His Majesty's Government.

The effect on the Fabian Society, and indeed on the whole Labour political setup during the twenties, was rather curious. The Society, largely, no doubt, owing to the deflection of its poten-tial thinkers mentioned above, became less and less the fountain head of Socialist thought; during the whole decade, 1919–29, it produced only forty-six pamphlets (of which six were com-missioned by an inquiry into the co-operative movement and three were reprinted lectures), as against nine in the single year, 1911. Its earlier propagandist role was almost entirely absorbed in the activities of the I.L.P., which also embarked to some extent on policy-making;[1] and, apart from local government, in which it maintained a continuing interest, as an organisation it effectively resigned its policy-making in favour of Sidney Webb's unique influence in Labour Party counsels. Its individual members, insofar as they contributed to local Labour Parties, contributed on the organisational side, not on the policy-making side. One of the major weaknesses of the second Labour Government was that its constituent bodies had done so little hard thinking on the problems which it would have to solve. *Labour and the Nation*, its official election programme, was woolly and fuzzy beyond measure in comparison with Sidney Webb's earlier *Labour and the New Social Order ;* the great bulk of *facts* used in the election

[1]During the 1924 Labour Government and afterwards, this policy-making process gradually produced a definite and separate programme to be forced upon the Labour Party—which development eventually resulted in the self-destruction of the I.L.P.

campaign was drawn from Lloyd George's *Liberal Yellow Book*. The Fabian Society, apart from its organisational interest in divisional Labour Parties, functioned mainly as an educational body recruiting some middle-class members to the Labour Party ; the Webbs' direct interest in it diminished correspondingly, and they made little active effort (as they had done in pre-war years) to bring young intellectuals into contact with it.

All these tendencies were greatly accelerated during the following decade. After the first few enthusiastic months, the second Labour Government (1929–31), began to cause acute disquiet among its most active Socialist supporters ; the diminishing I.L.P. made a quasi-Opposition inside the Party, and many other Labour supporters were seriously discontented. But neither the Webbs, nor the Fabian Society with Sidney on its Executive Committee, could canalise this discontent into effective channels, since Sidney was Colonial Secretary in the Labour Government.[1] As a matter of history, both Beatrice and Sidney were all this time steadily losing faith in the prospects of democratic Socialism in Britain ; even before the ignominious fall of MacDonald's second government Beatrice was interesting herself more in the " Socialist Sixth of the World " ; and almost immediately afterwards they both began to prepare themselves for the tour of the Soviet Union which resulted in the production of *Soviet Communism*, the most enormous political guide-book which has ever been published. The effect of their defection, and of the change in political interest and affiliation, may be judged from the fact that between 1930 and 1939 the Fabian Society, abandoned by its leaders and by most of its rank-and-file, produced only seventeen tracts and pamphlets, of which the last was appropriately titled *Our Ageing Population*. There was, it is true, an annual Fabian Summer School, attended year by year by much the same faces ; there were the Fabian Lectures, collecting at the Kingsway Hall a crowd which paid to listen to Bernard Shaw ; there were some book-boxes of outmoded works on economics, etc., somnolently circulating ; and that was all.

The Fabian Society itself was in the doldrums. But the Fabian tradition was vigorously alive. It was in the early months of 1931 that the efforts of C. R. Attlee, Stafford Cripps, G. D. H. and

[1]See Chapter XIII.

Margaret Cole, and others, resulted in the foundation of the New Fabian Research Bureau, whose General Secretary I became in 1933. The purpose of the N.F.R.B. was to revive the old Fabian tradition of hard thinking and respect for facts under modern conditions ; the Webbs played no part in its foundation, though they, along with Arthur Henderson, Secretary of the Labour Party, gave it their official blessing at its inauguration.

The point to grasp is that it was the N.F.R.B., staffed by a group of eager young Socialist thinkers (many of whom had received their Socialist baptism in the very practical test of the 1926 General Strike), which carried on the Fabian tradition during the thirties, and not the Fabian Society. The men and women who staffed the N.F.R.B. and its committees realised only too clearly that the lead given in *Labour and the New Social Order* had never been effectively followed up, that it was imperative to work out anew, and in detail, Socialist plans adapted to the changing conditions of the post-war world. The disastrous last months of the second Labour Government showed only too clearly the clamant need for the work of the new body—very tiny at the moment, but including in its membership most of those who were really prepared to put in long hours of hard unpaid work thinking out the new approaches to the new problems.

As the N.F.R.B. got into its stride, the Webbs began to show a kindly interest in its work. Having now retired from active political life to settle in the country at Passfield Corner and being preoccupied with Soviet Russia, their interest was at first intermittent. Perhaps also their experience in the nineteen-ten's made them a little chary of trying to influence yet another younger generation ! I well remember, however, a surprise descent of Beatrice upon the small N.F.R.B. office one day in 1934, soon after I had become General Secretary, to find out exactly what the Bureau was up to. She not only insisted on discussing all the research projects which the N.F.R.B. then had in hand, but she cross-examined all the members of the small staff as to what they did and wanted to know all about the active voluntary research workers. No doubt she encouraged her favourite nephew— Stafford Cripps—in the interest he then took in the work of the N.F.R.B. Certainly she was pleased when his son, John Cripps, put in a year's work as its Assistant Secretary (1935–6).

N.F.R.B., however, was for a long time a very small, though hand-picked organisation. In 1933 it had only 130 members, though these members, following the Fabian tradition of the 1880s, almost all played a perceptible individual part in its work. During the ensuing years the membership increased gradually, up to about 800 in the last months of 1938. It was then suggested that we should amalgamate with the older Fabian Society, whose General Secretary (F. W. Galton) was on the point of retiring. This idea commended itself both to the Webbs and to Alderman Emil Davies, Treasurer of the Fabian Society, who had just succeeded in liquidating the debt of the latter ; and Beatrice was particularly keen on it. The influence of herself and Sidney weighed a great deal in persuading the members of the then Fabian Executive Committee to vote in favour of the amalgamation.

Negotiations were drawn out during 1938, and a final meeting of two sub-committees to consider the amalgamation proposals was held on the afternoon of 26th September, when the Munich crisis was at its height. How Beatrice laughed at the account I gave her of the speed with which they reached agreement under pressure of outside events. Once agreement had been ratified by special meetings of both organisations, she held a lunch party at the London School of Economics, at which Shaw, Pease, Emil Davies and Galton met the Coles, E. F. M. Durbin, Hugh Gaitskell, W. A. Robson, and the leading members of the N.F.R.B. Executive. With her usual attention to detail Beatrice had herself planned Shaw's vegetarian lunch. Healths were drunk to those who had rendered long service to the old Fabian Society. These included Edward R. Pease, one of the founder members of the Society who, on his retirement at the end of 1938, had terminated a period of fifty-five years as Secretary, Hon. Secretary, and E.C. member of the Society, and E. J. Howell, the retiring bookshop manager who had served the Society forty-nine years as man and boy.

Early in the Second World War, soon after the amalgamation had been completed, Beatrice called at the Fabian office to find out what changes had resulted. Once more the staff was put through a detailed cross-examination as to the Society's work. She insisted on my going down the rather dark stairs from my office at 11 Dartmouth Street, Westminster, in front of her. Luckily I did so, for she tripped and fell and I caught her in my arms, amazed to find how light was this rather terrifying old lady. To assist the amalgamation Beatrice accepted for a couple of years the position of President of the Fabian Society. This was indeed a revolution, as the Society had had neither President nor permanent Chairman before. In fact the chair at meetings, both of its Executive and various other Committees, had been taken in rotation. Between 1939 and her resignation as President in 1941, less than two years before her death, Beatrice continued to take an active interest in the Society's growing research work.

Increasing age and the "blitz" made it more and more difficult for her to come to London. She made a practice, therefore, of sometimes inviting the General Secretary or officers of the Society to visit Passfield Corner for a talk, or else asked leading members of the Fabian Summer School over for a short visit from Frensham Heights. I remember on one occasion receiving a special summons to come and tell her about everything happening in Parliament— and particularly in the Parliamentary Party. What were the younger members of the Party—and of the Fabian Society— thinking? Having thought out the answers, I arrived at Passfield Corner to be greeted with the remark " Sidney and I are very anxious to know what the younger members of the Party are thinking." She then sat down on the fire curb facing me with her back to the fire and told me for the space of two hours what the younger generation ought to think—particularly about the Soviet Union! I hardly had a chance to get a word in edgeways. As I left she remarked, " I am so glad you were able to come. Sidney and I are very anxious to know what the younger members of the Party are thinking."

The last time I saw her, a few months before she died, Sidney had recovered remarkably well from a stroke and seemed in full possession of his faculties, although he found speech difficult. Beatrice said that he was perfectly happy as he was fully occupied with reading. She was obtaining for him fifteen books a fortnight from the London Library and he was enjoying himself reading Trollope, Thackeray and all the novelists he had never had time to read when he was a young man. She saw nothing surprising in the fact that he got through more than one book a day ! She

BEATRICE WEBB AT PASSFIELD CORNER, JUNE, 1939

BERNARD SHAW, PHOTOGRAPHED FOR THE FABIAN SOCIETY

was anxious to know exactly what powers the Government had taken for cutting down trees during the war. On being told, she insisted on visiting a small piece of woodland belonging to the Webbs which adjoined the house and, fondly regarding some young oak trees, stated firmly, " They are not going to cut down any of my trees ! " She had obtained a silk parachute which had come down nearby on their land during a recent raid and insisted on inquiries being made from the Minister concerned as to whether she could keep it for making up into a dress. In the course of the conversation she commented that Sidney still remained a convinced free-thinker whilst she had always been a " believer."

It is impossible to draw a hard and fast line between the work which the Webbs did for the Fabian Society and that which they did on their own or for other organisations with which they were from time to time connected. The work of the Fabian Society, Sidney once remarked, is the work of its individual members. It would certainly be true to say that Webbian and Fabian were even more synonymous than Shavian and Fabian. Wherein then lies the distinctive character which the Webbs more than anyone else gave to the meaning of the word " Fabian " and which they would have claimed showed itself in all their written work and generally in their political activities ?

It has frequently been stated that the term " Fabian " refers to a particular policy. When I was an undergraduate in the late nineteen-twenties Left-wingers hurled " Fabian " as a term of abuse at the heads of all they considered weak-hearted believers in the " inevitability of gradualness." Yet in the early days of the Society it had adopted as its motto " For the right moment you must wait as Fabius did, but when the time comes you must strike hard or your waiting will be in vain and fruitless." Founded in reaction against the very frothy revolutionary Socialism of the eighteen-eighties, the Fabian Society insisted on the need for working out practical schemes for applying Socialist ideas to particular problems that had to be faced. During its early days the Society laid down certain essential points of belief summarised for many years in a document called " The Basis " and subsequently modified and incorporated in the Society's rules after the amalgamation with the New Fabian Research Bureau in 1939.

I

Apart from these basic beliefs members of the Fabian Society have always been left to hold whatever views they liked on particular questions, and the Society has frequently published work by individual members or committees which represented the authors' views without in any way binding other members of the Society. This policy has enabled the Society to carry on its important work of thinking out suggestions for dealing with difficult problems from a Socialist standpoint and putting these ideas before the politically minded public in general and the Labour Movement in particular so as to influence both Government action and Party policy. It is true to say that without this wide freedom to differ within its ranks the Fabian Society could not have made its distinctive contribution to British political thought.

The Webbs always supported this general view of the work of the Fabian Society and its members. Nevertheless, it would be true to say that the influence of the Webbs and of Shaw upon their fellow members for many years was so great that the greater part of the work published by the Society was closely in line with their views ; this was largely due to the Society's method of working in early days. When *Fabian Essays* was edited by Bernard Shaw, he was not content to leave it as a collection of individual essays by separate authors. The contribution of each writer was fully discussed with the other contributors and largely reshaped and rewritten to meet their criticisms, which in the case of the Editor were frequently very extensive and forthright. *Fabian Essays*, therefore, had a real unity, which collective volumes rarely have, due to the fact that its authors were expressing their common point of view. There is no doubt that it owed a very large part of the influence it has had on political thought to this unity, and the same system of intensive discussion was applied to many other early publications. Thus, whilst it would be wrong to say that there was a distinctive Fabian policy save on certain essentials, the work of the Society for many years had such a strong element of unity that there was a great deal, in fact, to justify the common view of " Fabian " policy.

It is however true to say that there has always been a definite Fabian approach to political questions. The Webbs and their critics in the Society alike always insisted upon the need for thorough and accurate research. Propaganda and Socialist education have always been an essential part of the Fabian Society's work. They have, however, been based on factual research in the first instance. The Society, like the Webbs, has always taken a very strong stand against the prostitution of research in order to establish points of view already held before the research was started ; and its reputation both during their heyday and since depends in the main on the extent to which it has stood by its first principles.

In the more restricted field of the general trend of opinion of the majority in the Fabian Society at any particular time the Webbs' influence was also profound. For example, the *Minority Report* on the Poor Law (1909) was the work of the Webbs ; but it won general support in the Society, whose members threw themselves enthusiastically behind the campaign for breaking up the Poor Law. The 1918 programme of the Labour Party, *Labour and the New Social Order*, was written by Sidney Webb. It has frequently been described as a Fabian programme and certainly would have commanded general agreement among members at that time. In fact, the Webbs, like other active members of the Society since, first circulated their ideas among other interested members of the Society, for they found criticism to be frequently very helpful ; they then sought to put their ideas across in the wider political world.

In the late Victorian and Edwardian worlds the most effective method of getting ideas across was the dinner party and there important political figures and Civil Servants could be got together for friendly discussion. In this the Webbs were past-masters.[1] Even at that period, however, there was a larger interested public, apart from the " high-ups " of the London political world. The Fabian pamphlet has always been written to appeal to the limited public generally interested in some particular problem. In appealing to all those who were actively politically minded the Society in the long run has had a bigger influence than by direct approach to the great, although the Webbs by that method sometimes achieved spectacular successes. A gradual moulding of opinion within the Trade Unions and the Labour Party on Socialist lines was in the main achieved by this wider form of permeation. The Webbs, however, for a long time sought to influence all the main political forces of the country and were

[1]See Chapter V.

only gradually driven to recognise that the main changes which
the building of a Socialist Society would entail could only be
carried out by a Party, such as the Labour Party became in 1918,
which was fully pledged to a Socialist Programme. Their identification then, not only with the Fabian Society, but also with the
Labour Party undoubtedly lessened their influence in other
quarters. Whilst they regretted this, the Webbs realised that it
was an inevitable stage in political development.

Many have wondered how the Webbs reconciled their great
interest in the Soviet Union with their life-long interest in the
Fabian Society. Beatrice Webb once told me that so long as the
Russian Revolution went in for any kind of nonsense like Workers'
Control they had no interest in it. Once Lenin scrapped any
element of Workers' Control in Russia the Webbs began to show
some interest in the great Revolution.[1]

They had had no great love for the British Party system and
tended to look at party politicians from the bureaucratic angle of
the administrator. They genuinely admired the one-party system
in the Soviet Union. Mrs. Webb sent for me on more than one
occasion to discuss the Turkish one-party system which I had
looked into at the time of my visit in 1939. They thought it likely
that the Russian Communist Party might in time allow a diversity
of views such as existed in the then ruling Turkish party.[2] They
strongly argued against my view that the existence of strongly held
diverse political views in Turkey, and possibly later in Russia,
would be bound to lead to the creation of more than one party,
given the free expression of political opinion.

I am inclined to think that the Webbs' enthusiasm for Russia
in the latter part of their life was due in the main to the disillusionment that the two minority Labour Governments, particularly that of 1929–31, had caused. Feeling that there was little prospect in their lifetime of seeing a democratic Socialist Government carrying out the main changes in which they believed, in this
island, it was only natural that they should turn their attention to
the great experiment being made in Eastern Europe, which they
believed was so closely in line with many of the ideas they had
already put forward in the Fabian Society.

[1] See preceding chapter for details.
[2] See *Modern Turkey*, John Parker and Charles Smith (1940).

Their preoccupation with the Soviets, however, did not prevent them from taking a continued and lively interest in the fortunes of the revived Fabian Society—even though Beatrice, at least, sometimes characterised some of its officials as " very reactionary "—because they refused to go all the way with her in support of the U.S.S.R. They recognised, nevertheless, that the new Fabian Society was upholding the old traditions of factual research and freedom of opinion within the four corners of general Socialist conviction. At this point, however, it may not be out of place to mention one or two aspects in which the Fabian Society of today differs, inevitably, from the Fabian Society of previous generations.

In the first place, as the world has developed and the different parts of it became so obviously interdependent, the scope of any Socialist society has correspondingly widened. Once, the Fabian Society could proudly announce that " it has no views upon the Currency,"[1] and for many years its lack of interest in international affairs and foreign policy was the despair of Bernard Shaw and a handful (only a handful) of others ; today no Socialist can possibly disinterest himself in either foreign policy or currency problems. This means that the field of research and propaganda in which the Society must work has been enormously widened, while at the same time the amount of printed and published information with which its writers and speakers must acquaint themselves has increased in more than equal quantity. Gone are the days when the Society could obtain great kudos, and not a little cash, by issuing a penny guide to Workmen's Compensation. Guides of this kind are now issued by Government departments, but the task of the Fabian worker is not thereby lessened ; he has to familiarise himself with the Government (and other) publications and statistics on whatever the subject may be, and from this basic knowledge proceed to the formulation of further suggestions.

Secondly, the amount of *leisure-time* available to the professional and intellectual groups which have always undertaken the major part of Fabian work, whether in London or in the provinces, has substantially decreased. All these groups work longer hours, and are harder pressed by out-of-work commitments, than they used to be in the days when Edward Pease answered inquiries in his own hand and farmed out those he could not answer to members of

[1] *Tract* 70 (1896).

the Executive Committee. Members of the Executive Committee, or of the various research committees, have to be given much longer time than formerly to do the work demanded of them ; in addition, they are liable to require also the services of questionnaires, questionnaire-analysers, clerks and typists, before they can produce any worthwhile result. This in itself makes " Fabian research " in the mid-twentieth century a far more costly affair than it was in the late nineteenth ; we are not the only organisation to experience this difficulty.

Thirdly, the gradual development of the Labour Party from being the only central political organisation representing the working classes to become after 1945 the government of the country, has itself affected the position of any political grouping such as the Fabian Society which works in affiliation to the Party. The Society was a founder-member of the Party, and as such was affiliated to it from 1900 ; but as long as the Party was nothing more than a loose federal organisation of Trade Unions and Socialist Societies, with neither individual membership nor any clearly laid-down policy, the connection affected very slightly the day-to-day working of the Fabian Society. Fabians were to be found in all political parties, and could even stand for Parliament and in municipal elections under all sorts of banners. The 1918 reorganisation, which gave the Labour Party a programme, a nation-wide organisation, and an individual membership, made so wide a political activity impossible to sustain ; after the dis-affiliation of the I.L.P. and the Socialist League it became clear that there was no place in British politics for a body which claimed the right, while remaining within the Labour Party, to pursue a private political programme of its own. Hence the modern " self-denying ordinance " of the Fabian Society (first stated in 1939), under which the Society, *as a Society*, promulgates no policy and mandates no delegates to any conferences or gatherings, but puts forward any suggestions which it may have to make under the names of the individual or group responsible ; hence, too, its refusal to admit into its membership Communists (or others advocating policies in opposition to the Labour Party) or to allow its name to be used, locally or nationally, by those who in one guise or another seek to work up agitation against the Party and against the Labour Government. This, it may be, is a narrowing of the fine freedom of Edwardian days : it is nevertheless necessary in the times in which we live today. " Permeation " has usually come to mean " permeation of the Labour Party " ; and I do not believe that, if the Webbs were living today, they would quarrel with the new meaning. At all events, Beatrice in her Diary described the N.F.R.B. as " a most helpful venture " ; and almost her last published writing was a leader for *Fabian News* which ended with the words " Long Live the Fabian Society." In the six years since her death, during which the membership of the Society, and of its local Societies, has greatly increased, we have tried our best to live up to the standards set by the founders.

POLITICAL THOUGHT AND THE WEBBS

by

LEONARD WOOLF

ɪ*

XVI

POLITICAL THOUGHT AND THE WEBBS

by LEONARD WOOLF

The political thought of the Webbs is contained in twenty volumes, which they wrote in combination, in two volumes of autobiography and *The Co-operative Movement in Great Britain* by Beatrice, and in two books by Sidney. Their major works are :

1. *The History of Trade Unionism*, published in 1894, and *Industrial Democracy*, published in 1897, in which they related the history and analysed the structure and functions of trade unions.

2. *English Local Government.* This is an " analytic and historical description of the structure and functions of English Local Government " (to quote their own words) in ten volumes. They began this work in 1899, published the first volume in 1906 and the last in 1929.

3. *The Consumers' Co-operative Movement.* This is an analysis of the history, structure, and functions of the Co-operative Movement. It was published in 1921.

4. *A Constitution for the Socialist Commonwealth of Great Britain.* To quote the authors, this is " not only a critical examination of the existing machinery of government and industrial organisation of the nation, but also a carefully worked-out scheme applying the principles of socialism in a practicable reorganisation of British industry and government, in all its phases and at all grades." It was published in 1920.

5. *Soviet Communism : A New Civilisation.* The first ten chapters and 943 pages of this work contain a description of the structure and functions of the social organisation of the U.S.S.R. The last two chapters and 170 pages deal with the philosophy and objects of the Communist leaders and the kind of society and life which the new system is producing. The book was published in

1935 ; two years later the Webbs published a second edition, substantially the same as the first, but with a postscript in which they expressed a conviction that Soviet Communism was producing a new civilisation.

6. *My Apprenticeship* and *Our Partnership* by Beatrice Webb. These two books of autobiography, the first published in 1926 and the second posthumously in 1948, are essential to an understanding of the objects, method, and effect of the Webbs' political thought.

It will be observed that in nearly every case in which one attempts shortly to state the contents of this immense output, these twenty-five formidable volumes, one has to say that their subject is the history, structure, and functions of some kind of social organisation. The Webbs themselves use the words again and again to describe the object of their work or the subject of their studies. The words are the key to the whole philosophy of their life and thought. What interested them and what they thought important was social organisation, the forms which it had taken and might take, the functions which it had performed and might perform. They regarded themselves as scientists, social scientists. Just as the biologist studied the living organism, so they studied the social organisation. Historical research, analysis and synthesis, enabled them to trace the origin and development of various organisations, like the trade union or the parish council, to classify them in their appropriate genera and species, to describe their structure and functions. The " scientific investigator," Beatrice wrote, is " concerned essentially to discover the truth about the working or development of a particular type of economic or political organisation." And she described their motives and method thus :

" Like other scientists, we were obsessed by scientific curiosity about the universe and its working. But, unlike the astronomers and the physicists, the chemists and the biologists, we turned our curiosity to the phenomena that were being less frequently investigated, namely, those connected with the social institutions characteristic of *homo sapiens*, or what is called sociology. We accordingly devoted ourselves as scientists to the study of social institutions, from trade unions to Cabinets, from family relationships to churches, from economics to literature—

a field in itself so extensive that we have never been able to compass more than a few selected fragments of it." [1]

And in the preface to the final volume of their great work on local government, looking back over the thirty years of their labours, they gave this description of their object and achievement :

" With the publication of these two volumes we bring to an end a task on which we have been engaged since 1899, the analytic and historical description of the structure and functions of English Local Government. Like our works on Trade Unionism and the Consumers' Co-operative Movement, though on a larger scale, these ten volumes are studies of the structure and functions, in origin, growth, and development, of particular social institutions. Such an analytic history of social institutions seems to us to stand, in relation to Political Science, in much the same position as Applied Mechanics stand to Theoretical Mechanics ; or a treatise on Mines or Bridges stands to Geology, Chemistry and Mechanics. Beside Economic or Political Science, as commonly understood, there is room for a detailed study of the form and life-history of the social institutions in which the theoretic conceptions are actually manifested. There seems at least as good a claim for exact and minute examination and description of the structure and functions, during a chosen period, and in a given country, of such a social institution as Local Government, as there is for the like study of a particular species of the animal world. As the one exemplifies and corrects our Biology, so the other may illustrate and refine our Political Science." [2]

The Webbs, it will be seen, unlike many political thinkers, knew exactly what they wanted to do and what they were doing. In the sphere chosen, and largely discovered by them, their achievement was tremendous and their influence upon the theory and practice of politics immense. It is doubtful whether many people have read the ten massive volumes on local government and it is said that even students find *The History of Trade Unionism* unreadable, but the attitude to society and politics of everyone who thinks seriously about those subjects has been profoundly affected by those works. No one before the Webbs had devoted to such social

[1]*Our Partnership*, p. 16.
[2]*English Local Government. English Poor Law History*, Part II, Vol. I, p. vii.

institutions as trade unions and local government intensive analytical study based upon the scientific collection and classification of vast numbers of facts. Their claim that they were applying the methods of science to the framework of human society was, with certain reservations, justified. Our knowledge of the institutions which they studied became for the first time, through their work, scientific. This had effects of great significance.

The first effect was upon the methods of political or social thought. No one after the Webbs could ignore the profound influence of social institutions and organisations, the impact of their structure and functions, upon human life. Most of their successors have been so completely permeated by their method of thought that they do not realise that their minds have been politically processed by the Webbs. It has been pointed out that the Webbs, in their investigations, did not merely analyse and dissect the trade unions and organs of local government, they actually discovered them.[1] This is literally true, and it is almost true that they not only discovered, but invented them. Neither governments, nor civil servants, nor politicians, nor trade unionists themselves understood, before the publication of *The History of Trade Unionism* and *Industrial Democracy*, what the form of the trade union movement was, what it had achieved, and what its functions had been and might be. The political thinker had been no less ignorant; he had indeed never regarded such organisations as functional institutions whose morphology and physiology were the proper study of mankind. Sociologists, since the time of Plato and Aristotle, had recognised and analysed certain forms of government, like monarchy and democracy, but they regarded them as the static products of human history. The Webbs taught us to regard all social institutions as the natural genera and species of communal life, to study their dynamic history, and to classify them according to the functions which they performed. The mere fact that the trade union or the Rural District Council was given this dynamic status altered its nature. This new status and nature of the institution was the Webbs' discovery. It altered the whole complexion of political thought, at any rate in Britain, for the theorist and the

[1] See *The Webbs and their Work*, by Donald G. Macrae in the *Political Quarterly*, January–March, 1948.

statesman adopted the Webbs' axiom that the structure of social institutions was of primary importance in political theory and practice and that if you made up your mind what the function of an organisation should be, all that was necessary was to create the appropriate structure.

We are all, however bright or dull our minds may be, psychologically the products of our age or environment. The minds of the Webbs were extraordinarily bright, but they were conditioned and polished by the age into which they were born. It was the scientific age. Sidney was born in the same year as *The Origin of Species* and Beatrice only twelve months before. As a young woman she came under the personal influence of that eccentric philosopher and sociologist, Herbert Spencer, who wrote enormous volumes of fairy tales in the mistaken belief that he was applying scientific method to the interpretation and explanation of every department of human life. Beatrice was much too intelligent not to see eventually the absurdities in Herbert Spencer and his system, but she remained in part profoundly influenced by him. He himself was both cause and effect in the communal psychology of the last half of the nineteenth century. It was characteristic of that psychology to believe in the efficacy of science. It was, therefore, natural, indeed inevitable, that sooner or later some one should apply to Cabinets, trade unions, and parish councils the methods which had revealed so much about rocks, apes, and earthworms.

The *Zeitgeist* helped the Webbs to find the subject as well as the method of their investigations. The last half of the nineteenth century was perhaps the first period in human history in which the machinery of human life became more powerful and more important than life itself.[1] Hitherto social organisation and institutions had been almost always primitive and simple, and usually inadequate for the life which people were actually leading. At no time, except perhaps under the Roman Empire and in China, was there any real danger of people, including the ruling classes (a crucial point), becoming slaves to the machinery of life and government. But that was precisely what was taking place

[1] I am talking about civilised peoples since say 1000 B.C. Prehistoric man, primitive peoples, and savages have usually become the slaves of their own institutions and social beliefs, but the process is quite different from the one which I am here considering.

when the Webbs turned their scientific eye upon human society. It was that period of economic revolution in which the earlier individualist stage of capitalism was making way for the later stage which has been called monopoly capitalism. This meant the organisation of industry, commerce, and finance in very large, powerful units requiring an elaborate machinery for operating and often for regulating their relations with one another. Though the captains of industry and finance who controlled the factories and banks and worked this system were nominally inflexible adherents of unadulterated *laissez-faire*, they were themselves creating conditions in which *laissez-faire* would have made not only their own activities, but life itself impossible. Hence the growth of organisation, both intensive and extensive, in the sacred citadel of capitalism was inevitably accompanied by the same kind of growth in every nook and cranny of society. Everywhere—and not least in Government departments—every day and in every way the organisation, the regulation, the institution became bigger and better. New organs of organisation with new functions and new structures sprang into existence, while even the most ancient of institutions, like the parish council, suddenly found itself given by Act of Parliament a new status and powers.

It was therefore not unnatural that the Webbs, when they decided that society or sociology was the right object of scientific study, should have immediately been attracted by this new and gigantic phenomenon, this pullulation of organisations and institutions, continually increasing in size or extending the tentacles of their control over new spheres of life. The phenomenon itself was to a very large extent chaotic, and in urgent need of scientific investigation and treatment. The Webbs were pioneers in the work of investigation, but they were not merely scientific researchers into the morphology and pathology of society and its institutions, they were also, at the same time and all the time, intensely interested in clinical treatment, in the practical problems of how to make the institutions work efficiently—in fact, they were practical politicians as well as social scientists.

This dichotomy in their interest and work had a great effect upon their political thought and its influence. The period of their greatest activity was a time in which facts and events were making individualism impossible in one department after another of human life, in which communal control of or interference in, not merely the economic, but a vast number of the non-economic activities of man was inevitable. Socialism is a convenient name to describe the process, though it should perhaps properly be limited to the process operating upon the economic system. The significance of the often quoted remark of Sir William Harcourt— one of those Liberals whose profound conservatism has done so much to destroy European civilisation—" We are all Socialists today " is that at the end of the nineteenth century even the most rigid opponents of socialism recognised that socialism was essential to the efficient working of modern society and for the extension and consolidation of modern civilisation and that all that they could do was to obstruct the necessary socialist evolution until they themselves were dead or, still better, until it was too late even for socialism to be effective. These Liberals were largely successful ; unfortunately for those who survived them the corollary of their success has been two world wars, fascism, and communism.

The Webbs were, as Beatrice saw, temperamentally Conservative, but they took exactly the opposite view to Sir William Harcourt. This is not really surprising. It is the Conservative-Liberal who has a blind hatred of socialism and who destroys liberalism rather than admit socialism ; there is in socialism nothing inherently antagonistic to the Liberal-Conservative. The Webbs saw the necessity, the inevitability of socialism. What is more they liked the idea of it. They were not interested in, because they were not moved by, the larger and vaguer political and social ideas. They mistrusted ideals, and still more the idealists. They would have claimed to be intellectually upon the side of democracy, liberty, and equality, but they had no enthusiasm for that kind of thing and seemed to treat all such ideas as words which might at the appropriate time be used to induce people to organise society in the way in which the Webbs considered that it should be organised. The work of the Webbs as social scientists was inextricably entangled with and profoundly affected by their work and objects as practical politicians. For years Sidney spent an enormous amount of his time manœuvring in the London County Council ; Beatrice's long struggle on the Poor Law Commission is an epic story of practical politics ; all through the long years of their astonishing mental activity they were perpetually pulling strings and weaving their webs in order to get a Bill passed or rejected, to lure a Minister from one path into another, to " condition " the mind of some one who had the power to do or not to do something. They knew exactly what they wanted. They were convinced of the desirability and inevitability of what they called socialism. This, they thought, required the scientific planning of social life ; the adaptation of the structure of social institutions, both public and private, to the functions which the social plan required ; the training of a political élite who would be capable of running the machine efficiently and intelligently ; the education of the " ordinary " individual citizen so that he could be fitted squarely and fairly into an appropriate place in the social, but primarily economic, machine.

These were the objects which the Webbs consciously placed before themselves as practical politicians. They constantly pursued them with the greatest energy and pertinacity, and on the whole with very considerable success. They themselves made a clear distinction between their work as practical politicians and their work as writers of social science, and Beatrice, as her autobiography shows, was often torn between the two, doubtful whether it would not be both wiser and pleasanter to give up all the manœuvring and wire-pulling and devote themselves entirely to research and social science. This is a point which it is essential to be clear and frank about if one is to understand the Webbs and their minds and work. Their politics and political actions were directly determined by their political theory, but their politics had a reciprocal—and often unfortunate—effect upon their political thought. No one who knew and worked with them could fail to recognise and admire their complete personal disinterestedness ; I have never known any one less " on the make " or with greater personal integrity than they were. This applied to their own personal interests and to the ends which they were convinced were desirable. But they were so certain of the rightness of the ends which they were pursuing that they did not worry very much about the means which they used to attain them. The first time I worked closely with Sidney I was puzzled and troubled by this extraordinary mixture of scrupulousness with regard to ends and an almost ingenuous unscrupulousness with regard to means.

All this had a great, and by no means simple, effect upon their politics, their political thought, and upon their influence as thinkers. Beatrice liked to say that they both had second-rate minds, but that they were powerful in combination because complementary. There was a good deal of truth in this. Their integrity and unscrupulousness, the clearness with which they saw their limited objectives, the pertinacity or even ruthlessness with which they pursued them, the extraordinary quickness and subtlety of Sidney's mind when applied to administration or the day to day politics of bills, clauses, and committees made them a very formidable combination. Their influence upon the Labour Party, the trade unions, and the co-operative movement was immense, but it was not limited to the " Labour " side of British politics ; it permeated the Conservative and Liberal parties, the machinery of local government, and not least the higher ranks of the Civil Service. Their effect upon social evolution in the twentieth century was as powerful as Bentham's had been in the nineteenth.

Their ruthless concentration upon a limited field of human life and a curious habit of open-minded dogmatism gave to their thought and influence a dangerous narrowness, which showed itself in many different ways. I have said above that their politics had a reciprocal effect upon their political thought. It had a narrowing effect. They were entirely honest researchers and social scientists ; they would never have manipulated facts in their books in order to support the practical policies which they were sedulously pursuing in the L.C.C., the Poor Law Commission, or the sitting-room in Grosvenor Road. Yet to a great extent they regarded the object of their research work and books, even the ten volumes on local government, to be to provide them with material for permeating and persuading practical men to do what the Webbs thought ought to be done or for blowing them up if they refused to be permeated or persuaded. This had a narrowing effect upon their minds and thought and encouraged the open-minded dogmatism which was perhaps natural to them. It was easier to feel than to describe this apparently contradictory, but really logical, mental habit of theirs. If you talked to them about any subject, your first impression was that they were the most open-minded people imaginable. And so they were ; that is to say, they would give serious consideration to any statement, however wild or foolish, which you might make and to any objection which you might make to their statements or arguments. But the more intimately you knew them, the clearer it became that, though the open-mindedness was a very real thing, it was superimposed upon a rigid dogmatism which frequently made it completely ineffective. They had drawn for themselves a circle which enclosed certain subjects and departments of human life. Those subjects were *their* subjects ; they studied them closely and continually ; they had a theory and a policy with regard to them ; there were certain things which they wanted done with regard to them. They were open to consider attentively any view or argument bearing upon their subjects. But though they would consider objectively and attentively anything which you might say to them, nothing which you said could penetrate or affect the kernel of their dogmatic beliefs. Suddenly one realised that they were so strongly convinced of the soundness of their central beliefs that the consideration of any fact or argument conflicting with them was purely formal and that their combined brain was being unconsciously used as a powerful instrument for by-passing inconvenient truths. This process applied to " their subjects." Anything outside the circumference of their circle was treated differently. It belonged to a " subject " which was not theirs. Their opinion upon it was therefore irrelevant, and in some way or other the subject itself was irrelevant. They would discuss it intelligently, soberly, and seriously, as they would any subject, but in the end one was left with the impression that the subject itself was not a serious one.

The circumference of this circle which they had drawn in their own minds was a rigid barrier in their political thought, and in combination with some of the other mental characteristics to which I have referred above it accounted for some of the curious gaps in their minds. It is a remarkable fact that, although they spent the whole of their long lives upon the theory and practice of politics, devoting their great intellectual gifts to investigating the causes of what was good and bad in modern society and to the practical job of encouraging what was good and preventing what was bad, they paid no attention to two of the major problems of modern society, the problem of imperialism and the problem of war and peace. What interested them, as I have said, was social organisation, and they believed that, if you knew the kind of society which you wanted, you could get it by constructing the appropriate institutions and framework of government. Graham Wallas said that they were interested in town councils, whereas he was interested in town councillors. But there was more to it than that. They were concerned with the structure and functions of government, not with individuals, and therefore neither with the rulers nor the ruled. They were both exceptionally humane and civilised people and their object was to produce a civilised society, but they were doctrinaires and their doctrine led them to concentrate their attention almost exclusively upon the structure and functions of government and institutions.

The problems of imperialism, international relations, and war and peace cannot very easily be stated in terms of the structure and functions of institutions or reduced to mere questions of organisation. They have been the major causes of disorder, misery, and evil in the world for the last 100 years and they have made the orderly and civilised life for which the Webbs worked so devotedly impossible. They cannot be reduced to the terms of the Webbs' doctrine of structure and function, because in the very heart of them are blind passions and obstinate beliefs, the ideas and ideals of ordinary individuals. No doubt questions of organisation and government enter into them, but they have to be considered in terms of passion, fear, hatred ; the passion for power ; the belief in democracy or liberty or equality ; the ideas, ideals, delusions of nationalism and nationality. The problem which confronted us in India or South Africa, the international situation which caused the war of 1914, the phenomenon of fascism and Adolf Hitler cannot be investigated by the methods which the Webbs applied to trade unions and town councils and cannot be covered by any formula limited to social organisation.

The result was that the Webbs were not really interested in them, and, as they were outside the circumference of their circle, they were not included among *their* subjects. The first time that I ever worked closely with them was in fact on one of these subjects —in 1915 on war and peace. It is significant that it was only when the possibility of some kind of League of Nations began to be discussed, when the problem of the form of international government appeared, that they became interested in it. They asked me to write a book for the Fabian Society on international government, and, on the basis of my investigation, to work out with Sidney a draft constitution of an international organisation for preventing war. I admired enormously Sidney's mastery and ingenuity in everything connected with the intricate and often delicate task of fitting the League's structure to its appropriate functions, but I was also amazed at his lack of interest in any of the larger issues, which were not connected with organisation alone, but must have a profound influence upon the maintenance of peace, e.g., sovereignty. In dealing with sovereignty, you had to allow for psychology as well as organisation; psychology was not one of Sidney's "subjects"; it had therefore to be ignored.

The same causes produced other limitations in their thought and sympathies. Their conversion in old age to Marxian socialism and their admiration of the Soviet system followed logically from their fundamental social philosophy, their belief in the overwhelming importance of social structure and function. Marxian socialism or modern communism is the *ne plus ultra* of such a philosophy. In their earlier days the Webbs had never been interested in pure Marxianism, mainly because their minds and methods were typically British; the abstract, Talmudic argumentation of the true believers was antipathetic to them, and they believed that all the advantages of a planned economy and organised society could be obtained in Britain by the gradual transition from capitalism to socialism; the transition would be accomplished by a series of *ad hoc* hops and compromises, directed by the Webbs and the Fabian Society. Their change of view was due to two facts: first, their conviction that the change might be too gradual, that in many parts of Europe the sands were rapidly running out, and that a revolutionary reorganisation of society on socialist lines was the only alternative to chaos. Secondly, the Webbs were always realists, and they saw in Soviet communism not a theory, but a reality. Here was an organised society, a socialist society, based upon a conscious adaptation of the structure of institutions to their required functions, of the kind which they had always believed in and dreamt of. Naturally they were intensely interested in its organisation and welcomed it as a new form of civilisation. The fact that they condoned, or at least found excuses for, the Soviet "purges," the labour camps, the suppression and regimentation of opinion, the denial of freedom of thought, freedom of speech, and freedom of the press, in fact all the paraphernalia of modern authoritarianism and of the police state, shocked many people. This curious gap in their social conscience or consciousness was not due to any inhumanity or even insensitiveness, but to their doctrinairism and the consequent narrowness of their vision when they observed human society. It was the government, not the governed ; the Soviet system, not the Soviet citizen ; the machinery, not the psychology of civilisation, with which they were concerned. The idea of liberty and all large, vague political ideas and ideals (except, perhaps, those connected with equality) which have stirred men's communal emotions since the Athenians fought at Marathon and Pericles showed his fellow-citizens how free men should live in a free city, meant very little to them. They were convinced that if the machinery of society was properly constructed and controlled efficiently by intelligent people, if the functions of the various parts of the organisation were scientifically determined and the structure scientifically adapted to the functions, if the round pegs were then fitted into the round holes and the square pegs into the square holes, then we should get an adequately civilised society in which we should all be adequately healthy, wealthy, and wise.

It would be wrong and misleading to end this short analysis of the Webbs' political thought upon a critical note and in a minor key. The narrowness of their outlook was a very real thing, and in estimating their achievement and influence it is essential to deal candidly with it. But they were not the narrow and rather inhuman characters which many people who did not know them well assumed them to be. They were two very remarkable individuals ; as they became older, they developed the kind of eccentricity which is characteristically British ; they exaggerated and humourously caricatured themselves. It was impossible, if one knew them, not to feel for them great affection as well as admiration. As for their achievement, it was tremendous. They discovered and explored a whole new province of vital importance in sociology, and their influence upon politics and political thought was so extensive and profound that many of those who belittle them are unaware of what in fact they owe to the Webbs. They were specialists, and like nearly all great specialists, they had to narrow the range of their vision. That accounts for the limitations and holes in their political thought to which I have had to draw attention. Darwin had to forego and atrophy his appreciation of music in order to concentrate all his attention upon apes and earthworms, and we owe *The Origin of Species*, in part, to this sacrifice. The Webbs devoted to the study of social institutions the same kind of unremitting concentration ; they made similar sacrifices, and their achievement is not unworthy to rank with those of other great scientists.

BEATRICE WEBB AS AN ECONOMIST

by

G. D. H. COLE

XVII

BEATRICE WEBB AS AN ECONOMIST[1]

by G. D. H. COLE

In one sense, Beatrice Webb was not an economist at all ; for she denied entirely the value of any "self-contained, separate, abstract Political Economy." She was in fact a sociologist, and concerned herself with economics only as a branch of sociology. In the 1880's, while she was still feeling her way towards her life's work, she spent much time and effort on the study of both classical and Marxian economics, and came to the conclusion, which she never found cause to retract, that they were alike fundamentally, unrealistic and wrong in their approach to the study of social facts. At that time, when Socialism was just reviving in Great Britain after its long sleep, a vigorous controversy was being raged between the adherents of classical economics, mainly after the schools of Mill and Jevons, and Marxism, which was still known in this country mainly through highly simplified abridgments and expositions of Marx's works. The neo-classical economics of Marshall were just being born : the Austrians were very little known ; and most students of Marxism stopped short at the first few chapters of Volume I of *Capital*, which alone were available in an English translation. The Fabians had not yet formulated their own socialistic version of the utilitarian economic doctrine derived from Jevons rather than from Marx : they were feeling their way slowly towards this new formulation, and Bernard Shaw in particular was greatly under the spell of Marxism, as appeared in his famous controversies with P. H. Wicksteed. This was the atmosphere in which Beatrice Webb wrote, in the middle 'eighties, a series of notes " On the Nature of Economic Science " ; and the gist of these unpublished memoranda is given in an appendix to *My Apprenticeship*. " I see few advantages, and many disadvantages, in collecting together all the activities concerned with the production and consumption of wealth, in all the various stages of

[1] Adapted by permission from a paper written for the Royal Economic Society.

social evolution, and in all the different varieties of social organisation by which this function is performed ; and in making this object or purpose the subject of a self-contained science styled Political Economy, apart from the study of human behaviour in society—that is to say, of social institutions, or Sociology." And again, " Political Economy, as professed and taught, deals with only one of many social institutions engaged in or concerned with wealth production ; and it is misleading to ignore those other social institutions by which wealth has been, and is now being produced among hundreds of millions of people unacquainted with the ' big business ' or profit-making capitalism, for which Ricardo sought to formulate the ' laws ' that his successors have been, during the past century, so diligently refining and elaborating."

This frontal attack on abstract, deductive economics leads straight on, in Beatrice Webb's notes, to a constructive formulation of the tasks which, she considers, the student of social questions ought to attempt. " What need to be studied are social institutions themselves, as they actually exist or have existed, whatever may be the motive attributed to the men and women concerned ; and whatever may be the assumed object or purpose with which these institutions are established or maintained . . . The study of profit-making capitalism or modern business organisation would take its place alongside the separate studies of other social institutions, such as the family ; consumers' co-operation ; the vocational organisations of the various kinds of producers ; local government ; the State (or political organisation) ; international relations ; the intellectual, aesthetic and religious interests of man, and possibly a host of other departments of what can only be regarded (and may one day be unified) as Sociology."

Beatrice Webb went on to write that this view would involve an abandonment of the abstract, deductive method, " without the possibility of precise verification of its inferences, which Ricardo's authority imposed on successive generations of British economists." It would imply a very different method. " Whether competitive profit-making or capitalism promotes greed and oppression, and depresses public spirit—like the analogous accusations that State employment favours slackness and lessens initiative, and that vocational organisation favours exclusiveness and stale technique —*are all alike questions to be investigated*. ' By their fruits ye shall know them '—I would add, more especially by the spiritual fruits, i.e., by the characteristic state of mind which any particular institution brings about in the individual and in the community, the character which it produces, as manifested in the conduct of individuals and organisations."

Then, further on, " A necessary implication of this new classification would be that what would have to be investigated, described and analysed are the social institutions themselves, as they exist or have existed, not any assumed ' laws,' unchanging and ubiquitous, comparable with the law of gravity, any failure of correspondence with the facts being dismissed as fiction. A second corollary is that these social institutions, like other organic structures, have to be studied, not in any assumed perfection of development, but in all the changing phases of growing social tissue, from embryo to corpse, in health and perversion, in short, as the birth, growth, disease and death of actual social relationships. And their diseases may even be the most interesting part of the study ! "

Further on again, Beatrice Webb defined one part of her objective as " the study of the economic *behaviour* of particular individuals and classes." In another note, written in the 'eighties, she pleads for " a body of students who will seek truth for its own sake, with the single-minded desire to present a true picture, and if possible an explanation of social life." In this note she goes on to plead for a combined technique of " personal observation and statistical inquiry," on the ground that " in social science, as in all other sciences of organic life, quantitative and qualitative analysis must go hand in hand." Then follow papers on " The Method of the Interview " and " The Art of Note-taking "—the germs from which grew the Webbs' practice through many years of diligent social investigation and their summary of this experience in the volume *Methods of Social Study*, published in 1932.

What these notes make clear is that Beatrice Potter, even before her meeting with Sidney Webb, knew very well what she was setting out to do, and had already formulated for herself both a critique of Political Economy and a constructive view of the functions and methods of Social Science. She was not, at this time, a Socialist : Socialism was, for her, the outcome of actual practice of the methods of social investigation which she had defined for her own use ; and it follows that the Socialism at which she arrived was undogmatic, relativist, and regarded rather as an instrument of action than as a theory. She was as impatient of the dogmatic Marxism which took its stand on the labour theory of value as of orthodox economics. Her own theory of value she defined in terms of " a correspondence or union between economic faculty and economic desire." " It is," she wrote in 1892, " so to speak, the marriage settlement of economic life, and like many other matrimonial arrangements it is not always to the advantage of both parties. And moreover, in this vale of tears many faculties and many desires do, as a matter of fact, remain unmarried ; and thus fail to generate exchange value. Indeed, it should be one of the main objects of applied sociology to bring about the largest measure of unbroken continuity and mutual satisfaction in an ever-increasing stream of marriages between the economic faculties and economic desires of the human race."

Beatrice Webb linked this sociological theory of value to her conception of the integration of social structure. " Was it fantastic to suggest that this idea of the democratic government of industry as a joint affair of consumers and producers had some affinity with the idea of exchange value being the result of a correspondence or union between economic faculty and economic desire ? The proper relationship of Trade Unionism and Co-operation is that of an ideal marriage, in which each partner respects the individuality and assists the work of the other, whilst both cordially join forces to secure their common end—the Co-operative State."

This passage was written in the actual year of Sidney and Beatrice Webb's marriage, and after his influence had begun to fuse itself with her thought. I think it is possible at this point to discover what was each partner's principal contribution to their long and latterly indistinguishable collaboration. Sidney Webb was already the mainstay of the Fabian Society, the principal source of the stream of social information which was being poured out through its tracts and lectures, the very embodiment of the quantitative study which Beatrice had said should go hand in hand with qualitative study of social affairs. Her experience had been in this qualitative field, especially her work for Charles Booth's great London Survey. She had already published her small, but remarkable study of *The Co-operative Movement in Great Britain* ; he

had written on *Socialism in England*, on *The Eight Hours Day*, and
on *The London Programme*, and, in addition to *Facts for Socialists*
and numerous other Fabian Tracts, had contributed to *Fabian
Essays* the study of *The Historic Basis of Socialism* in which he
gave the essence of the Fabian doctrine of Utilitarian Collectivism as
the social structure appropriate to the age of machine production
and surveyed the growth of the activities of the State as an organisation for the promotion of social welfare. He had moreover been
very active behind the scenes in creating the Progressive Party on
the newly formed London County Council, and was already deeply
engaged in the study of local government as an agent for the provision of collective services for the people.

Thus, even at the time of their marriage, the work that lay before
them as the outcome of their union was already defined. Sidney
Webb drew from Beatrice a new interest in the achievements and
possibilities of voluntary organisation and a conception of the need
for a wide diversity of studies of forms of social and personal
behaviour. She learnt from him to think more of the rôle of State
and local government in the promotion of welfare, as well as a
clearer appreciation of the forces of social evolution and the value of
historical studies. In practice, she left the statistics to him, and
he left the individual " case-work " largely to her ; and they
joined forces in an immense amount of documentary research
which resulted, over a long period of years, in the great series of
volumes on which their combined literary reputation securely
rests.

In giving these studies their initial direction, Beatrice Webb
evidently took the lead. Her relatively slight study of *The Co-
operative Movement* (1891) was followed in 1894 by their joint
History of Trade Unionism—the first, and still the best, book that
attempts any careful survey of the phases of Trade Union growth
and of their significance. *Industrial Democracy* (1897) was the
sequel, studying and analysing in detail the current activities of
the Trade Unions in the fields of collective bargaining, social
insurance, and the promotion of legal enactment, and in its concluding sections attempting an evaluation of the place of working-
class producers' associations in the society of the coming era. The
companion pieces, following up Beatrice Webb's historical study
of Co-operation, were long deferred. A part of them appeared in

the special supplements on *Co-operative Production* and *The Co-operative Movement* issued in 1914 by the *New Statesman*—itself one of their children ; but *The Consumers' Co-operative Movement*, the big volume in which they attempted to do for the Co-operative Societies what they had done in *Industrial Democracy* for the Trade Unions, was not published until 1921.

In the meantime, Sidney Webb had had his turn, of which the fruits appeared in the massive series of volumes on the history of *English Local Government* from the seventeenth century up to the reform of the Corporations in 1835. Unrivalled as history, in this field, these volumes were much more than a mere survey of the past. Although the story was not, save in the case of the Poor Law, carried beyond 1835, it was presented essentially as an introduction to the later development of local government as an instrument of collective welfare. The series culminated in the volume, unattractively and misleadingly called *Statutory Authorities for Special Purposes* (1922), in which, after recording the growth of the special Commissions which were the real fore-runners of modern local government agencies, the Webbs attempted a social evaluation of the place of local governing institutions in the life of society. With this series of volumes go also their more specialised studies of modern local government, including the *New Statesman* supplement of 1914 on *State and Municipal Enterprise*.

During the years through which the Webbs were pursuing their intensive studies of Trade Unionism and local government the Labour Party was in the making, and the Fabian Society, which was one of its original constituents, was pouring out tracts and lectures developing its gospel of evolutionary Socialism. Sidney Webb, in addition to his work on the L.C.C., to which he had been elected in 1892, played a large part in the activities of the Society: Beatrice Webb but a small one, typified in her Fabian pamphlet on *Women and Factory Acts* (1896) and her editorship of *The Case for the Factory Acts* (1901). She, though she had joined the Fabian Society in 1893, still preferred for some time to stand rather apart from Labour politics, following up her special concern with the conditions of working women and her close connections with Trade Union and Co-operative leaders. This was the epoch of Fabian " permeation," when she and Sidney, in their several ways, were trying to influence the younger and more hopeful members of

BEATRICE AND SIDNEY WEBB AT PASSFIELD CORNER

This picture was painted by Sir William Nicholson for the London School of Economics, where it now hangs

BEATRICE AND SIDNEY WEBB WITH BERNARD SHAW,
HILL FARM, 1930

the existing governing class, and were still sceptical of the power of the working classes to create a powerful political party of their own. His field was primarily that of politics, local and national : hers, that of social reform, especially in connection with the growing agitation against sweated labour and the demand for a " national minimum " of wages and working conditions.

It was at this point that the appointment of a Royal Commission to inquire into the working of the Poor Laws gave them both a fresh field of social activity adjacent to the social studies which they had made their own. Beatrice Webb was made a member of the Commission ; and she and Sidney Webb proceeded to devote the next few years of their lives to making the reform of the Poor Laws the point of focus for their practical social policy. The famous Minority Report of the Poor Law Commission (1909) was written mainly by Sidney Webb ; and into it they put a large part of their social policy. Not content with proposing the abolition of the Boards of Guardians and the break-up of the Poor Law so as to merge it in with the developing duties of the local governing authorities in town and country, they proceeded in the second half of their report to deal at length with the problem of unemployment, advocating public works for the maintenance of the level of employment in bad times, State measures for the rehabilitation and training of the long unemployed, and many of the proposals which are now embodied in projects for the maintenance of " full employment " and the recognition by the State of responsibility for " social security " among the people. They flouted convention by publishing, in face of official protests, their own annotated and edited issues of the Minority Report ; they founded the National Committee to Promote the Break-up of the Poor Law (subsequently renamed the National Committee for the Prevention of Destitution) to spread abroad the doctrines of the Report. They appealed for support to men and women of all parties, or of none ; and they carried on together what was probably the most highly organised social campaign since the days of the Anti-Corn Law League. They addressed meetings and founded branches all over the country ; they called in London a great conference at which they made the most of the support which they had been successful in enlisting from all parties and from public men in a wide variety of spheres : they founded a

K

journal, *The Crusade*, out of which developed the *New Statesman*. For several years their activity was unremitting ; and Beatrice Webb, who had hitherto taken little part in the work of propaganda, took her full share in all these labours, and also made their home at 41 Grosvenor Road a centre of all manner of plots and entertainments. Their efforts were abortive. John Burns, the President of the Local Government Board, would have nothing to do with their proposals ; and Lloyd George was following the different line that led to the National Insurance Act of 1911. The Poor Law remained unreformed, save in secondary ways, right up to 1929. John Burns was able to boast that he had " dished the Webbs," though in fact the main responsibility was not his.

From 1911, when the Insurance Act became law and was accepted by the Trade Unions for the sake of their share in its administration, the failure was evident ; and the Webbs had to decide what to do next. What they did was to found a Fabian Research Department, which they set to work on a series of inquiries relating their earlier work on Trade Unionism and Co-operation to the new winds of doctrine that were blowing about the working-class movement and making themselves manifest in waves of strikes, often against the wish of the Trade Union leaders, and in a widespread disillusionment with the achievements of the Labour Party, which had first appeared in force in the Parliament of 1906. They set on foot a new study of the control of industry, designed to further the idea of a partnership between the producers and the consumers, and to counteract on the one side Syndicalism and on the other the too exclusively political bias of the Labour Party leaders. Out of this new venture, in which Beatrice Webb played the leading part in organisation, while Sidney Webb took his full share in the writing, came the series of special supplements to the *New Statesman*, not only dealing with Co-operation in its various aspects but also embodying the first real study ever made of the forms and methods of organisation in the skilled professions—an exceedingly valuable pendent to their earlier account of the Trade Unions.

The outbreak of war in 1914 interrupted, though it did not wholly suspend, these researches. The Fabian Research Department found itself overwhelmed with current activities arising out of the war, and called up to serve as a daily adviser on emergency problems to the working-class movement. The Webbs themselves became immersed in war work—Sidney as a leading spirit of the War Emergency Workers' National Committee, Beatrice especially in connection with problems of women's employment and war service. When problems of reconstruction began to be taken into account, Beatrice Webb played an important part both on the War Cabinet Committee on Women in Industry and on various committees attached to the Ministry of Reconstruction—especially the Maclean Committee on the machinery of Local Government, which enabled her to revive their proposals for the break-up of the Poor Law and for a reorganisation of the departmental structure designed to improve the equipment of the State for its task of promoting social welfare. Out of her work for the War Cabinet Committee arose her book, *Men's and Women's Wages : Should they be Equal?* published in 1920. At the same time she and Sidney Webb made use of such time as they could call their own to complete their series of books on local government, to begin work on their great history of the development of the Poor Laws, and to follow up Beatrice's earlier study of the growth of Co-operation with a full study of the contemporary development of the consumers' Co-operative movement.

The end of the war confronted them with the need to restate their social gospel of partnership between producers and consumer as the key to the right adjustment of social relationships. This they attempted to do in *A Constitution for the Socialist Commonwealth of Great Britain* (1920)—the least successful of their major books. Sidney Webb had been mainly responsible for drafting the new Socialist programme with which the Labour Party, reorganised under his and Arthur Henderson's influence, appealed to the electors at the end of the war; and *A Constitution for the Socialist Commonwealth* was in the main an attempt to influence the formation of Labour opinion at a time when political and economic institutions alike seemed to be in the melting pot. Its proposals for a Social Parliament, distinct from the Political Parliament dealing with the affairs of government in the traditional sense, was an attempt to meet the attacks of Syndicalists and Guild Socialists on orthodox Fabian Collectivism without sacrificing the ultimate supremacy of the consumers in economic affairs. But its proposals were generally deemed too artificial ; and it exercised little influence on the shape of public opinion. It appeared, indeed, at a time when the foundations of Syndicalist and Guild Socialist influence were being undermined by the post-war depression ; and its ignoring of the challenge presented by the development of the Soviet system in Russia deprived it of any appeal to the working-class " Left " or to the new generation of Socialist intellectuals who were looking, still bemusedly, to Russia for inspiration.

In 1923 the Webbs followed up this unsuccessful essay in constitution-making with a very much better book, *The Decay of Capitalist Civilisation*, in which they analysed relentlessly the signs of capitalist decline and the growing tendency of capitalism in decay to resort to restrictive devices which were a blank denial of its claim to rank as a promotor of adventurous enterprise. Immediately thereafter, the accession of the first Labour Government to office drew them both away from writing to active participation in public affairs. Sidney Webb became President of the Board of Trade ; and Beatrice Webb constituted herself hostess to the members of the new governing class and especially to the wives of the Labour Ministers and M.P.'s, for whose benefit she founded the " Half-Circle Club " in an endeavour to protect them at once from social isolation in London and from the insidious risks of patronage.

The fall of the first MacDonald Government at the end of 1924 gave the Webbs opportunity to resume their writing. In 1926 Beatrice published *My Apprenticeship*, the fascinating record, based on her diaries, of her mental and political development up to the time of her marriage. *My Apprenticeship* gave a wide public an idea of her personality quite different from that which had prevailed before among those who knew the Webbs only by their political writings. They had been dismissed often enough as inhuman, mechanistic, mere schemers of social projects into which men and women must be made to fit regardless of personality or private desire. Such a view of Beatrice Webb's outlook could not survive the publication of her candid and engaging record of the earlier phases of her pilgrimage. There were some who drew the conclusion that the inhumanity was Sidney Webb's, and that Beatrice was a great spirit thwarted by marriage to a machine. But none who knew Sidney Webb could have endorsed this judgment. Inhuman he never was, even if his part in their partnership was mainly that of quantitative analysis, while Beatrice attended to the qualitative elements in the social situations which they surveyed. They were too closely bound together in spirit for their thoughts and attitudes to be thus divided. In private conversation, either of them could at any moment begin a sentence with " We think " without fear of violating the other's mind. The character of their collaboration comes out clearly in *Our Partnership*, the sequel to *My Apprenticeship*, published in 1929 after the death of both the partners.

The pause which followed the fall of the first Labour Government also gave them the opportunity to finish their great *English Poor Law History*, of which the first volume, dealing with *The Old Poor Law*, appeared in 1927, and the second and third, carrying the record from 1834 to the end of the system then inaugurated, in 1929. *Methods of Social Study*, to which reference has been made already, followed in 1932.

At this point it seemed to many as if the Webbs had completed their life-work. The second Labour Government, in which Sidney Webb, now Lord Passfield, was Colonial Secretary, had called them back to politics in 1929 ; and Beatrice, who strongly objected to being called " Lady Passfield," had resumed her position as Labour hostess. The fall of the Government in 1931 had released them from these, on the whole, uncongenial tasks ; and they withdrew from London to spend their latter years at their house, Passfield Corner, near Liphook, Beatrice announcing her intention of setting to work on *Our Partnership*, which was to be the sequel to *My Apprenticeship*, but was to be published only after their death. Their story was, however, to have an ending very different from that which most of their friends and admirers had anticipated. Experience of Labour politics over the dozen or so years since the end of the war had taught them much, and had above all roused in them an intense curiosity about the real significance of the immense Socialist experiment which was being made in the Soviet Union. In 1932, when Beatrice was seventy-four and Sidney seventy-three years old, they set off together to see for themselves what was really happening in the one country in which capitalism had been definitely overthrown and a form of Socialism set up in its place.

On the eve of their departure I was invited to write for an American magazine, *Current History*, a forecast of what they would make of the Russian experiment. Despite their reputation as " moderates," and their lifelong association in Great Britain with the cause of evolutionary Socialism—despite the association of their names with Sidney's *mot* about " the inevitability of gradualness," I was in no doubt what their conclusions would be. I felt sure they would come back enthusiastic for Soviet Communism, as it was working itself out in Russia, and that they would find in it something essentially consistent with their social ideals. I said so, and I was right ; but I was taken by surprise by the thoroughness with which they were able to apply their methods of social investigation to the unfamiliar conditions of a new country and an unknown language. The two volumes of *Soviet Communism : a New Civilisation?* published in 1935, were an astonishing *tour de force* for two ageing Fabians whose lifework many had deemed to be at an end. Astonishing, yes ; but entirely consistent with the corpus of their previous writings. In the Soviet Union, Sidney Webb found the planned Socialist economy which he had been advocating steadily for the best part of fifty years ; and Beatrice found a fascinating proliferation of social activity which she was able to interpret in terms of her interest in social behaviour and to study as a release of motives inhibited under capitalism but set free under Socialism to achieve miracles of individual and collective social effort. Neither of them was in any way appalled by the absence of many of the institutions which most people in England regarded as the essential hallmarks of political and social democracy. There were some who said this was because the Webbs preferred order and method to democracy ; but anyone who reads their book can hardly fail to be struck by their continual insistence on the emergence of new forms of popular self-expression, on the efficacy of the appeal to new popular motives of collective service and aspiration in evoking new responses, and on the sheer number of persons actively participating in the work of government in the Soviet Union in comparison with supposedly more democratic countries. In effect, the Webbs, though they put a question mark at the end of their challenging title, believed that they had discovered in the Soviet Union a new kind of democracy, capable of serving as the basis for a new civilisation with values essentially different from those of the capitalist era.

It is only necessary to look back to Beatrice Webb's notes from which I quoted at the beginning of this chapter, to see how precisely, in her account nearly half a century afterwards of the new civilisation of the Soviet Union, she was seeking, and as she believed finding, answers to certain of the questions she had posed to herself right at the beginning of her career. " The study of profit-making capitalism," she had urged, would, in a true arrangement of the social sciences, " take its place alongside the separate studies of other social institutions." She had written in those early days that " one of the many mischievous results of the abstract and deductive method (in Economics) has been the underlying assumption, used as a premise for its deductive reasoning, that pecuniary self-interest is, in fact, the basis of modern business enterprise, all else being ignored as merely ' friction '." She had gone on to deny that this was a true picture even of capitalist society, and to stress the contributions made by " public spirit and personal vanity, delight in technical efficiency and desire for power, political and social ambition, the spirit of adventure and scientific curiosity, not to mention parental love and pride of family, and even racial prestige." In the Soviet Union she was studying at first hand a quite different pattern, in which these motives were finding room to work, not to the exclusion of " pecuniary self-interest," but so as to relate it quite differently to the other motives, with quite different results. The spectacle of this new civilisation in the making fascinated her ; and the thought of it came so to dominate her mind that in her last years she could hardly talk for more than a few minutes about anything without bringing it in. The " democratic centralism " of the leaders of the Soviet Union did not perturb either her or Sidney : indeed, they seemed hardly aware of it. They never, indeed, regarded either the structure of the Soviet State or the " one-party " system on which its government rested as at all appropriate to British conditions and ways of life. They were scornful to the end of British Communism ; but they believed that the Soviet Communist type of social organisation was both right for Russia and consistent with the fundamental requirements of democracy.

It is no part of my task in this brief study to write of Beatrice

Webb as a person, or much that I should like to say would come in at this point. My affair is only with her contribution to economic studies ; and yet I cannot keep the two things entirely apart. I first met Beatrice Webb personally just at the point of transition between her work on the National Committee for the Prevention of Destitution and her creation of the Fabian Research Department as an agency for inquiring into the problems of the control of industry. I was then a very cocksure young graduate, deeply impressed by Syndicalism and Industrial Unionism and in process of developing into a Guild Socialist in an attempt to reconcile the claims of the producers to freedom and self-government with the claims of the general consuming public to the highest possible standards of living and freedom of choice. In my cocksureness, I very thoroughly misunderstood Beatrice Webb, regarding her and Sidney as the quintessential representatives of bureaucratic collectivism, and brushing aside the large concessions made in *Industrial Democracy* and their other writings to the claims of the producers. I was not, I think, *wholly* wrong ; for the Webbs, both in their dislike of disorder and untidy thinking and in their opposition to Syndicalism, were disposed in those days to lean over towards bureaucracy. But it took me a long time to discover that, at all events in Beatrice Webb, this leaning over involved an effort, because her natural sympathies were on the side of voluntary organisation, of producers as well as of consumers, and she was very much alive to the need for variety and diversity of experiment in social structure. Gradually, I came to understand better her fundamental point of view, and to appreciate how much closer my own was to it than I had for a long time believed. During the period of antagonism—combined always with reluctant admiration of her outstanding quality—I was exceedingly rude to her ; for I had more than my share of youthful arrogance. She—and Sidney too—were entirely unmoved by my rudeness. They went on treating me just as if I had been charming to them, helping me to find my way along roads which they had travelled together, behaving to me as if the cause we had equally at heart was much too important for mere personalities to be allowed to get in the way. They were exceedingly good to me ; and the end of it was an abiding friendship as well as a firm assurance that Beatrice Webb was the greatest woman I had been privileged to know.

I am but one among very many—a great diversity of creatures—upon whom her influence has been very marked. I got much more from her directly than from Sidney because it was more her way to move the talk on to the plane of fundamental ideas. Sociologically, her opinions had much in common with those of J. A. Hobson, to whom also I owed a great deal. His *Freethought in the Social Sciences* works out many of the notions which underlay her social thinking, though she never set them down in the same formal way. There is the same insistence on the unity of the social studies; the same refusal to recognise as valid a separate body of economic theory based on abstractions, the same determination to study directly the practical *behaviour* of persons and institutions, where the " economic" appears only as an aspect of a working unity spreading out over the whole of social life. I have never been much influenced by the Webbs' practical " tips " about method. Each researcher, or at all events each team working together, must, I think, largely make up a personal technique of interviewing, note-taking, and the like. For that reason, *Methods of Social Study* appeals to me much less than most of the Webbs' books ; and I can regard it only as an account of their methods, and not as a guide to my own or anyone else's—save, of course, that anyone can pick up from it many useful hints. The essence of the Webb way of social study was not in the particular technique they devised for it, well as that technique may have served their ends. It was in their whole approach, their belief that the significance of social structures could be understood only by direct, systematic and laborious investigation of their actual *behaviour*, past as well as contemporary, and that the quality of any society had to be measured by assessing, not its theoretical perfection, but its practical succes. in eliciting constructive loyalties and playing upon socially desirable motives.

The Fabians have often been called " the modern utilitarians," as having taken the doctrines of Bentham and Mill and converted them from individualist to collectivist terms, using them to justify the extension of State activity in the social field and applying the " greatest happiness " principle in new ways corresponding to the changing technical conditions of the modern age. Thus stated, the Fabian doctrine is Sidney Webb's, rather than Beatrice's, contribution to the common stock. She, accepting it broadly,

K*

extended its meaning both by recognising that collective social action for happiness could manifest itself quite as fruitfully in voluntary as in statutory forms, and by insisting that the search for happiness must involve the creation of many-sided opportunity for the successful exercise of constructive faculties and the expansion of personal motives in socially productive actions as well as for the satisfaction of passive consumers' needs or desires. Her curiosity about social *behaviour* had always the invigorating quality of a curiosity about individuals : it never reduced itself to a study of the institutions merely as social *mechanisms* apart from the motives which drove them on. That was why the Soviet experiment so deeply stirred her imagination—not mainly because it seemed to her to be solving the mechanical problems of productive organisation and releasing society from the inhibitions and restrictions characteristic of capitalism in decay, but principally because she believed it was finding out new ways for the successful exercise of human faculty in the creative service of mankind.

THE WEBBS IN RETIREMENT

by

KINGSLEY MARTIN

XVIII

THE WEBBS IN RETIREMENT

by *KINGSLEY MARTIN*

In writing about Sidney and Beatrice Webb, I find it difficult to explain why I remember them with so much affection. Admiration for their capacity and disinterested industry will be taken for granted, but it is much easier to recall the traits which make them the natural butt of satire than the human qualities which are completely left out in the caricature that Wells drew of them in *The New Machiavelli*. Nothing that I ever saw of them in more than twenty years' acquaintance would for a moment justify his charges of personal ambition and malicious gossip. I start by putting it on record that they were kind and friendly people who could only be represented as small-minded by a novelist who had quarrelled with them and whose literary revenge was sharpened by the knowledge that he had been in the wrong. They bore him no malice, told people to read his book and in the end persuaded him to forget his animosity. It is true that my own memories of the Webbs have a comic edge to them and that visiting them in their dignified old age had in it an element of pilgrimage. But the gods did not disappoint. They were all of a piece ; hostile critics looked in vain for the feet of clay and their laughter in the end was respectful and even affectionate.

I only got to know the Webbs well after 1931, when they had retired from active politics and lived at Passfield Corner. Before that our acquaintance was spasmodic. I remember the excitement of the first occasion when I met them at one of those hopeful Socialist gatherings in the early 'twenties. It was the first time I had seen the intelligentsia at work. I travelled from Cambridge with W. H. R. Rivers, the anthropologist and psychologist, who had joined the Labour Party and wanted to get into the House of Commons in order, he told me, to psycho-analyse Lloyd George as well as his Labour colleagues. The meeting was at a country house in Sussex. There were the Webbs and the Bertrand Russells and the Laskis, Eileen Power, Barbara Wootton and others who have made their mark in socialist politics since.

The occasion had memorable moments. There was a violent argument about Guild Socialism, which had then caught the imagination of us younger Fabians. Mrs. Webb, who was then keen on " professional representation," as she was later on popular " participation " as the basis of government, declared that if representatives were elected, not geographically, but functionally by Guilds, they would be the "creatures" of their constituents. It was an argument that was to bubble over continually in those post-war years; it only ended with the General Strike in 1926, the climax, as the Webbs, always collectivists, declared, of a foolish syndicalist phase. During this period the Webbs took all the slaps and scoldings of the younger Left, who denounced them as the arch-bureaucrats, with a good-humoured detachment. They watched the Communist wing of the Guild Socialist movement with a smile. In deference to criticism they added workers' management councils to their model constitution for industry and, when hard pressed, said " Don't worry so much about our wickedness ; look at what's coming up behind you on the Left." They were true prophets : it was the Communists who broke up the National Guilds League. But this is to anticipate. On the occasion I am describing, it was Bertrand Russell, recently back from the Far East, who took up the cudgels on behalf of the absent Guildsmen. He was adept at pulling Mrs. Webb's leg. The argument wandered off into a dispute about China and Japan. Russell said that the Webbs only liked the Japanese because they were efficient and sanitary and read the Webbs' books ; he liked the Chinese just because they were dirty. Mrs. Webb got very angry ; her claws came out as they sometimes did when she was roused. Sidney, as usual, refused to be drawn.

After that I met the Webbs at Summer Schools, and once or twice lunched with them at the famous house in Grosvenor Road. If the food was really as plain as H. G. Wells declared, it was quite good enough for me. My pride in being entertained by the Great, plus the importance of the conversation, would have satisfied me if the food had been bran and sawdust instead of boiled mutton and rice pudding. After lunch Mrs. Webb asked me whether I was going to stand for Parliament. I had a feeling of being nobbled, and sheered off with evasive replies. At that time I still thought the world my oyster, to be opened with my own swaggering sword. I had no idea of a political career, especially if someone else was making it for me. I think Mrs. Webb formed a correct impression, which she never lost, that I was too intellectually flighty, too exploratory, to be much use to the Party.

Before leaving I asked Webb, who looked a little surprised, if I could use the lavatory. Harold Laski and I walked away together. Harold declared that my request had been an extraordinary act of courage which no one had ever dared perform before in the Webb household. He said that the week before he had dined there with Ramsay MacDonald, and that he and the Premier had had to make use of a timber yard on the way home.

A few years later I joined the staff of the *Manchester Guardian*, and in 1929, when Webb was a peer and Colonial Secretary, he suggested I should come and see him about colonial policy. I recall the fantastic obtuseness with which I suggested to C. P. Scott that this was rather a flattering invitation. C.P.'s look reminded me that he thought it would be bestowing a great favour on any Minister to allow him to talk to any *Manchester Guardian* representative. However, I went to Passfield Corner, where I found Webb in the throes of the Palestinian controversy. The pro-Arabs had been seducing him, and Jos Wedgwood had just left after a heated altercation about Zionism. Webb was as nearly ruffled as I have ever seen him. My interest was in Kenya and the native question and the demands of the settlers. Webb had decided to publish his remarkable White Paper following up the Devonshire Report. Although, he said, he was always averse from " religious exercises," he thought we ought to make a really stable promise to the natives, guaranteeing them security. The White Paper promised them that the lands they then had should be theirs " for ever." A rash promise which was broken with many others before long. Webb was not very successful as a Minister ; his presence never inspired awe in the Lords or the Commons ; his beard was the subject of jest and his voice was too weak to impress. He found it difficult to make up his mind. He had written so many superb memoranda in the past, weighing up pros and cons, that he had not acquired the habit of final responsibility : he was the ideal Civil Servant and not used to the job of deciding on a policy for which he would be attacked and which he would have to defend in debate.

II

After 1931 the Webbs were disillusioned about the Labour Party. They decided to leave active politics to younger people, and to retire to Passfield Corner to finish their literary labours. Mrs. Webb was delighted to have got Sidney to herself. She had always been doubtful about the wisdom of Sidney going into Parliament, as we know from *Our Partnership*. She knew that he was better as an *eminence grise* than as a public figure, and the compromises and over-simplifications of party warfare morally disgusted her. At last she had Sidney all to herself. Years before, she had written :

"One sometimes wonders whether all this manipulating activity is worth while : whether one would not do almost as much by cutting the whole business of human intercourse and devoting oneself to thinking and writing out one's thoughts. It would certainly be far pleasanter, because a far less complicated life, with fewer liabilities for contraventions against personal dignity, veracity and kindliness. It is so easy to maintain these qualities in a vacuum ! In rubbing up against others, one's vanity, one's self-will and any strain of spite get uncovered and revealed in all their ugliness to oneself, one's friends and one's opponents. But someone has to do this practical work . . . If one frankly realises one's own moral incapacity during spells of activity, it makes one more careful not to admit unworthy desires and thoughts in the times of withdrawal from the world —and the whole level of one's mental life is raised and supported by the wholesome fear of the eternal fall of the man of action.

The Webbs had begun to doubt whether the Labour Party would ever be the efficient instrument they had tried to create for making England into a scientifically managed collective state. They talked about the "aristocratic embrace," which our astute ruling class knew to be so much more effective than the frank opposition of Conservative Parties on the Continent. Mrs. Webb had always understood the importance of social contacts in British politics, and had tried, by entertaining and instructing the wives of Labour Ministers, to make them more at home when meeting the aristocracy, thereby immunising them against both the embarrassments and seductions implicit in dining and hob-nobbing with the socially experienced ruling class. This experiment had not been very successful, and Beatrice Webb, herself a member of the ruling class, was well aware that she and Sidney had been politically effective just because they were not impressed by money and position, and were never tempted to confuse the small change of courtesy with the real payment of political concession. They loathed J. H. Thomas ; he was an even worse example of the effect of contact with " great personages " upon a weak character. How could a party led by such people carry out a social revolution ? It may be remarked here that the Webbs were in some intellectual confusion. They were contemptuous of the British Communist Party ; I remember their caustic comments on the self-destructive nature of a party of cabals and intrigues, where one small group was set to spy on another, and intellectual integrity sacrificed to doctrinal orthodoxy. It must be added that Webb did not think MacDonald dishonest in creating the Coalition Government of August, 1931, though he deplored the secretive method by which he had divided and destroyed his party. Until 1931, they had dismissed the Soviet Revolution ; " we are not interested," they said, " Russian methods and problems are too dissimilar to ours." But they changed their mind in 1931. Mrs. Webb was immensely impressed by Bernard Shaw's description of the Soviet Union on his return from his famous visit to Moscow with Lord Lothian and the Astors. Perhaps after all, they were living to see their dream of the socialist state translated into reality ? They decided to devote the rest of their lives to the study of Soviet Socialism. They visited the Soviet Union and, with the help of translators, read innumerable documents and books. They interrogated visitors to Russia of any nationality who could be induced to make the journey to Passfield Corner. They set to work on their last great body of research which matured in the two big volumes on Soviet Communism. " Old people," they remarked, " are always absorbed in something, usually themselves ; we prefer to be absorbed in the Soviet Union."

This concentration of interest did not mean that they lost desire to keep contact with events in England. They worked intensively all the week, and liked people to go down on Saturday afternoons for a week-end of sustained conversation. They regarded people like me, I think, as useful channels of information. In my case, there was the additional reason that I was associated with two of their most successful experiments. I had been a junior lecturer at the London School of Economics, which they had founded a generation before, and which had grown to greatness on lines they had not anticipated, but whose welfare still remained for them a subject of perpetual concern. And in 1931, I had become editor of the journal they had founded in 1913 as the vehicle of Socialist thought. At one time or another, I heard from them a lot about the origin of the *New Statesman* which, under Clifford Sharp, had become Liberal-Imperialist rather than Fabian. Indeed, when Massingham, their old friend and enemy, had turned into the Socialist editor of the Liberal *Nation*, Sharp, in charge of the Fabian *New Statesman*, had fallen under the influence of Asquith whom he praised to the skies, and conceived a detestation of Ramsay MacDonald, the Labour Prime Minister. The Webbs' view of MacDonald was probably not very different from Sharp's. Mrs. Webb's earlier diaries show that they never had any liking for his woolly speeches and intriguing, ambitious mind. " When things were difficult," Webb said to me, " MacDonald always had neuritis." And then, fair-minded as always, he added, " He does really get neuritis, you know, just because he's worried." But that did not make things easier for his colleagues when he shut himself up and refused to make up his mind about anything.

It was characteristic of the Webbs that having founded the *New Statesman* and worked like slaves to put it on its feet, they then left it alone to run its own course. Just how much work they put into it is revealed by some extracts from Mrs. Webb's diary that were published in its twenty-first birthday number. Their big task of " historical research " had to be put aside to plan " this organ of Fabianism."[1]

In my day the Webbs were not, I think, satisfied with the paper, but they seldom criticised. They saw the value of the amalgamation with the *Nation*, though it represented a force in politics with which they had never been sympathetic. As Desmond MacCarthy wrote years later, " The *New Statesman* with its high, dry detachment from personal and (above all) from self-delighting emotions,"

[1] See Chapter IX.

was certainly austere, though bracing. " The *New Statesman* invariably emphasised the least gratifying reasons it could for any generous policy. In this respect it contrasted with its rival, the *Nation*, now happily united with it in holy wedlock. Both papers had often moved in the same direction, but while the *Nation* supplied arguments which encouraged its readers to feel that they were the salt of the earth, the tone of the *Statesman* in arguing the same point would be, ' if you *want* to escape being a short-sighted fool, this is the line you must take.' "

Mr. MacCarthy is here hitting an important nail on the head. If I sometimes fell into inconclusive arguments with the Webbs, it was because like Shaw, they totally lacked that strain of liberal morality which is so strong an element in the British character and in the Labour Party in particular, and which has never been more faithfully expressed than by H. W. Massingham. The Webbs' central idea, with which I heartily concurred, was to turn government into a science. Like others who have had the same idea, however, they seemed to me to oversimplify the factors and sometimes to forget what government was for.

They were interested in the economic and political structure of society ; they were disinterestedly, and I would even say passionately, desirous of social improvement and of greater human happiness as they conceived it. Their watchwords—and they are very good ones—were " measurement and publicity." That is to say, they wanted to substitute quantitative for qualitative arguments ; to find a solution instead of gassing about justice and liberty. And they agreed that in order to avoid the danger of tyranny, there must be freedom of criticism and " public accountability " for all state action. From the political point of view they were never really at all interested in liberty—that is to say in the intractable complexity of individuality. People must be placed in categories for the purposes of government, and they were apt to remain in categories even when they did not fit. The Webbs acknowledged, theoretically, that there was a category of artists who might have their value, but whom they did not understand. What they did not appreciate was the element of the artist in each of the individuals whom they put into categories. Shaw never fitted anywhere ; so Mrs. Webb put him into a special category of " sprites." The functions of government must be performed by detached people, who are above human weaknesses and moved by the desire for public service, unencumbered by slogans of morality. Shaw may have regarded the Webbs in their old age as the nearest human equivalent we are likely to know to the Ancients in the last act of *Back to Methuselah*. The adventurous and artistic and other disturbing human elements were childish nuisances to be got out of the way as early as possible. Perhaps I can best summarise the point if I recall that Lowes Dickinson, philosopher and poet, anarchist by nature, told me that he decided not to be a member of the Fabian Society when he heard Mrs. Webb say that marriage is " the waste-paper-basket of the emotions." To people like Lowes Dickinson, love, intensifying through life, was the supreme object of living, and the test of good government was the opportunity it gave for love to achieve its most creative potentialities.

Once it is understood that the Webbs' basic desire was to turn the pragmatic art of ruling into an impersonal science, it is easy to understand their enthusiasm for the Soviet Union. They admitted that Russia suffered from " the disease of orthodoxy " ; they agreed that there were many growing pains in the Soviet Union ; that the Communist Party, which they rightly saw was the energising force which held together the vast scheme of producers' and consumers' organisations, was often autocratic and unnecessarily intolerant. They were prepared to admit defects. But that the whole system was a model application of state socialism, that in Russia only was there an assured hope for the future of the world and the birth of a new civilisation of abundant vitality and promise, they were immovably convinced. They declared that in Russia the socialist world was being built by realists. They agreed with Bernard Shaw that two- or multiple-party government had become an absurdity. Mrs. Webb was particularly interested in the conception of a new ruling aristocracy, based on popular consent. The idea fascinated her all through her life and after her discovery of the Soviet Union, it took a far more mature and realistic form than that conceived by H. G. Wells, for instance, in *The Research Magnificent*.

Mrs. Webb decided that the necessary mechanism for carrying through social change is a disciplined, poor and devoted body such as the Jesuits were in the days of Loyola, and such as the Communists were in the days of Lenin. In such arguments one always recalled that the Webbs, and Mrs. Webb in particular, themselves belonged to a governing class. Shaw writes somewhere, contrasting the journalists and ideologists and talkers with the " governing people " who know the methods and the compromises that have to be used to rule. In her early diaries, Mrs. Webb studied the minds of this class with an intensity that would have surprised the politicians if they had known the scrutiny to which they were subject. She studies her father, outlines his innumerable good qualities, lists occasions on which he refused money-making where it involved dishonourable conduct. But she noticed that in his business deals he was ruthless to competitors, and actuated by a desire to make money, without any consideration of the public interest. She remarks : " As life unfolded itself, I became aware that I belonged to a class of persons who habitually gave orders, but who seldom, if ever, executed the orders of other people." And later she writes :

" Deep down in the unconscious herd instinct of the British governing class, there *was* a test of fitness for membership of this most gigantic of all social clubs, but a test which was seldom recognised by those who applied it, still less by those to whom it was applied—*the possession of some form of power over other people*. The most obvious form of power, and the most easily measurable, was the power of wealth. Hence any family of outstanding riches, if its members were not actually mentally deficient or legally disreputable, could hope to rise to the top, marry its daughters to Cabinet Ministers and noblemen, and even become in time itself ennobled."

She was sure that this British ruling class was inefficient and irresponsible. Socialism she saw as the application of science and public spirit to social organisation ; capitalism as the survival of an emotional and selfish attitude in matters which are inevitably in their effects public, and which should be efficiently organised as public services. A society founded on private enterprise the Webbs regarded as anarchy ; and to take more out of society than one put into it was quite literally theft. The job of the intelligent and self-respecting was to build an efficient, incorruptible and non-acquisitive society. To do so they must be blameless in their private lives as well as realistic in tactics. Here there was some differ-

ence between Beatrice and Sidney. In a mild way, Sidney could be
called Machiavellian. Mrs. Webb was always concerned about the
choice of means, and troubled in her conscience when they seemed
to her immoral. The Webbs were, however, completely together
in believing that their task was first to analyse society, to divide
the population into categories, and then so marshal and publicise
facts and the policy arising from them that argument and opinion
would eventually defeat the vested interests in anarchy.

The Webbs were never moved from their main objects by any
individual examples of blundering, or by stories of cruelty or
hardship. Individual and national liberty had never been important items in their creed. They were interested in carrying out the
changes which alone they believed would make a good life possible
for the masses. Mrs. Webb became furiously angry with anyone
who suggested that Soviet Communism was losing sight of its
objectives, and that the Communist Party might be too much
concerned with power and too little with its just use. She wrote
angrily denying the statistics of the dead in the vast peasant
tragedy of the Ukraine in 1932, and during the great purges of
1937 she defended the Soviet Government in a memorandum
which was afterwards embodied in the introduction to a new
edition of *Soviet Communism*. She used, I believe quite correctly,
the argument that after revolutions it is never possible for those
who are successful to grant full liberty to those whom they have
overthrown. She cited as an example the treatment of Catholics
in this country after our own mild revolution in the seventeenth
century. She pointed out that 150 years passed before they received full civil rights. I tried, I am afraid vainly, to persuade her
that even granted that the parallel was relevant, it did not absolve
democrats from the duty of criticising, when the suppression of
the old order went to unnecessary or dangerous lengths. To me it
has always seemed clear that Protestant England was justified in
the seventeenth century in excluding from governing positions
Catholics who were frequently allies of an enemy power, and
certainly disloyal to the revolution. But I can never see that this
justified the flogging and execution of Titus Oates and his friends,
nor can I see that it would have been anything but to the advantage
of England if Protestants who accepted the Revolution had criticised
these hysterical excesses.

III

The pilgrimage to Passfield Corner was sometimes exhausting. The Webbs had been working intensively all the week, and their immense fund of argument and conversation was bottled up inside them. One arrived for tea on Saturday. Mrs. Webb met one very graciously at the door. Sidney gave you a rather perfunctory handshake. You were taken upstairs and your part of the house, including your bathroom, was very firmly indicated. You went down to tea where there were probably other guests. Serious talk began at once. The condition of the world and of the Labour and Socialist movement in particular, and immediate topics of the day, were systematically dealt with. One could almost hear Mrs. Webb putting a mental tick after each item, when it had been discussed and nothing more of importance was likely to be said on the subject. The long, meaty conversation could continue at night by the fire. At 10.30 you went to bed. At half-past eight next morning you would be having breakfast and Mrs. Webb, who had already been up for several hours and done a lot of work, would be standing between you and the window, lecturing you—as I remember on one occasion—on the defects of the Douglas credit scheme. You were released for an hour after breakfast, but you started promptly at eleven on the walk over the heather and through the sunken lanes of Hampshire. Mrs. Webb would usually remark that " the English climate is the best in the world, because it is never too hot or too cold to work or to walk." Since the Webbs did both tirelessly, and had no desire to sunbathe, there was no object in arguing the point.

There was always the strange and to me incomprehensible incident with Sandy, the white dog in Nicholson's portrait of the Webbs. Just before the walk started, he began to bark at Mrs. Webb, while she hit the ground with a walking stick. While she shouted loudly and repeatedly, "Sandy ! Sandy !", Sidney stood silently by, watching. I could never make out who won this odd battle of wills or why it had to be fought. Dogs do bark with excitement when they are going out. I never dared to question Mrs. Webb on the subject. It was a ritual behind which lay some mysterious emotional satisfaction. In the end Sandy made a final and tragic rebellion. I suppose he reached the end of his patience. Anyway he bit Mrs. Webb and had to be destroyed.

At lunch there would be some distinguished visitor, for years almost invariably an authority on Russia. He would be scientifically cross-examined, and the information he provided would be used to elaborate or correct some passage in the still unpublished *Soviet Communism*. Russia would have been the main topic of talk the night before ; it would have overflowed during the morning walk, and would still be pursued during tea, when a taxi would arrive to take one home, so full of mental food that even the strongest digestion was somewhat exhausted.

The endless argument about Russia, however, was not all, or even the most memorable, part of one's visit. After supper on Saturday night, it was possible, if one was dexterous, to switch the conversation into another gear. The car steered by capable hands along the road towards the scientific socialism of the future could be put into reverse, and, with pleasing jolts of memory, carry one back along amusing by-roads peopled with interesting characters, like the young Lloyd George, and Haldane, and Winston Churchill, whom the Webbs had entertained during the early years of Fabian permeation. Mrs. Webb, with her skirts turned back over her knees, and her fine hands extended over the fire, as you will see them in Nicholson's picture, would allow herself to relax, and talk about her family, and the early days of their marriage, and to reveal passages from the diaries, many of which can now be read in *Our Partnership*. The dog Sandy sat now quiescent by the hearth, and Sidney, looking absurdly like a cockatoo, perched on a chair with his tiny feet scarcely reaching the ground and a high feather of hair standing up on his huge head, would break in now and then to correct or embroider an anecdote from a still more accurate memory.

The contrast between these two never ceased to fascinate me. One needed no very great discernment to know that they were deeply in love with one another. Many have poked fun at their " love among the blue books." Mrs. Webb has told us indeed of early matrimonial disagreements about the administration of the Poor Law in the early seventeenth century and such-like, and of how they " ended in kisses " with Mrs. Webb sitting on Sidney's knee. How, people ask, does this fit with a courtship in Epping

Forest reading Wordsworth, who was Sidney's favourite poet ? Beatrice confesses she could read no poetry. The answer is that those early kisses, and the spirit of their courtship amongst the blue books somehow or other survived through fifty years of married life. Their love was as happy and commonplace and human as that of any couple who ever lived. They hated separation, even for a few days. And when they overwhelmed one by their dual personality, each beginning and interrupting with a pontifical " we think . . . .," it was because they had genuinely thought out each problem together, and come to a joint decision which was the result of the truest marriage of two minds that has ever been achieved.

And yet two minds were never less alike. Sidney was really the man of pure reason. He once told me he had " no inside " ; he had never had a headache, never an attack of physical or spiritual indigestion. His mind was stored with accurate and valuable information, neatly arranged and strung together on a single strong thread. He read and digested books at a superhuman rate : it was said he could read and remember 200 pages an hour, and a story is told of his reading the whole of Chambers' *Encyclopaedia of English Literature* in the train between London and Edinburgh. He seemed to remember everything that was useful to his purpose and to know nothing that was not. After his death a correspondent wrote to describe a walk with Sidney Webb in the garden at Passfield Corner. He halted at the end of a row of fine sweet peas, and said, " Those are very pretty ; I don't know whether they are the sort we eat, do you ? " His notions of literature and art were rudimentary in the extreme. When, after his death, tributes were paid to him in the House of Lords, one speaker recalled the sole occasion on which it is known that the Webbs went to hear a Wagner opera, Webb was asked if he had enjoyed it. "Oh, yes," he said, " we had a most enjoyable evening. We happened to be sitting just behind Herbert Samuel. I was able to have a most useful conversation with him in the interval on the incidence of sickness in pregnancy."

It would be a complete mistake to imagine from such incidents that Webb was inhuman, a man of blue books and statistics. He was, on the contrary, full of accurate and unusual information on any subject outside the arts. He was never patronising, never superior, always kindly and particularly helpful and encouraging to the young. He was not human only in the sense that he possessed to a higher degree than anyone I have ever met the quality of disinterested reasonableness. That is certainly an unusual human quality. Because he was single-minded and infinitely kind, he was a better person to go to in difficulty than Beatrice, who was a complex mixture of aristocratic superiority, intellectual impatience and puritanical morals. Perhaps his outstanding quality was this disinterested generosity. When we summarise his life, we see the closest parallel in the life of Jeremy Bentham. Like Bentham he studied English law and institutions and social customs, judging them always by the criterion of their utility to society, and in every case suggested, with an astounding fertility, the reasonable alternatives which a wise legislation could substitute. From this intellectual cornucopia everyone was free to pilfer. From him, as from Jeremy Bentham, it may be truly said that all the world borrowed and left him rich.

I recall a conversation which precisely illustrates the contrast between the Webbs, and the way in which their joint conclusions were so often reached. Her violent reactions would be modified by his reasonableness, and the conclusion would be common to them both. On this occasion Mrs. Webb was pouring her particular scorn on a well-known contemporary woman who, she said, degraded her name by selling it for advertising purposes. She was riding so high a horse that Maynard Keynes, who was also of the company, gently pulled her leg : " But surely you are too severe ; we should all sell our names if only we were offered enough. You yourself would do it for a million pounds." Before Mrs. Webb could utter her indignant denial, Sidney, always on the alert and quick to see the commonsense reply, said, "Oh, yes, of course we should if we were offered a million pounds, my dear. But we should do the advertisement in our own way, so that we should not be ashamed of it." " You mean," said Keynes, " You would say, ' This is the best cigarette you can hope to buy until the industry is nationalised.' "

Beatrice Webb was as complex as Sidney was simple. Her two personal books, *My Apprenticeship* and *Our Partnership*, reveal with the help of the diaries which she wrote in long, sleepless hours during the night, that she was endlessly troubled by emotional conflicts and sought a personal religion as well as an impersonal solution for the world's problems. She was intensely interested in people and human character ; she would like, she tells us, to have been a novelist, and regretted, when some of the younger generation, her eight sisters' children or grandchildren, proved ultra-modern, that she had not had the opportunity earlier of seriously studying the new science of psychology. She was, in point of fact, thoroughly Victorian in her attitude both to sex and to the younger generation. She was immensely interested in her innumerable grand nephews and nieces—I say innumerable because she tried to keep up with the proliferation of their families and took a pride in thinking, even after the 150 mark was passed, that none had been missed—and she tried hard to be tolerant and understanding about their personal problems. When one of her nephews read a clever play he had written, which gloated, in the manner of the 'twenties, over the sexual peculiarities of our society, Mrs. Webb was very much shocked not, as she explained, for herself, but because others, less used to frank speech, were also among the audience.

The problem of sex became mingled with the problem of Soviet development. She had been, I recall, perplexed by the sexual freedom at first encouraged in the Soviet Union, and was fond of emphasising that puritanical discipline which the early Bolshevik Party imposed on itself. She was relieved when a new abortion law was passed, explaining that in imposing severe penalties the Soviet Government was actuated not so much by a desire to increase the population, as by its discovery of the social evils that resulted from excessive sexual freedom.

Quite early in our acquaintance I learnt that Mrs. Webb was more interested in religion than any other topic. The extracts from her diary published in *Our Partnership* reveal how large a part prayer played in her life. Her formula was that " the two big forces for good in the world were the scientific method applied to the processes of life, and the use of prayer in directing the purpose of life." Mrs. Webb read a great deal of philosophy, and found temporary satisfaction in a variety of thinkers, including General Smuts, whose Holism seemed to her valuable. But I doubt if any of these philosophers satisfied her for long. What she knew was that prayer was of practical value to her. She records on many occasions that it was " the habit of prayer which enabled her to survive and to emerge relatively sound in body and sane in mind." Prayer was not to her a petition, but a consecration of purpose and a purifying of motive. She believed, I think rightly, that in discarding contemplative prayer as one of the superstitions of religion, her rationalist friends had lost an important technique of the good life. What is perhaps more surprising is that the adolescent struggles which she recalls in *My Apprenticeship* continued into her middle years. In girlhood, she constantly records in her diary her regret for wasting time at parties and in flirtations and in showing herself off in pretty frocks amongst clever people. These temptations still continued twenty years later, when in her diary she excuses the brilliant dinner parties which she gave or attended by saying, only too truly, " our social adventures always have a purpose."

One reason, I believe, for Mrs. Webb's happiness in old age was that all this ascetic conflict which had played so large a part in her private life was over. The manœuvrings of politicians, the outwitting of dull people on Royal Commissions, the attractive glitter of social occasions, exhilarating for the moment and regretted afterwards, the waste and distraction of entertainment, the moral problems and enforced Machiavellism of political achievement—all these interferences with personal dignity, veracity and kindness, were over. She and Sidney could devote themselves to thinking and writing out their thoughts. Sitting by the fire, Mrs. Webb would occasionally talk of such matters. Sidney said little ; he did not need to pray because he had no chance desires to overcome. Lacking all vanity, and enjoying all the pleasures of life simply and in moderation, asceticism tempted him no more than excess. Mrs. Webb once hazarded the view that he too " believed," but I never could detect that he had any religious views ; the subject bored him, since there were so few established facts on which to form a hypothesis. The concentrated life of research and public service had demanded, it is clear, great sacrifices of Beatrice Webb, but none of Sidney. They had set out together, as they would tell one, with great advantages, £1,000 a year of unearned income, unusual experience and knowledge, and a remarkable coincidence of purpose. They had accomplished " the considerable work " which they had set themselves to do fifty years before. They were not dissatisfied. Even after Sidney had his first stroke and could no longer remember consecutively or talk easily, I had no impression that he felt frustrated or unhappy. His life's work was done ; he would re-read all the Victorian novels. Beatrice also gave one the impression of conscious success ; she had never been sympathetic with failure, and liked to remember what the Webb partnership had achieved and to speculate about the future. But there was always an undercurrent, a restless dissatisfaction, about her. She saw that their chief mistake had been " to reject the Marxian theory of the decay of capitalism." But I think what really perplexed her was a growing doubt whether any reorganisation of society which she and Sidney had envisaged or Soviet Russia carried into effect, would satisfy the needs of human beings if, as seemed possible, most of them were, like herself, complex and emotional and not, like Sidney, simple and rational.

INDEX